How to profit from your divorce

P.A. Ross

London | New York

Published by Clink Street Publishing 2017

Copyright © 2017

First edition.

ISBN: 978-1-911525-33-2 paperback
eISBN: 978-1-911525-34-9 ebook

Inspired by a true, unique and financially proven story of how to regenerate your wealth during and after your divorce; using the principles of a management buy-out.

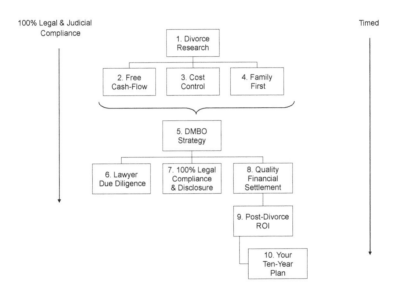

'An application of common sense and not an application to the courts'

Written by PA Ross

"The greater danger for most of us lies not in setting our aim too high and falling short; but in setting our aim too low, and achieving our mark."

Michaelangelo

A tribute to my mum who lost her husband and devoted father at the age of 29 years old; proudly raising myself and my two younger sisters. She was my life's inspiration, a role model in achievement and everyone's friend. My mum never complained and was resilient to the day she was taken from us in 2006; she is no longer in pain, suffering from Alzheimer's.

With gratitude and thanks to our world class dementia care system who nursed my mum during her years of need and help.

Disclaimer

This book is based on the author's true story and factual experiences; it is written and designed to share information and author opinion only. This information and the author's unique divorce experiences are original and fully authenticated which are provided and sold with the knowledge that the publisher and author do not offer any legal or other professional advice; this book is written from a layman's perspective and opinion. In the case of a need for any such expertise, please consult with the appropriate legal professional in your country of residence; divorce laws do vary by country. This book does not contain all information available on the subject. This book has not been created to be specific to any individual's or organisations' situation or needs; individual divorce cases have their own circumstances and requirements. Therefore, the book is provided with the understanding that the author or publisher is not engaged to render any type of legal or any other kind of professional advice. The personal content of each chapter is factually correct and true; the content of this book is at the sole expression and freedom of opinion of its author, and not necessarily that of the publisher. No warranties or guarantees are expressed or implied by the publisher's choice to include any of the content in this volume. Every effort has been made to make this book as accurate as possible; however, there may be typographical and or content errors. Every effort has been made in the non-disclosure of 3rd party names, organisations, non-confidential and confidential documents. Therefore, this book should serve only as portraying the author's own true life experience and opinion and not as the ultimate source of subject information. This book contains information that might be dated and is intended only to educate and inform; all information is factually correct and can be fully substantiated. The author and publisher shall have no liability or responsibility to any person or entity regarding any financial loss or damage incurred, or alleged to have incurred, directly or indirectly, by the information contained in this book. You are responsible for your own choices, actions, and results. Please consult with a legal professional for your own counsel.

Contents

Chapter Two – The Divorce Management Buy-out (DMBO)

Page 117

Chapter Three – Select your lawyer very carefully

Page 133

Chapter Four – It's your financial settlement

Page 205

Chapter Five – In to recovery

Page 213

Chapter Six – Building your 10-year Plan

Page 245

'Never ever let anyone tell you that you can't do something' – 351

Preface

Following nearly five years of acrimonious divorce; four divorce lawyers, three barristers, six court appearances, four different judges, acting as a 'litigant in person', the threat of bankruptcy and even a penal notice, finally topping everything with a successful complaint to the Legal Complaints Service. Being totally exasperated; there had to be another and better way to complete a divorce, draw a line and move on with life.

The cost of divorce in the UK adds up to a massive £5.7 billion a year; the average cost of divorce is £44,000,[1] which is an increase of 57% between 2006 and 2014. One in three lives is affected by divorce[2] with many divorcing couples now struggling to pay their legal bills; 47% of couples were not expecting the bill they eventually got. For the majority, 90% of couples were surprised by their legal bill, the charge was higher than they expected[3] – there really has to be another way to reduce the cost and financial pain of family breakdown?

Ironically, and almost five years on; we finally and independently achieved an out of court financial settlement, taking a matter of weeks to complete. Achieved by removing our respective divorce lawyers and not returning to court for the seventh occasion. The court legally ratified our settlement; enabling us to draw a line and, at long last, to move forward with our lives – with hindsight showing the many salutary lessons learnt about how to legitimately manage your divorce as a management buy-out and at a fraction of the cost.

---

[1] AVIVA report 'Cost of Divorce reaches £44,000 for UK couples' 19 August 2014 – http://www.aviva.com/media/news/item/uk-cost-of-divorce-reaches-44000-for-uk-couples-17337/

[2] Mail Online 'British family under threat as 1 in 3 lives are affected by divorce' 11 September 2007 – http://www.dailymail.co.uk/news/article-481292/British-family-threat-lives-affected-divorce.html

[3] YouGov report 'The cost of splitting up' 20 June 2013 – https://yougov.co.uk/news/2013/06/25/potential-surge-diy-divorces/

Metaphorically, I could say 'the jury is still out – did the UK family law system help or hinder my divorce?'

As a decent, law-abiding and hard-working family man, who lost his dad at the age of seven years old. With Yorkshire blood running through my veins; man and boy who learnt to take responsibility from an early age and worked hard all his life, not only as a loving and devoted parent also to make his mum and dad proud. My motivation for writing this book; I candidly look at divorce purely from the client's side and from a challenging yet new and different perspective, which hopefully can be of help, inspiration and reward to some of the 42% of the UK marriages that end in divorce.[4] Further, I do so hope that my book will expedite some change in our adversarial divorce system; then there is the human side helping and safeguarding over 500,000 children and families who are affected as a result of family breakdown.[5] Quantifying divorce by numbers; around 20 million people in the UK are already living in the shadow of divorce,[6] there are just under 115,000 new divorce cases each year (13 per hour) in the UK, and just under one in five (19%) of couples believe their marriage will end in divorce.[7] In other countries, the divorce rate is even higher in the US it is an estimated 50%; that's around 814,000 divorce cases and annulments per year.[8] In China, it is estimated 5,000 couples divorce every day.[9]

---

[4] Data released 9 February 2013 by the Office for National Statistics (ONS) 'Divorces in England and Wales 2013' – https://www.ons.gov.uk/peoplepopulationandcommunity/birthsdeathsandmarriages/divorce/bulletins/divorcesinenglandandwales/2013

[5] Family Justice Report Interim Report released March 2011 –https://www.gov.uk/government/uploads/system/uploads/attachment_data/file/217357/family-justice-review-interim-rep.pdf

[6] Data released by state funded 'Fathers Direct'; by the Daily Mail 11 September 2007 – http://www.dailymail.co.uk/news/article-481292

[7] Data released by Inside Divorce' Monday 8 January is Divorce Day for Britain' 8 January 2007 – www.insidedivorce.com/.../InsideDivorce.com%20D-Day%20press%20r...

[8] Provisional source of statistics CDC/NCHS National Vital Statistics System. Excludes data for California, Georgia, Hawaii, Indiana, and Minnesota. http://www.cdc.gov/nchs/nvss/marriage_divorce_tables.htm

[9] Statistical source Xinhua (publication date N/A)

Many books are written by family lawyers, mediators, counsellors and legal professionals on the subject of divorce, some even write about divorce 'dirty tricks'. My own book, uniquely, looks at divorce differently and firmly from the client's side of matters; I take a strategic, sometimes confrontational yet constructive approach to planning your divorce, as if it was a management buy-out (MBO). It's a new and alternative approach, which can not only co-exist and fully comply with existing UK divorce procedures and legislation; it can complement them. I genuinely hope that family lawyers who may read my book see my opinions and research as balanced and constructive client feedback and make some changes to improve the client experience. Perhaps it could be an opportunity for family lawyers to put themselves in their client's shoes; enabling a deeper understanding of client's concerns and anxieties.

I believe that this is something that hasn't been done before, and some even said 'it couldn't be done'. The Divorce Management Buy-out (DMBO) works using the following ten-point plan, hopefully an easy to follow step by step practical plan;

1. Divorce Research
2. Free-cash-flow
3. Cost Control
4. Family First
5. DMBO Strategy
6. Lawyer Due-diligence
7. 100% Legal Compliance + Disclosure
8. Quality Financial Settlement
9. Post-divorce Return on Investment (ROI)
10. Your 10-year Plan

Using the above 10-point plan; my DMBO resulted in the achievement of:

✓ A successful, transparent, fully disclosed and legally binding buy-out agreement significantly below the demands of the other side
✓ 100% retention of my new 'fledgling' company
✓ 100% retention of the matrimonial home and all contents
✓ Saving £55,000 in conveyancing, removal and stamp duty costs

- ✓ No future maintenance costs
- ✓ My total divorce costs were 65% lower than the other side's costs and 50% lower than the UK average total cost of divorce
- ✓ All my legal costs were paid in full – without going into debt
- ✓ 100% full disclosure and legal compliance – 'no dirty tricks'
- ✓ Compelling and factual divorce evidence
- ✓ Over 500% financial return on DMBO investment, over 5 years

I found my DMBO was tax efficient. Avoiding having to sell the marital home and not having to purchase a new home, I legitimately saved money on not having to pay stamp duty, VAT due on estate agent fees, conveyancing and legal costs, new furniture, fixtures and fittings, surveyors and removals. I passionately take into account what is important to the client and their family; divorce does not mean the loss of family values it can make them and you stronger. Looking at the 'big picture', some of the opportunities and the processes, which can be missed by family lawyers?

The following chapters describe each practical step-by-step part of the DMBO process, which I was able to integrate and link to prevailing divorce procedures and legislation; finding it complementary and 100% compliant with the existing UK law and the legal divorce process. The DMBO resulted in a sustainable long-term profit, which any good management buy-out should. I provide numerous personal examples, anecdotes and research at each stage of the process; allowing you, however, to personally select and create your own bespoke DMBO, which meets your own individual divorce needs and family circumstances. The process avoids legal jargon and puts the client and family needs at the heart of the divorce. The DMBO further considers the 'bigger picture' from initial divorce research to the ten years after the financial settlement has been agreed. Looking ahead, the process takes into account future market and economic conditions, which may impact on your financial settlement; an example of such economic change and financial uncertainty would be the UK's decision to exit from the European Union and the possible impact on house prices, inflation, interest rates, investment and employment. By direct comparison, my own divorce and financial settlement was completed during deep economic uncertainty and the worst recession for 80 years. I hope from my own first hand experience and using the 10 point plan will help you navigate your divorce through potential uncertain times ahead – as I discovered, divorce during uncertain times can be to your financial advantage.

Wearing my client's hat, I have complete respect and 100% compliance with the family law system and legalities. In fairness, there are many UK family law firms who provide good customer service and legal value for money. In my opinion, it is without any doubt that market and client needs have changed; parts of the UK divorce system are now in need of reforming so as to become less adversarial, which would not only reduce client's costs it would potentially save a significant amount of tax payers money. Within the chapters ahead, the weight of shared and compelling research provided by many legal, official and academic institutions supports and justifies the need for change within our divorce system. I again acknowledge that there are many family law firms who have an excellent reputation and pride themselves on the highest standard of service. But I believe family lawyers now need to re-segment and better understand client needs; build new and additional skills as market, client, social and ethnic shift takes place. Potentially, changes and new skill sets could reduce the level of client complaints made to the Legal Ombudsman, which we candidly discuss at length in the book, challenging the status quo – by the way it is reported by the Legal Ombudsman that divorce related cases are the second most complained about area of law in England and Wales.[10.] Whilst researching my book, I posted several social media discussions to lawyers and family professionals asking their opinion on the current UK divorce system. A number of UK and international lawyers responded to my posts, agreeing that the divorce system and fellow lawyers need to change; one UK lawyer replied to me saying:

> *"It is really no longer about getting the brief and then running with it right through the legal system."*

As the legal aid budget is cut, and due to the high cost of divorce, there will be a growing number of divorcing couples representing themselves; the

---

[10.] Legal Ombudsman Media and Communications informed the author 8 March 2016 that "Conveyancing is the most complained about area of law at 23%, with family law now the second highest at around 14%." The latest data is available http://www.legalombudsman.org.uk/raising-standards/data-and-decisions/#complaints-data.

legal term known as acting as a 'litigant in person'. As a result of government cuts; the *Telegraph* and BBC news report that some law firms estimate that, following the cuts, there could be 200,000 fewer cases each year which will qualify for Legal Aid.[11] Therefore, in my opinion, family lawyers may need to re-think their financial models to enable them to offer more cost efficient ways to deal with divorce; it would also provide family lawyers a competitive advantage in a changing and crowded market place. One of the more immediate areas that could be improved and used more by family lawyers is better use of available technology and connected communication in an attempt to reduce legal costs and duplication, which in turn would improve productivity and client service. Many other professional service industries such as financial services, management consultants and insurance lead the way in technology and communication. I am sure that many divorce law firms may follow other industry practices and learn when it comes to legal efficiency, time saving and improving service through the use of technology; if nothing else to reduce the mountain of paperwork and letters some lawyers can churn out, which client's end up footing the bill for. At the last count, I hold almost a library of 15 files full of divorce-related paperwork.

Recently, it was the Legal Ombudsman who said:

"… as the legal services market continues to change, with the arrival of commercial giants and big high street brands, and the increasing cross-selling of financial, legal and other services by banks and insurers, it is the lawyers who show that they can adapt their traditional view of clients and put customers at the heart of their business who stand the best chance of prospering."[12]

Living almost five years of divorce acrimony; I am in complete agreement with the Ombudsman's opinion and would challenge many of the more

[11] Reported by BBC News 9 April 2013 and Telegraph 4 July 2013 – http://www.telegraph.co.uk/news/politics/10160022/Legal-aid-overhaul-may-lead-to-lack-of-legal-representation.html
[12] Legal Ombudsman Report "Costs and customer service in a changing legal services market" March 2012 – http://www.legalombudsman.org.uk/downloads/documents/publications/Costs-Report.pdf

traditional divorce practices and procedures. However and in my opinion, there are some simple and immediate things, which could be done to put the client at the heart of their business, such as a commitment by family lawyers to having round table meetings and to 'thrash out' divorce settlement common ground, before heading off to the divorce courts; as I said many times in my divorce years, to 'make an application of common sense and not an application to the courts' is putting the client's interests first. At the time of my break up, 80% of all UK divorce cases ended up in front of the judge.[13.] Further, the cost of heading off to the divorce court is a significant burden on UK taxpayers. It is estimated the total cost to the government of family breakdown in the UK is a whopping £47 billion a year;[14.] a reduction in court costs and time would play some role and contribution in reducing this massive taxpayers' bill. Savings could be re-invested in building more hospitals, and recruiting and training much needed doctors and nurses. As I see it from the client side, there are six key strategic issues facing the future of the family law market, which I will be discussing in some detail throughout the following chapters.

During in my years of divorce, I did propose 'tongue in cheek' to both my lawyer and barrister that I should pay a percentage of their fee based on the results they achieve. In business, it is common practice to remunerate on the basis of performance, which makes business accountable to their shareholders; so why should the same principle and accountability not apply to lawyers, making them more accountable to their clients? In my own 25-year professional business career a part of my remuneration was always performance related; if I didn't achieve my personal performance targets, I didn't get paid – it's as simple as that.

Before researching and writing my book; I was under the impression that my personal divorce experience of acrimony and legal complaint would be

---

[13.] Evening Standard 'Divorce lawyers 'steer couples to court for profit' 2 March 2007 – http://www.standard.co.uk/news/divorce-lawyers-steer-couples-to-court-for-profit-7254123.html
[14.] The Christian Institute 'Family Breakdown costs taxpayer £47bn a year' 18 February 2015 http://www.christian.org.uk/news/family-breakdown-costs-taxpayer-47bn-a-year/ and the Mail Online 'The £50 billion price of failed families' 13 February 2015 http://www.dailymail.co.uk/news/article-2953053

in the minority, or even an isolated example. Since researching and finding new insights; I have become surprised at the scale of divorce-related complaints particularly connected to family lawyer's costs and customer service; I am certainly not alone. Such insights and supporting research, most of which are in the public domain, has given me further confidence in writing my book, but also 'there has to be another way' to reduce divorce hostility and the current adversarial system. The Legal Ombudsman reports that divorce is the second most complained area of law only after conveyancing.[15] A report published by the Legal Ombudsman and in the public domain "challenges lawyers to raise their game and make the divorce process less painful for clients".[16]

I was told by a close family member way back in the 1970s, that the most expensive purchase you will make in your life is your family home. Well, how wrong this can be; the true cost of divorce, including the loss of your home can be many times greater. Your hardearned cash, worked for and saved over many decades, can be quickly eroded in expensive and acrimonious divorce battles along with paying maintenance well into your twilight years.

It was Groucho Marx who said:

> *"Paying alimony is like feeding hay to a dead horse."*[17]

In contrast, my book shares a fully legally compliant story of how I had a tight and disciplined control of my legal costs, negotiated wisely my

---

[15] Legal Ombudsman Media and Communications provided direct to the author 8 March 2016; advising that "Conveyancing is the most complained about area of law at 23%, with family law now the second highest at around 14%." The latest data is available http://www.legalombudsman.org.uk/raising-standards/data-and-decisions/#complaints-data.

[16] Press release issued by the Legal Ombudsman report 'The price of separation: Divorce related legal complaints and their causes' 2012 – http://www.legalombudsman.org.uk/downloads/documents/publications/The-price-of-separation-LeO-report.pdf and BDRC study 'Individual consumers legal needs'. The Ombudsman report is available online at www.legalombudsman.org.uk released 28 February 2013.

[17] Brainy Quote http://www.brainyquote.com/quotes/quotes/g/grouchomar128095.html accessed 27th April 2016

financial agreement, selected and 'sweated' my share of the marital assets after divorce; and engaged in forward and targeted planning by evaluating and understanding the external market conditions, which would impact on my divorce settlement. How I saved costs was resourceful; how I legally represented myself as a 'litigant in person', stepping up to the plate in the courtroom battles against my ex-spouse's barrister. After my divorce, how I invested my remaining marital assets in high growth markets resulting in a quality financial settlement with a legal and legitimate net gain four years on of over £1 million. Contrary to many stories that divorce leaves you financially much worse off; it's an opportunity, as I discovered, to make a profit. With high respect and regard for any lawyers who may have the opportunity to read my book, I provided full disclosure, supported by forensic investigation of all marital assets, transparency, honesty, respect and integrity throughout my divorce. In keeping both the legal and moral high ground at all times I can certainly sleep easy in my bed at night.

You could say it was serendipity; I found a new and stronger relationship with my daughter as a result of my divorce. During divorce, relationships with your children journey into uncharted waters, however with any journey into the unknown you can make new discoveries, as I did with my daughter. Also, like any responsible father, I would have put my life on the line to protect my daughter during the years of divorce. As a 'litigant in person' I independently and proudly stood up in court to vigorously protect her; I found a deep inner strength – despite the court ruling against me on one particular issue – I knew that my principles and values were the right ones; I think everyone was aware that I was trying to protect my own daughter.

When my daughter completed her university studies; we gave her the choice of which of her parents she would choose to live with, whilst saving to buy her own home. She was completely free to choose and was under no pressure or influence from either myself or from my ex-spouse. Her choice was to live with her dad. I do believe in principle, that children from a certain and sensible age prior to their eighteenth birthday should be respected and given more independent choices, to meet their changing wishes and needs when parents divorce.

The consequences of divorce can not only result in the marital assets you have worked so hard for over many years being potentially lost quickly through a poor divorce financial settlement and high legal costs; divorce can also result in long-term health problems, stress and emotional trauma. Divorced people are three times more likely to commit suicide than married people; in the US, divorce ranks as the number one factor linked to suicide rates in major cities.[18.]

There are dozens of pitfalls during divorce, such as not having enough cash to pay legal fees and day-to-day living costs; selecting the wrong lawyer; failing to thoroughly prepare; losing control of the divorce; protracted and costly divorce procedures; lawyers who may fail to put their client's interest first, allowing emotion and acrimony to distract you and losing your fair share of marital assets; and selecting a lawyer who may fail to explain legal terms and jargon that would enable you to understand what is going on and what you are charged for (I was told in the early days of the divorce process "it is possible a case could go to a final hearing, where you could be cross-examined in the witness box", and my immediate thought was I felt that I had broken the law and was heading for a criminal trial). This book not only discusses the many pitfalls and how to avoid them; it also translates some of the legal jargon and processes into layman's language.

To overcome such challenges, and the potential loss of decades of hard work, requires not only a good strategic plan and compelling evidence, but also 'bloody-minded' determination and belligerence, resourcefulness, resilience and pride – a positive 'can do' attitude; never giving up on your hard-earned assets. I discovered that you become a stronger person when you reach the light at the end of the divorce tunnel.

[18.] National Institute for Healthcare Research Rockville 'Suicide and Divorce' reported by Divorceinfo.com – http://divorceinfo.com/suicide.htm

It was Thomas Jefferson who said:

> *"Nothing can stop the man with the right mental attitude from achieving his goal; nothing on earth can help the man with the wrong mental attitude."*[19]

My divorce began in early 2006 and the final settlement was reached nearly five years later, in 2010. In 2006, not only did my 25-year marriage end, my mum passed away after several years of battling with degenerative Alzheimer's disease, and finally I left my near lifetime corporate career working for some of the world's biggest companies to start my own business; 2006 was without any doubt my nemesis year, requiring deep inspiration.

The divorce process requires loads and loads of positivity and inspiration to keep you going; it is important to find your own personal and sometimes deep sources of inspiration inside in order to maintain motivation, self-esteem and sheer determination, to keep going through months and possibly years of divorce. Sources of inspiration need to come from your very own deep and self-beliefs, values and spirit.

As Winston Churchill once said:

> *"If you're going through hell, keep going."*

My sources of inspiration

Having lost her husband at the age of only 29 years old and raising three very young children I thank my mum for passing to me her values, inspiration and her belief in what can be proudly achieved through hard work, resilience, determination and never complaining; she just got on with life. My mum passed away on the 19th July 2006; due to her loss of cognitive skills she left us not knowing that her son was starting his divorce, which is as I and my mum would have wanted after 25 years of marriage; she left us with the positive and happy memories of our marriage and grandchild.

---

[19] Brainy Quotes http://www.brainyquote.com/quotes/quotes/t/thomasjeff120994.html accessed 27th April 2016

In writing many of these chapters, I have taken further inspiration not only from personal divorce years, but also from my world travels to over 60 countries; including visits to five of the Seven Wonders of the World and the 'darker side' of some cities across the globe. Travelling has provided the opportunity to re-evaluate human spirit and the 'people facts of life', from a Third World living with poverty and poor health and education, to highly developed economies and lifestyles; these experiences have taught and helped me better understand cultural needs and diversity. Later in my book I will share many more original stories and photographs of experiences and things learnt after meeting some fascinating people from all corners of the globe and cultures; their human spirit has truly inspired me through my divorce years and well beyond.

Visiting several Third World African countries; being privileged to visit and meet the people of Soweto, South Africa after years of apartheid. Watching a small girl visit the local shop with a returned empty Coca-Cola bottle; the Soweto shop keeper gave the little girl one rand for the returned bottle, with which she bought a single Cadbury Chocolate Éclair – the shop keeper told me this was all she could afford. The same shopkeeper taught me how to use a special handshake when meeting the locals of Soweto; the handshake would show that I came to visit as a friend. Visiting Nelson Mandela's small and humble home, whilst in Soweto. Living and seeing many original artefacts and photographs of his imprisonment on Robben Island during the years of apartheid. How his wife, Winnie Mandela had to sleep on the kitchen floor at night, out of view and firing line of the local snipers, the external walls of their home peppered with holes from gun shots and blackened from fire bombs.

Visits to Zimbabwe, Ghana and Kenya; experiencing the devastating effects of HIV, malaria, poor education, poverty, crime, corruption and past slavery; visiting a tribal camp and meeting a witch doctor, whilst at Victoria Falls, Zimbabwe. Contrasting life in Africa with the fast changing cultures, poverty and growth in China and Asia, visiting The Great Wall of China on a very cold December morning; looking out through the freezing cold air to follow it snaking into the distance, as far as the naked eye could see, and trying to figure out how such an achievement was completed without modern construction equipment and technology. However, remembering it is called 'the longest cemetery on earth' because, reportedly, one million Chinese workers died building it.

Early one peaceful Sunday morning; standing on the memorial bridge, a few metres above the *USS Arizona*, Pearl Harbour. Looking down on the watery grave of some 1100 sailors entombed in the Arizona; watching a stingray majestically glide through waters towards us as small bubbles of engine oil rise to the surface from the vessel's fuel tanks, it is said that each bubble of oil represents a tear for the crew who died on 7th December 1941, following the Japanese attack. Later, taking a helicopter ride and following the route across the Hawaiian island, which the Japanese fighter planes took to Pearl Harbour in 1941.

On my very first business trip to Australia; before getting down to business, being given a grand tour of the Melbourne Cricket Ground (MCG) by my Australian hosts. The Aussies taking great pride, as a sporting nation, telling me of the number of times they had beaten the English cricket team or the 'poms' at the MCG. Following the MCG tour, as an equally passionate and competitive sportsman, we had many hours of sporting banter over a cold beer after business hours. You know, after visiting Australia, my next stop was Auckland, New Zealand; my Kiwi hosts did precisely the same; this time it was a visit to Eden Park, the venue of so many All Black rugby triumphs; rugby is almost a religion in New Zealand. Playing rugby in my early days; turning to competitive squash for 40 years has been a big part of my life; without any doubt my values of competing hard and fair were a natural asset to have in my divorce armoury.

I have been so lucky to live and breathe such rare experiences, which have taught me so much about people and the relativities of life; keeping me inspired through almost five years of divorce and enabling me to write this book.

Writing my book frequently reminded me of the quote from Jim Lovell, Captain of Apollo 13, whilst listening to him speak at a dinner in Boca Raton, Florida, in the late 90s. Jim Lovell told the story – as the stricken Apollo 13 reappeared from the dark side of the moon and came back in to communication with mission control, he looked through his small cockpit window and placing his thumb up to it, at which point his thumb nail completely blocked and covered planet Earth, yet he still had a perfect view of the entire solar system. At this point of his speech he said "everything in life is relative". Which is a profound thought to keep throughout your divorce, and the life beyond.

As Jim Lovell and his crew defied death; so have the people in many parts of the world I have visited, in the aftermath of natural disasters and disease; people continue to struggle after devastating hurricanes, tsunami and crippling diseases, such as malaria, polio and HIV. I have learnt how local people living in such countries adapt and try against adversity to get on with life with a tremendous human spirit. During the years of divorce, visiting Sri Lanka with my daughter in May 2009; in the same month the Sri Lankan Civil War had just ended, with the Sri Lankan army defeating the Tamil Tigers. It was only five years after the tsunami; the island had not recovered. We remember driving past buildings, which had been destroyed by the tsunami, still in ruins five years on.

The tsunami was one of the worst disasters ever recorded in Sri Lankan history. It is estimated over 30,000 people lost their lives, and many more were left homeless. In addition to the human loss; the tsunami had widespread impact on the environment and natural habitat. We talked to the surviving local people in 2009, who have had to adapt and try to rebuild their lives. The locals told us that ten days before the tsunami hit the island, wild and domestic animals seemed to know what was about to happen and fled to safety. According to eyewitness accounts; herds of elephants headed to higher ground, insects were seen, almost in a military fashion, marching to higher ground and dogs refused to go outdoors. The belief is that wild and domestic animals have a sixth sense and know in advance of impending disasters through vibration in the Earth. Talking with Sri Lankan locals at a tea plantation in the northern part of the island, they told me that since the tsunami have seen a noticeable change in climate conditions, resulting in periods of drought. Sri Lanka relies on the rainy season to help drive their hydro-electric power stations; due to the lack of rain the island was preparing for long power cuts, which would affect both residents and industry.

All of my experiences and stories from around the world have shown not only how people and even animals cope and adapt when faced with adversity and disaster, but also, in their cultures and values, what is relatively important to them. I have taken such first-hand experience of global tragedies and loss to consider my own life; thinking entire populations face much more adversity than I ever did during my divorce years.

As Jim Lovell said in Boca Raton in the late 90s:

"Everything in life is relative."

My good fortune of visiting many diverse cultures, values and religions across the globe has provided me with a respect and appreciation of the UK's multicultural society in which we now live. Such cultural and religious diversity in the UK no doubt has an impact on attitudes and people's sensitivities to divorce. While understanding that country divorce laws always prevail and must be respected, this is an area of societal and community change that family lawyers may need to develop new soft skills, sensitivities and better understanding – enabling them to respond and deal with the changes in society and culture. In London, there are over 270 nationalities alone;[20] the world has certainly moved on.

Before closing on this particular part of the introduction to my book – as a refresher, sources of inspiration need to come from your very own deep and self-beliefs, values and spirit. Look deep into your own individual and personal beliefs – we all have them – and search out the ones which are going to inspire you; it maybe a special person in your life, a vivid memory that navigated you through adversity or a hero who overcame significant challenges and setbacks in order to succeed.

It was Bill Clinton who said:

"If you live long enough, you'll make mistakes. But if you learn from

---

[20] Evening Standard '270 nationalities and 300 languages' 1 March 2011 – http://www.standard.co.uk/news/270-nationalities-and-300-different-languages-how-a-united-nations-of-workers-is-driving-london-6572417.html

them, you'll be a better person. It's how you handle adversity, not how it affects you. The main thing is never quit, never quit, never quit."[21.]

The quote from Bill Clinton is not only a reminder of how to inspire one's self through adversity; it is also an appropriate introduction to the next part of my book.

The Divorce Management Buyout (DMBO)

I quickly discovered, I guess from my business background, that planning your divorce settlement can be managed as if it were a legitimate and legal company 'Management Buyout' (MBO). As touched on a little earlier, I believe this is something that has not been done before.

When seeking the definition of a company MBO, there are many parallels and principles which can apply to the way you manage your divorce. Depending on where you search online or which dictionary you choose, the definition of a company MBO broadly reads as follows:

"A transaction where a company's management team purchases the assets and operations of the business they manage. A management buyout (MBO) is appealing to professional managers because of the greater potential rewards from being owners of the business."[22.]

Source: Investopedia

The key principles of a successful company MBO are:

1. A vendor who is willing to explore a sale of their assets.
2. A vendor who will accept a realistic price and a fundable deal structure.

[21.] Brainy Quote – http://www.brainyquote.com/quotes/quotes/w/williamjc454937.html accessed 27th April 2016
[22.] Investopedia 'What is a Management Buy-Out (MBO)' – http://www.investopedia.com/terms/m/mbo.asp

3.   A committed team of people.
4.   Good future prospects of a return on investment without high risks.[23]

Source: Managementbuyout.co.uk

When applying the principles of an MBO to your divorce, rather than buying the company's assets you are buying the marital assets. You are negotiating to buy all or part of the marital assets, at a realistic price, through a fundable deal structure and a committed team of people. Your spouse is the 'vendor' who is seeking an 'exit strategy' from the marriage by selling the marital assets, also at a realistic price. Post-divorce; you are able and must invest in the retained marital assets, which provide the best long-term financial returns, profit and value without too much risk.

Achieving the best possible and quality financial settlement to fund your 'Divorce Management Buyout' (DMBO) requires research, resourcefulness, due-diligence, complete and unconditional legal compliance, strong and effective negotiation plus robust strategic planning. Also after your divorce has reached a legally binding 'clean break' financial settlement, you must be able to maximise the financial returns on your assets. Legally, you should protect yourself by closing every single door of opportunity, in order to prevent your ex-spouse returning years later and trying to claim for more money from you as your assets increase their value. An early point to make at this moment; a 'clean break' agreement can only be achieved in certain divorce circumstances; a legal professional would provide you with the correct advice, depending on individual and family circumstances.

As a key element of your research, and a leading principle of the DMBO, it is crucial to assess the strengths and weaknesses of your own position as well as those of your spouse. Being resourceful and keeping costs under control is a further key principle, and discovering ways to find free cash to contribute to the legal costs of divorce. Rarely, if ever, is the cost of divorce built into the household budget; you will require many powers of resourcefulness and imagination to financially fund the months, and even years of divorce, without heading into debt. In my opinion and from experience, some family

---

[23.] Strategic Corporate Finance Transactions Limited – www.managementbuyout.co.uk

lawyers may think you have tens of thousands of pounds hidden under the mattress, waiting to pay their fees. This is just one example of how some family lawyers may fail to understand the budgetary needs and constraints of their client; we are not a corporate business with tens of thousands of pounds sat in the bank account. Some family lawyers can request advanced payment to be paid by the client 'on account' to help the lawyer's cash-flow. In my experience, having now spent over 25 years in business and working with lawyers all over the world, I haven't come across a law firm who hasn't enjoyed a healthy cash-flow; it's an industry that generally does not carry high capital overheads and one where cash-flow is usually positive.

As touched on a little earlier, divorce or family law-related cases, are the second most complained about area of law in England and Wales. In the main, complaints relate to cost. In one case, a woman's bill exceeded the original estimated expenditure by £40,000 because the firm 'had neither sought to challenge the clients approach nor inform the client of the mounting costs'.[24.]

> *The Legal Ombudsman states that "this is a pressing issue for*
> *consumers and legal services providers alike".*[25.]
>
> Source: *Legal Ombudsman website*

I ask myself the question; if so many recorded complaints are made to the Legal Ombudsman relate to divorce or family-related cases, how many further family legal customers are there who would have justified grounds for complaint, but who – maybe for the reason of feeling fearful, stressed or intimated – do not make a formal complaint against their family lawyer? In my opinion, I would imagine there would be a significant number who would be justified in complaining but fail to refer matters to the Legal Ombudsman. Perhaps the Ombudsman could think of ways to remove such customer fears and reticence; the actual number of complaints received by the Legal Ombudsman could be just the thin end of the wedge.

[24.] Guardian 'Divorce costs warning issued to lawyers' 28 February 2013 – http://www.theguardian.com/law/2013/feb/28/divorce-costs-warning-issued-lawyers
[25.] Legal Ombudsman report 'The price of separation: Divorce related legal complaints and their causes' December 2012 – http://www.legalombudsman.org.uk/downloads/documents/publications/The-price-of-separation-LeO-report.pdf

Also, we now live in a world where we share our frustrations, opinions, sometimes anger and even our private moments with an ever-growing network of people and friends through social media; we need to remember in divorce proceedings what we instantly share with our 'friends' could end up in the hands of the other side, who could use those personal feelings and private moments against us in court. Social media and digital technology are playing an increasing part in divorce proceedings, Facebook postings, online chat and tweets are now being used as evidence in the court room. With technology increasing, and with friends and peers, it's important to remember that anything you post on social media could come back and 'bite you' and find its way to divorce evidence against you.

The digital world continues to grow at pace with seamless advancement in new technologies and mobile innovation; at the time of writing this book it is forecast that 10% of **UK GDP**[26.] will come from the digital economy in 2016, and without doubt will continue to increase further in the following years. I can personally see the increasing use of legitimate digital data in divorce cases not only as courtroom evidence, but also in marital financial analysis, connected communication, e-services and divorce case research. However, and in contrast to market forces and trends, some family lawyers, in my opinion, have been slow to take up and use digital technology as a tool to assist customer service, procedures, divorce modelling and cost efficiencies.

Being totally candid, and hopefully not wanting to be too critical; it is my view that change *per se* has been generally slow in the family law sector. In this day and age where innovation is a constant and digital is ubiquitous, change is inevitable, and embracing it is necessary to the overall success of the legal process. The landscape of how to conduct business in the legal industry has moved significantly, requiring new legal and business models. Lawyer's clients are using digital technology daily in their own lives at work and at home; client's expect their lawyers to have and use the same. Family law firms who effectively manage innovation and technology in their practice can expect to benefit the client, become more efficient, improve

---

[26.] Department of Business Innovation and Skills 'Growth Dashboard' report 22 January 2015 – https://www.gov.uk/government/publications/growth-dashboard

productivity, reduce costs, improve marketing, obtain real-time client feedback, make better and more informed decisions, create a point of difference against their competitors and grow their business faster.

In context, the Reports Research Director James McCoy of YouGov says: "In order to survive in this market environment, law firms must innovate and look for new ways to provide legal support outside of traditional divorce proceedings."[27]

If we were to make comparisons with other professional services such as finance we would find countless examples of companies and complete industry sectors adapting to changing market, competition and customer needs. An example could be the 'wealth management' market. A report recently published by PricewaterhouseCoopers states:

"New regulations on suitability and compensation, as well as the demands of clients for tailored solutions and digital access to financial information, are forcing banks to rethink how they bundle products and services in tiered service offerings that appeal to different client segments and enable the wealth manager to control the cost-to-serve appropriately for the different segments. These packages should include digital client communication elements including "post-advisory services" such as notifying clients when a product drops off the bank's recommendation lists."

The report goes on to say:

"The industry also needs new pricing models. Clients want to know exactly what they are paying for, and regulators want clients to have the ability to compare prices across the industry. Transparency is the name of the game. This will fundamentally change how wealth management services get priced. Two-thirds of banks believe that pricing will shift from fee- and transaction-based models toward "pay for advice" or flat-fee arrangements. In fact, some banks have already introduced such pricing models, particularly in the U.K., where new client protection and suitability laws are

---

[27] YouGov UK 'Potential surge in DIY divorces' 25 June 2013 https://yougov.co.uk/news/2013/06/25/potential-surge-diy-divorces/

already in effect. Though the U.K. experience suggests that pay-for-advice pricing will become more widespread."[28.]

In my opinion, legal services need to provide family solutions, delivered by lawyers and out of court. Family lawyers need to continually raise the value of their services while better controlling the client's costs; clients need to know what they will be actually paying for. We will be discussing in depth all of these issues and more from a client's opinion and need in a later chapter.

You know, preparing and writing this book I have discovered there is a depth of official research written and published by legal and professional bodies – plus my own experiences and personal research using social media tools – which consistently highlight the high cost of divorce, the negative impact on families and children, highlight adversarial processes and practices, and examine raw emotion and stress; yet, with the utmost respect to the profession of family lawyers, in my judgment and experience nothing of significance seems to change to help the client reduce costs – I passionately hope and believe there has to be another way, and change will take place. This is underpinned by my earlier research; the cost of divorce has increased by 57% between 2006 and 2014[29.].

The DMBO model – a brief introduction

Purely as a means of introduction and preliminary outline the fundamental principles of an MBO, led me to create the following 4 leading platforms from which I built the DMBO model; the 4 platforms are numbered and correlate to Diagram 1:

1. Create a research-led divorce fact-base.
2. Find free-cash to pay for your divorce.

[28.] PricewaterhouseCoopers report – 'Global Wealth Management Outlook 2014-2015 – New Strategies for a Changing Industry'. The report was originally by Booz & Company in 2014 – http://www.strategyand.pwc.com/reports/global-wealth-management-study2014

[29.] Aviva 'Cost of divorce reaches £44000 for couples' 19 August 2014 http://www.aviva.co.uk/ media-centre/story/17337/cost-of-divorce-reaches-44000-for-uk-couples/

3.   Tight cost control.
4.   Your family and children, unconditionally, must come first.

These 4 platforms provide and lay a robust foundation for stage 5, which is the 'DMBO Strategy'. In real-time, the strategy can last for many months or even years, during which time circumstances will inevitably change. Therefore the strategy has the flexibility to adapt to changing and, sometimes, unforeseen circumstances. Within my book, we use the DMBO model as a structured framework; throughout and continually describing step by step each stage of the process – demonstrating with, not only my own personal experiences, but also many other examples of divorce cases, and plenty of interesting and relevant research.

The DMBO model is different from other models; it is designed by the client and from the client's perspective. Providing you with a 'road map' to navigate and follow, it allows you to have control over your own hard earned marital assets; further, the DMBO model is objective and financially compelling. It protects your best interests – if you are going to make money it's best to make it after divorce. So it is financially client friendly.

It was Winston Churchill who said:

> *"Let our advance worrying become advance thinking and planning."*[30.]

[30.] Brainy Quote http://www.brainyquote.com/quotes/quotes/w/winstonchu156920.html accessed 27 April 2016

The DMBO Model

Diagram 1

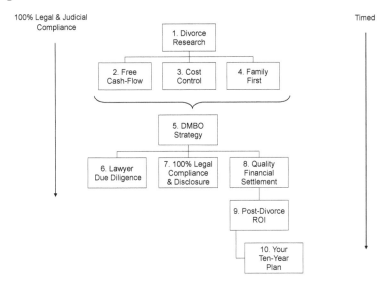

Based on my experience and mistakes, at stage 6 we discuss in detail the lawyer interview, recruitment and selection, also how to undertake lawyer due-diligence. The overriding factor when selecting your family lawyer is that they must provide you with the best legal service, advice and value. There are hundreds if not thousands of lawyers who want your business; it's a competitive market. Research them, and take your time – don't rush the selection of your lawyer, treat the selection like an interview. Ask to see your lawyer's CV their track record, ask as many relevant questions as you can – what are their qualifications? When did they qualify? Seek testimonials and references, check a shortlist of lawyers with the Legal Ombudsman, ask your lawyer if any complaints have been made against him or her. This was my first big mistake; I chose the wrong lawyer, who I eventually 'dismissed' and had to refer to the 'Legal Complaints Service'. I won my claim and a reduction in my legal bill.

Some family lawyers can fail to see the 'big picture' they pre-judge the outcome of the divorce case based on similar or past cases. Here's a reminder of the previous social media comment sent to me by a UK family lawyer;

"It is really no longer about getting the brief and then running with it right through the legal system."

This reminds me of the old cliché, 'no longer does one size fit all'. Coincidentally, and at the time of writing this book – I was watching a family lawyer on breakfast TV providing their opinion on a case, which was due to be heard in the High Court that very day. I asked myself how the lawyer could pass opinion and pre-judge any part of the case if they were not privileged to have heard all of the detailed evidence of the case. Moreover, the judgement hadn't yet been presented; perhaps the family lawyer had a crystal ball.

We discuss in a later chapter the choice and merits of legally representing yourself as a 'litigant in person' and of purely using your lawyer in an advisory capacity, which can save significant costs. In my own case, my final legal costs were a little over £16,000 compared to my ex-spouse, whose costs, I believe, were estimated to be more than three times higher. Being a 'litigant in person', stepping up to the plate in court and making your case to the judge and the opposing barrister, is, without doubt, a steep and fast learning curve; it takes you well out of your 'comfort zone'.

In my view and experience, achieving the best possible financial settlement is a protracted process, and I learnt in the latter stages of the divorce procedures that removing lawyers from the negotiating table can expedite the conclusion of a financial settlement at little or no cost. Both myself and my ex-spouse became so exasperated with our respective lawyers and their failure to reach a settlement that we removed them completely from the negotiating table to enable agreement; we achieved a financial agreement in a matter of weeks.

Moving on with the process; akin to an MBO; evaluate the prevailing market conditions, which can impact on your DMBO strategy during the divorce years. Be prepared to adjust your strategy to respond to changing external economic conditions and future market trends.

It was Charles Darwin who said:

> *"It is not the strongest of the species that survive, not the most intelligent, but the one most responsive to change."*[31.]

In my own situation, in 2008, the wider market and economic changes we were experiencing were affecting most people; we were entering economic recession, house prices were set to fall 20% over the following four years and interest rates were at an historic all-time low; such economic conditions can legally be to your advantage when negotiating the financial settlement. Timing and patience are crucial to the success of your negotiated financial settlement; 'keeping your powder dry' – using your negotiating currency at the most effective time and place. Plan when to use wider economic conditions, respective strengths and weaknesses, financial circumstances and available negotiating collateral.

> *"Negotiation is not a policy. It's a technique. It's something you use when it's to your advantage, and something that you don't use when it's not to your advantage."*[32.]
>
> *John Bolton*

Only a minority of divorces are simple and easy with both spouses agreeing on everything, no hassles, no harsh words or ill feeling, no problems with money, property, child custody, cars, house, etc. Ironically, in the early days of our divorce myself and my ex-spouse had the intention of and commitment to negotiating and settling our divorce fairly and amicably – best laid plans.

After full legal due-diligence and the interviews, you are able to choose your own lawyer. However, and with the greatest of respect, you are not able to choose a lawyer for your ex-spouse. In my opinion, I genuinely felt that her selection was a lawyer whose style and approach was somewhat confrontational. We returned to the divorce court on no less than six occasions – such

---

[31.] Tatoeba https://tatoeba.org/eng/sentences/show/2295
[32.] Brainy Quote – http://www.brainyquote.com/quotes/quotes/j/johnbolton455671.html accessed 27th April 2016

a situation of embattlement required a plan which channelled all the hostility and emotion into a positive and favourable outcome for my future, while acting professionally and with respect throughout. On one occasion, my ex-spouse's barrister congratulated me on being 'adept under cross-examination', which I took as a compliment. However, I didn't tell him that I had plenty of practice and experience at being cross-examined in business, by some heavyweight companies and directors across the world. Also, I was tempted to say, being married for 25 years you become well practiced to cross-examination and interrogation.

Do not be afraid to challenge your own lawyer, not only on costs, but also on the quality of legal service. I successfully referred my first lawyer to the 'Legal Complaints Service', receiving the compensation of a £1175 reduction in my legal bill; in my view, the lawyer's service was simply unacceptable. In my honest opinion, some lawyers can overlook the fact that you are entrusting them with everything you have worked hard for over many years.

In my full, honest and respectful opinion, parts of the UK divorce procedure now require overhauling and reform. The system can be adversarial, disproportionately expensive and protracted – in some cases the legal bill swallows up the remaining value of the marital assets; leaving you and your spouse with very little or even nothing. Divorce cases should be judged and planned on a cost vs. benefit evaluation. Many married couples spend years of hard work and long hours building the value of their marital assets, only to see them fast disappear in a matter of months through high legal bills. Within my book there are many third party examples of extraordinarily high legal costs, leaving very little for the respective spouses.

Divorce procedures, form filling, petitions, affidavits need overhauling; divorce procedures spend so much time looking at the past and not at the future. This creates even more confrontation and animosity as many 'skeletons are brought out of the cupboard', which is non-productive and achieves very little. In my opinion, conflict could have been resolved between our respective lawyers by having a round table and 'grown up' discussion to find common ground, rather than continuous threats, litigation and court hearings. This alternative approach would save on legal costs, taxpayer's money, valuable court time and stress. To quickly recap on what I would say during my divorce years 'an application of common sense and not an application to the courts'.

Unconditionally, during the divorce procedure your children's interests must be put first. During one of the many visits to court, whilst representing myself, I genuinely felt that everyone recognised and acknowledged my fair and legitimate reasons for wanting to protect my daughter. In my opinion, the issue in question could have been resolved given a little more time and without referral to the court. You know, despite losing this argument and at a cost, I – or I am sure any other responsible and loving parent – would not hesitate in doing the same, protecting their children no matter what the cost is.

I am sure there are many family lawyers who show genuine sensitivity and understanding to divorcing families and their children. From my experience and vested opinion it would help if some family lawyers practiced a better emotional understanding and the use of improved 'soft skills' when it comes to the sensitivities of children, no matter what the children's age. In my own judgement, some lawyers may need to be better equipped, and lead with empathy when handling family issues and family values, through training and coaching; perhaps lawyers may need an improved understanding and practice of what is meant and known as 'emotional intelligence'.

> *Wikipedia's definition of 'Emotional Intelligence':*
> *"Emotional intelligence is the ability to monitor one's own and other people's emotions to discriminate between different emotions and label them appropriately, and to use emotional information to guide thinking and behaviour."*[33.]

Research in the US recommends that future lawyers should be screened and trained for empathy. It was found that student lawyers in the first instance are logical thinkers and have low levels of empathy. Further, it was found that training of US law students can cause an 'erosion of empathy', and the more empathetic students tend to drop out of law school at a much

---

[33.] wikipedia.org definition of 'Emotional intelligence' – https://en.wikipedia.org/wiki/Emotional_intelligence

higher rate. Furthermore, some US law firms have used an assessment metric when hiring new recruits; the metric has a scale to measure sociopaths on a scale of 0 to 40, with higher levels being extreme behaviour in their hiring practice, preferring to employ lawyers with sociopathic index close to 29.[34.]

Now, I am not advocating, in any way at all, that 'emotional intelligence' should overrule the letter of divorce law, for which I have the utmost respect, and aim to comply with 100%. However, I feel more family lawyers could practice and take into greater consideration emotion when dealing with family sensitivities – to confirm, this is my very own personal opinion. Taking this a stage further; perhaps new policy needs to be considered to take account of a changing social and ethnically diverse world that families and children now live in. At the time of writing this part of my book we have just re-elected a Conservative government, who appear to be younger family MPs – some are lawyers. I do hope this will expedite change and wake up MPs to the new more actively social family world of expectation, emotion and family safeguards.

In saying all of this and looking at the bigger picture – divorce is only one small part of your whole life; there is a magnificent opportunity after divorce to start a brand new life. A new life, after divorce, requires lots of positive thinking, changing habits and the opportunity to build new skills; doing things you haven't done before and perhaps didn't think you could do.

Life after divorce, as with the divorce process, requires a long-term plan, setting new goals and ambitions. Make the retained marital assets from your divorce work as hard as financially possible; I call this 'sweating the marital assets'. Through 'sweating my assets' after my divorce financial settlement my healthy financial returns have come from legitimately investing: in property, art and emerging markets; something I probably wouldn't have done in my married years.

[34.] 'Future lawyers should be screened and trained for empathy' by Mark Baer Mediator, Family Law Attorney, Collaborative Law Practitioner, Speaker, and Author 27 August 2015. Posted by Huffington Divorce – http://www.huffingtonpost.com/mark-baer/future-lawyers-should-be-_b_8046278.html

Life after divorce also provides the opportunity and freedom to spread your wings, travel, meet different and new people; to do things that you haven't or couldn't do before, to move outside your comfort zone. The opportunity to create multiple income streams, which builds new personal wealth and investment, in order to thrive and enjoy life after divorce.

Personally, I have had a 'blast' since my divorce was finalised – I would like to share my time with you along with many interesting facts, the humour, the mistakes and lots of anecdotes, which I hope will make you a stronger person, and inspire you to reach the light at the end of the divorce tunnel and the life well beyond.

> *"More marriages might survive, if the partners realised that sometimes the better comes after the worse."*
>
> *Doug Larson*

Although it will be difficult at times, try to keep a sense of humour throughout your divorce and see the lighter side of matters.

5 Rules to Remember in Life: [35.]

1. *Money can't buy you happiness, but it's more comfortable to cry in a Mercedes than on a bicycle…*
2. *Forgive your enemy or even your spouse's lawyer, but remember the bastard's name…*
3. *Help someone when they are in trouble and they will remember you when they are in trouble again…*
4. *Many people are alive only because it's illegal to shoot them…*
5. *Alcohol doesn't solve problems but neither does milk…*

On a slightly more serious note; it was Edmund Hilary who said:

> *"Good planning is important. I've also regarded a sense of humour as one of the most important things on a big expedition. When you're in a*

[35.] '5 Rules to Remember in Life' www.tumblr.com – https://www.tumblr.com/search/5%20rules%20to%20remember%20in%20life

difficult or dangerous situation, or when you're depressed about the chances of success, someone who can make you laugh eases the tension.''[36]

When your DMBO is complete; measure the success of your achievements each and every year after your divorce settlement – this will not only quantify your successes, it will provide a sense of achievement, satisfaction and reward.

Since my divorce, many have said to me 'how did you manage to do that', which always reminds me of the following quote:

> *"The most rewarding things you do in life are often the ones that look like they cannot be done.''[37]*
>
> *Arnold Palmer*

I also have a reminder sitting on my study shelf at home, which says:

> *"Mission Impossible – they said it couldn't be done."*

As with the preparation for the divorce itself, I have carried out much shared research when planning and writing this book with one or two more interesting and surprise findings, along with some of my own private anecdotes:

- Divorce lawyers have their busiest day on the first working day after the Christmas and New Year holiday.[38]
- More than 1.8million couples will have contemplated splitting over the Christmas and New Year holiday period.[39]

---

[36] Secrets of Great Leaders: 50 Ways to Make a Difference – https://books.google.co.uk/books quote number 15

[37] Brainy Quote – http://www.brainyquote.com/quotes/quotes/a/arnoldpalm386349.html accessed 27 April 2016

[38] The Independent 'Lawyers prepare for divorce day' 3 January 2015
http://www.independent.co.uk/news/uk/lawyers-prepare-for-divorce-day-as-christmas-holidays-take-their-toll-9955646.html

[39] The Independent 'Lawyers prepare for divorce day' 3 January 2015
http://www.independent.co.uk/news/uk/lawyers-prepare-for-divorce-day-as-christmas-holidays-take-their-toll-9955646.html

- Married couples who met online are three times more likely to divorce than those who met face-to-face.[40.]
- Social media is being cited in almost one in five of online divorce petitions.[41.]
- 66% of divorces were on the petition of the wife.[42.]
- 34% of marriages are expected to end in divorce by the 20th wedding anniversary.[43.]
- The average age of people divorcing in 2011 was 44 years old for men and 42 years for women, in England and Wales.[44.]
- Almost half of divorces involve children under 16 yrs.[45.]
- Only, 15% of divorces were granted as a result of adultery.[46.]

Source: ONS/Relate/Various Legal Surveys and Media Divorce Reports

The Office for National Statistics also said: "Once marriages survive for a decade, it is estimated that fewer than 31 per cent will end in divorce, and after 20 years, the proportion ending in divorce falls to almost 15 per cent. For marriages that survive to longer durations, divorce is rare." The ONS also said that "Those who marry more than once are more likely to undergo divorce in later marriages. Nearly one in five people who got divorced in 2012 were doing so for the second time, it said. The percentage of so-called 'double divorcers' has almost doubled since 1980. Those who have been previously divorced have higher proportions of marriages ending in divorce than those who marry for the first time or those who remarry following the death of a spouse."

[40.] The Telegraph 'Couples who met online are 3 times more likely to divorce' 26 September 2014 – http://www.telegraph.co.uk/news/science/science-news/11124140
[41.] The Telegraph 'Facebook fuelling divorce' 21 December 2009 – http://www. telegraph.co.uk/technology/facebook/6857918/Facebook-fuelling-divorce-research-claims.html
[42.] 'Relate – Fact Sheet: Separation and Divorce' January 2014 – https://www.relate.org.uk/files/relate/separation-divorce-factsheet-jan2014.pdf
[43.] 'Relate – Fact Sheet: Separation and Divorce' January 2014 – https://www.relate.org.uk/files/relate/separation-divorce-factsheet-jan2014.pdf
[44.] 'Relate – Fact Sheet: Separation and Divorce' January 2014 – https://www.relate.org.uk/files/relate/separation-divorce-factsheet-jan2014.pdf
[45.] 'Relate – Fact Sheet: Separation and Divorce' January 2014 – https://www.relate.org.uk/files/relate/separation-divorce-factsheet-jan2014.pdf
[46.] 'Relate – Fact Sheet: Separation and Divorce' – January 2014 – https://www.relate.org.uk/files/relate/separation-divorce-factsheet-jan2014.pdf

The ONS further reports that in contrast, since 1931, marriages have declined from around 300,000 per year to a little over 200,000 per year, whilst divorces have increased to well over 100,000 per year in England and Wales. Around half of couples who got divorced in 2012 had at least one child under the age of 16 who was living with them. More than 20% of these children were under the age of five, an age at which many will grow up to have little, or no, memories of their parents living together as a married couple.[47.]

Divorce and marriage in England and Wales 1931 to 2011 (000s)

Diagram 2

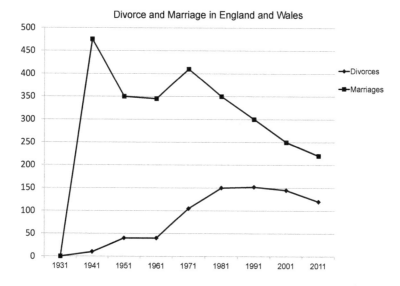

Source: ONS

[47.] The Office for National Statistics Report – 6 February 2014 'Divorce in England and Wales 2012' – http://www.ons.gov.uk/peoplepopulationandcommunity/birthsdeathsand marriages/divorce/bulletins/divorcesinenglandandwales/2014-02-06

More baby-boomers are getting divorced...

We live in a world where we are living longer; today we benefit from improved health, better and more varied and reliable diets. Medical care has improved and medicines have become more advanced while one-in-six of the UK population is currently aged 65 and over, by 2050, one in four will be. However, so-called "silver splitter" separations continue to increase at pace; the number of people over 60 who are divorcing is rising at 3% each year, equalling 45% over a decade. It is forecast by 2037, 10% of all divorcees will be aged over 60 years old.[48]

In 2015, the UK Government made radical pension changes, which could trigger a further increase in divorce from the "silver splitters", as couples thinking of divorce could access their pension pots to cash-in and start a new life after marriage. The overhaul, which came into force in April 2015, makes it much easier and cheaper for people to withdraw money directly from their pension pots rather than buying an annuity. Those who have been discreetly thinking about divorce in the past, but put off any decision, could now be encouraged to press ahead with divorce proceedings following the changes in pension rules.

Data published by the ONS in July 2015 states: "The increase between 2002 and 2014 in the percentage of the population who were divorced was driven by those aged 45 and over, with the largest percentages divorced at ages 50 to 64 in 2014; it is expected that this trend will continue."[49] Interestingly and in contrast, further research published by Prudential in June 2013 states:

[48] UK International Longevity Centre (ILC-UK) 'The Rise of the Silver Separators – Divorce and Demographics in Later Life' January 2015 – file:///C:/Users/paul../Downloads/The_rise_of_the_silver_separators%20(2).pdf
[49] The Office for National Statistics July 2015 'Population estimates by marital status and living arrangements: England and Wales, 2002 to 2014' http://www.ons.gov.uk/peoplepopulationandcommunity/populationandmigration/populationestimates/bulletins/populationestimatesbymaritalstatusandlivingarrangements/2015-07-08

"Divorce reduces average expected retirement income by around £2,600 or as much as 16 per cent a year, according to new research from the Prudential. People who are planning to retire in 2013 and have been divorced expect to retire with an annual income of £13,800 compared with £16,400 for those who have never experienced a marriage breakdown. The results have highlighted stark differences in expected retirement income between those who have been divorced and those who have not."[50.]

An unwanted Christmas present...

January is always the busiest time of the year for divorce lawyers; the long Christmas and New Year holiday takes its toll on thousands of relationships. Over Christmas, married couples are spending longer periods of time together; there's more opportunity to argue, particularly after a bottle of wine or two; all the grievances just pile up and the pressure cooker explodes. Just after Christmas 2015, I remember overhearing a conversation in my local supermarket between two middle-aged gentlemen; one of the gents was saying "I've had enough and can't wait to go back to work, the missus is driving me mad at home"; the familiar conversation brought a smile to my face, thinking how many other couples are saying the same? In addition, there is also the financial worry at Christmas with not only the cost of the festive season, but also higher everyday living costs. At New Year, people often make resolutions and think about divorcing in the year ahead. A recent study by the Family Mediation Helpline found one in four parents, or around 1.8m couples, consider divorce directly after the Christmas period.[51.]

For many unhappy partners, misdemeanours and even revelations of a fling at the office party could be the straw that 'breaks the camel's back', particularly now that smartphones have cameras and video recorders that can

---

[50.] Data by the Prudential 19 June 2013 – "divorce 'costs £2,600 per year in expected retirement income' – http://www.pru.co.uk/pdf/presscentre/divorce_cost_in_expected_retirement_income.pdf

[51.] 'Relate Policy and Research – factsheet: separation and divorce' and the Family Mediation Helpline January 2014 – https://www.relate.org.uk/files/relate/separation-divorce-factsheet-jan2014.pdf

upload pictures and videos to your tablet in minutes to be shared with friends and family. That said, adultery as a cause for divorce has dropped to an all-time low, accounting for just 15% of dissolutions granted across all genders in 2012. More than half of wives filing for divorce these days cite their husband's 'unreasonable behaviour'.[52.] Other grounds for a divorce at Christmas include verbal abuse, domestic violence, lack of sex and, believe it or not, disappointing presents. However, a case of genuine misunderstanding was recently heard on my local radio station; the husband had decided to unsubscribe from a speculative sales company, which was repeatedly sending him unwanted emails. When confirming his desire to unsubscribe and requesting that he did not want to receive any further annoying emails, the company sending the unwanted correspondence 'pinged' a final plea with the subject title "so does this mean it's all over between us?", which his suspicious wife apparently opened and read on their shared home PC. I hope the husband managed to redeem himself and explain any misunderstanding between them and what the email really meant.

Spotting the signs of a looming divorce...

A survey carried out by InsideDivorce.com of 100 UK law firms, as well as 2,000 people who were married, divorced or separated; found that nearly one in five of all marriages (19%) was 'on the rocks'. 44% of spouses surveyed said their sex lives had fallen flat, while 10% of marriages were entirely without sex at all.[53.] Following the recession, some couples trapped in unhappy marriages were waiting for the value of their house to recover before attempting to split their assets or, by contrast, the hardship of the economic slump temporarily encouraged them to pull together. In a later chapter, I will be able to explain how the recession, changing market and economic conditions played a key part of my DMBO.

[52.] 'Relate Policy and Research – Factsheet: separation and divorce' – January 2014 https://www.relate.org.uk/files/relate/separation-divorce-factsheet-jan2014.pdf

[53.] Survey of 100 UK law firms, and 2,000 people who were either married, divorced or separated carried out by Inside Divorce 26 October 2009 reported by Metro 'Christmas ends in divorce for thousands' – http://metro.co.uk/2009/10/26/christmas-ends-in-divorce-for-thousands-369834/

Irwin Mitchell LLP commissioned research, which report that one in four married couples are only together for the sake of their children and plan to divorce once they grow up, according to the recent study.[54] From my own experience, when my daughter had left home to study at university it was the time my marriage was heading for divorce.

The report further revealed the top ten reasons for staying in an unhappy marriage:

1. I have too much to lose.
2. Worried about the impact on the children.
3. I can't afford to move out/live on my own.
4. I can't afford to go through a divorce.
5. I want to give it some more time before making a decision.
6. Stigma of divorce.
7. For my partner's money.
8. Worried about how we will manage contact with the children.
9. I worry I won't meet anyone else.
10. We have too many shared financial interests.

One divorce lawyer even suggested that the 2012 London Olympics had an effect, with couples putting off the split until after the long Jubilee and sporting summer.

Divorce hotspots…

Looking around the UK, there are certain and unexplained locations that have a higher divorce rate than others – as yet no one has been able to give the reason for this.

The *Guardian* report that Weston-super-Mare has for some reason emerged as an unlikely capital for unhappily married couples. Normally this seaside

---

[54] Irwin Mitchell report 'Reasons Couples Stay In Unhappy Marriages' 15 December 2014 http://www.irwinmitchell.com/newsandmedia/2014/december/research-reveals-1-in-4-married-couples-staying-together-for-the-kids

town, which I visited many times as a child, is better known for its pier, beach and donkey rides. Recently, some 2,447 divorce petitions were lodged in Weston-super-Mare from a population of just 80,000 people – the second highest level of any city or town outside London. Many couples decide to move to this part of the country as they move into their retirement years, which could fuel the increase in divorce following the recent changes in pension rules with easier access to pension cash.

Birmingham topped the list with 2,799 couples applying for divorce in the past year, the Ministry of Justice said, but by contrast to Weston-super-Mare, Birmingham has a population of 1.1 million. Leicester County Court came third on the list of divorce applications with 1,831 petitions, followed by Romford County Court with 1,783 and Coventry Combined Court Centre with 1,766. However, the *Guardian* further reported, London is known as the divorce capital of the world; thousands of wealthy business people, investors and foreigners, many of whom work in the City of London financial district or own property in Britain, now end their marriages in the English divorce courts. In 2010, a Nigerian woman managed to increase her settlement to £275,000, almost 10 times the original settlement awarded to her in a Nigerian court, after bringing her case to the High Court in London.[55.]

Are prenuptial agreements going to avoid lengthy and expensive settlements?

It is not only the world of famous celebrities and the rich that couples associate with prenuptial agreements. More and more, prenuptial agreements are being used by ordinary individuals to help prevent costly, lengthy and hostile battles at court if the relationship comes to an end. A prenuptial agreement is a formal agreement, best drawn up by a lawyer before a couple get married that sets by agreement what will happen to their assets in the event of future divorce. There is much debate, whether prenuptial agreements are enforceable in the UK courts. As I believe, they are not enforceable or legally binding in the UK. The divorce court has very wide

---

[55.] Guardian online –Weston-super-mare divorce capital' 20 February 2013 – http://www.theguardian.com/society/2013/feb/20/weston-super-mare-divorce-capital

discretionary powers to distribute family assets as they see fit, so as to bring about fairness between the couple.

In 2014, the *Telegraph* reported proposals were made to ministers that would allow a couple to set the terms of a divorce even before they get married. The proposals included rules to combat 'gold-diggers', meaning that a bride or groom who brought their own assets into a marriage, such as a family-owned company or an inherited fortune, would not lose them in the event of divorce.

The *Telegraph* further reported that Ms. P, a former beauty queen, was battling to secure a divorce settlement of £2.6 million from her husband's £6 million fortune. Ms. P said that she had no intention of finding a job and was already looking for her third husband. The ex-beauty queen wanted £750,000 a year and had set her sights on a £5.5 million new home in West London, which required a mortgage of a mere £3 million with re-payments of £120,000 per year. Ms. P denied marrying her husband for money; she claimed that she thought he was a driver when they first met[56].

A case heard in 2010, where divorce proceedings issued were in England involving German heiress and her French ex-husband. A prenuptial agreement had been drawn in 1998 and signed in Germany, prior to moving to England later in the same year. The couple lived in London where they spent most of their married life and had two children. It was argued by the husband's legal representatives that the prenuptial agreement was not valid in England, although the agreement would have been valid in Germany had they divorced there. However, despite the legal arguments the Supreme Court judges decided that the German prenuptial agreement could be upheld despite the couple were divorcing in England[57].

---

[56] The Telegraph online 'Russian beauty queen awarded multi-million payout in bitter divorce battle' 4 June 2015 – http://www.telegraph.co.uk/news/uknews/law-and-order/11650701

[57] Guardian online 'Landmark ruling for prenups in battle of multi-millionaire heiress and her ex' 17 October 2010 – http://www.theguardian.com/law/2010/oct/17/prenup-divorce-legal-heiress

In Russia and some Eastern European countries, the story is somewhat different. A Russian friend of ours was married to an oligarch; when her marriage ended in divorce, whilst living in Moscow she received very little after the divorce settlement. She now lives in the UK and is married to an English academic. Another friend, who is living in a former state of the USSR recently divorced; after many years of marriage and raising a family her ex-husband kept the large matrimonial home overlooking the Baltic Sea and his oil business, whilst she retained a small apartment in which to live and her small beauty therapist business as the agreed divorce settlement; her ex-husband was a former member of the KGB.

Would you remarry your ex-spouse?

Statistics for restored marriages, where ex-spouses remarry each other, may be somewhat surprising and unusually odd. While statistics provided by *Psychology Today* suggest that in the US 67% of second marriages and 73% of third marriages end in divorce,[58] things seem to go a little better for people who remarry their spouses. It is reported as many as 6% of divorced spouses remarry. In my personal experience, I have only come across one couple who remarried after divorce; she was a teacher at my daughter's school. However, we have friends in Oxford who have an arrangement, where the ex-spouses share the same house with their new respective families. The arrangement, which seems to work well, allows their children the flexibility and freedom to visit or live with each parent as they so wish.

Would you invite your three wives (two ex-wives plus your current wife) to your 60th birthday party? Well, a friend and fellow squash player took the brave decision to do just that; despite the level of alcohol consumed the birthday celebrations were a success and all three wives 'hit it off' with each other and danced the night away.

---

[58] Article written by Mark Banschick, M.D., a psychiatrist and child advocate. Author of The Intelligent Divorce and posted in Psychology Today on 6 February 2012 'The High Failure Rate of Second and Third Marriages'.

Recent research carried out by OnePoll reported that 21% of divorcees regretted the way they conducted their divorce; in addition the research found 33% regretted the way it affected their children, and 24% wished they had avoided the financial consequences. Interestingly, only one in five had no regrets at all about their divorce.[59.]

Whilst the UK has a relatively high divorce rate; travelling around the world...

The divorce rate is even higher in the US at around 50%, increasing from around 13% in 1960. But Russia, Sweden, Belgium and Eastern European countries are worse off, with divorce rates higher than 55%.[60.]

In China, 5,000 couples divorce every day; Chen Yijun, an expert of sociology in the Chinese Academy of Social Sciences, was quoted saying: "Less communication between husbands and wives and increasing extramarital affairs are the big killers of marriage... Chinese men and women are becoming increasingly independent in terms of personality and finance."

Divorce can be extraordinarily expensive. Let's look at cases reported by many media channels from around the world:

Russian businessman Dmitry Rybolovlev divorced his wife Elena Rybolovl-eva, with an estimated price tag of $4.5 billion. Elena was also awarded ownership of two homes in Switzerland worth $146 million.

In 1999, the Rupert Murdoch ended his marriage to Anna Torv Murdoch, and spent a reported $1.7 billion. Soon after his divorce; Murdoch married Wendi Deng, from whom he is now divorced.

[59.] One Poll and Harrogate Family Law 'One in five regrets how they behaved through divorce' 10 February 2016 http://harrogatefamilylaw.co.uk/one-in-five-regrets-how-they-behaved-through-divorce/ and http://www.onepoll.com/?s=divorce
[60.] 'Worldwide Divorce Statistics ' Worldwide Divorce Rates: Top 20 Countries with Highest Divorce Rates per Capita' 'http://divorce.com/worldwide-divorce-statistics/

The 31-year marriage of Mel Gibson and Robyn Gibson ended in 2009. The Hollywood director and actor lost $425 million in the divorce.

The divorce map of the world below, which was produced by wikipedia draws the latest divorce data from each country.

Diagram 3

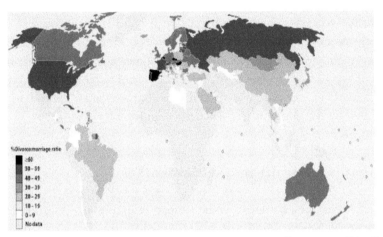

Source: en-wikipedia.org

The top 10 countries with the highest divorce rate are:

1. Russia
2. Belarus
3. Ukraine
4. Moldova
5. Cayman Islands
6. United States
7. Bermuda
8. Cuba
9. Lithuania
10. Czech Republic

Source: Huffington Post.[61.]

[61.] Huffington Post Divorce 'Highest Divorce Rates in the World 21 December 2010
http://www.huffingtonpost.com/2010/12/21/highest-divorce-rates-in-_n_798550.html

Russia has the highest divorce rate in the world. In 2015, I visited a remote town in Western Russia to find out why. Living with two different Russian families for seven days; my research found that not only deteriorating living conditions but financial difficulties and alcoholism was historically, and currently, a major reason for divorce. New economic sanctions imposed by many western countries, high inflation, low wages and Russian government policies further added to family breakdown and divorce. My research discovered how Russian education policies are developing the next generation of nuclear weapons design, which must be of concern to our western allies. Without doubt, there is growing evidence of a return to Cold War living standards and government policies. In the following chapters I share much more of my Russian research, my adventures and photographs of fast deteriorating living conditions and Cold War characteristics. I also share why I was told by Russian police to leave the country after seven days.

So what is a fair divorce settlement?

Divorce leaves men better off while women end up poorer, a study by the University of Essex has found. Researchers who monitored 10,000 divorced couples over ten years discovered that the ex-husbands' disposable income went up by an average 15 per cent. In contrast, the women saw their income drop by an average 28 per cent. The findings, from a University of Essex social science study, undermine beliefs that both sides suffer equal financial hardships from separation. The sharp difference is partly accounted for by the income gap between the sexes; it is estimated that unmarried women earn an average 14 per cent less than their male colleagues. Men tend to throw themselves into their work and do well, but women have to raise the children.[62.]

There are differing scenarios – individual and marital circumstances, plus

---

[62.] New Statesman 'Why do we still believe divorce leaves men worse off than women'http://www.newstatesman.com/economics/2014/09/why-do-we-still-believe-divorce-leaves-men-worse-women 30 September 2014 and Partnership dissolution: how does it affect income, employment and well-being? Authors Mike Brewer and Alita Nandi Publication 10 September 2014 – https://www.iser.essex.ac.uk/research/publications/working-papers/iser/2014-30

many more, sometimes complex, variables, which I do not plan to enter into. Every divorce settlement is different. However, to achieve the best possible financial settlement, you must have a divorce plan, a clear set of objectives and a strategy on how you intend to achieve your objectives.

Planning my divorce like an MBO held only one regret, I didn't start the plan early enough. Arguably, with hindsight you should start to plan the day you marry or even before by entering into a prenuptial agreement. Remember, your chance of divorce; the odds on a divorce are relatively high, 42% of marriages end in divorce England and Wales, with divorce rates at even higher levels in many international countries.

Having a clear game plan and a strategy built on the principles of an MBO paid real dividends during and in the post-divorce years. I have more than recovered my costs of divorce; in fact, my costs have been recovered several times over. As with a company MBO, after the acquisition of the assets is completed, you aim to recover your costs as quickly as possible; next, the assets you have bought you make work as hard as financially possible in the immediate years after acquisition. The returns you enjoy are then reinvested to continually increase your net worth and raise your personal financial bar.

An appropriate reminder of the earlier quotation by Michaelangelo:

> *"The greater danger for most of us lies not in setting our aim too high and falling short; but in setting our aim too low, and achieving our mark."*

To briefly recap, when your DMBO is complete; you are able to measure the success of your achievements each and every year after your financial settlement, this will not only quantify your successes, it will provide a sense of achievement, and probably bring a small yet deserved smile to your face after months or years of divorce proceedings and acrimony.

I have named these measures 'Divorce Key Performance Indicators (DKPIs)

My own DKPIs:

1. Increased net worth from £200,000 to £1.3 million from 2011 to 2014.
2. Transfer of my ex-spouse's share of the marital home; retained and invested in the marital home.
3. Retained and invested in the marital home contents.
4. No future divorce related payments.
5. Achieved a legally binding 'clean break' agreement.
6. Retained 100% shareholding and control of my company.
7. Successfully complete my daughter's university education.
8. Continued travelling the world – holidays in Maldives, Cayman Isles, Mauritius, Hawaii, Mexico, USA, Kenya, Sri Lanka, Paris, Venice, St Lucia and Russia.
9. Successfully represented myself as a 'litigant in person'.
10. Delivered my legal costs on budget, without borrowing money.

In business, I have always used the saying 'if you can't measure it, then don't do it' how else will you know, if you have achieved your objectives? The same principles apply to the achievement of your divorce and financial objectives.

To confirm my earlier qualification to any legal professionals who may read my book; my divorce was 100% legally compliant, transparent and fully disclosed, and was further ratified by the court with a 'clean break' and binding settlement.

> *"The ultimate measure of a man is not where he stands in moments of comfort and convenience, but where he stands at times of challenge and controversy."*
>
> *Martin Luther King Jnr.*

Chapter One
Prepare to plan – act quickly

My divorce began in February 2006; ironically in April of the same year, we were due to celebrate our 25th wedding anniversary. With hindsight the symptoms of a marriage breakdown had been there for at least three years prior. However, I guess, to be honest, I mistakenly chose to deny them; being 'an ostrich' by burying my head in the sand thinking the relationship would improve.

My first lesson was the failure to spot the symptoms early and to begin to plan for divorce immediately. The early symptoms of my imminent divorce were several:

- The humour and laughter in our marriage had disappeared.
- Our one-to-one communication was becoming strained, eventually almost non-existent.
- The physical side of our marriage had completely stopped.
- The chemistry had dissolved away.
- We had become disconnected with a lack of relationship respect.
- We had stopped loving each other.

Eventually, knowing my divorce was inevitable; I ceased denying my 25-year marriage was just 'on the rocks' and understood it would end in separation and finally divorce. I had to move quickly and make up for lost time during my period of denial.

First, I identified the marital assets that would have a long-term appreciation in value and would play an important part and be necessary after my divorce. For example, the long-term value of the marital home, my pension and, most importantly, my new company, which at the time of formation was co-owned through a 50% shareholding agreement with my ex-spouse.

In 2006, after almost 30 years of a successful corporate career, working my way up the career staircase with some of the world's biggest companies, I leapt off the corporate ladder to land at the very bottom again and begin building my own 'fledgling' company. With hindsight, I discovered that creating my own company just before divorce was actually not a bad move, although it was never part of my original divorce plan. Creating and building a new company had always been one of my lifetime ambitions. Again, hindsight is a wonderful thing; at incorporation, I should have registered my company to myself as being the sole shareholder with 100% personal ownership, rather than 50% ownership shared with my then spouse. At the point of no return when my divorce was inevitable, I recollect thinking how could I financially and legally justify the transfer of my ex-spouse's 50% share of the company to me, before we became embroiled in legal proceedings and divorce lawyers.

In the early days of separation, during one of the many heated and emotional arguments with my ex-spouse. I managed to turn the heat and the emotion down with a factual proposal – I obtained her agreement to sign a document transferring her 50% share of my new 'fledgling' company. My first goal had been achieved; I now had 100% control and ownership of my new company. As the company had just been established with a very small turnover, the company valuation was zero; hence passing my ex-spouse's share of the company to myself would result in no financial loss to her. Provision of my company accounts, which my accountant had prepared and filed with Companies House, legitimately confirmed the financial performance of my new 'fledgling' company. On signature, I immediately had all the formal paperwork drawn up by my accountant and informed Companies House of the share transfer. I knew at this stage my company was relatively safe and would provide a foundation and security to build and invest for my future. Later, in the divorce proceedings, as I expected the point was raised by the other side. A copy of my company accounts, the signed letter and joint signatures on the official transfer documents were provided to the other side.

As soon as divorce becomes inevitable, try to secure legitimate and justifiable 'quick wins'. If successful, ensure that you have signed written agreements; supported by official and legally binding documents, which you may come to rely upon later in the divorce proceedings. In the early stages of the divorce process, carry out as much planning and preparation as possible, it will save time and legal costs in the long-run. Further, it will provide a robust foundation for your divorce strategy, giving focus, objectivity, control and compelling evidence. Learn from my mistake of early denial – don't ignore the impending signs of divorce; take the lead initiative and act straight away. There is a well known saying in business 'first movers gain the advantage'.

As touched on a little earlier in terms of planning ahead, a few years before separation is not a bad time to think about building and launching your own company. For me after nearly 30 years, it was the opportune time to move off the corporate career ladder. If you do decide this is a route you wish to take pre-separation assess all the risks and be prepared to release all the corporate comforts, expect much less financial security with a much lower income and benefits during the early years of your new company. I had the idea to create my own company and developed the business plan some four years before my divorce started.

My other lessons from acting quickly in the early stages of divorce – keep a clear mind and keep your composure, channel emotion and energy towards securing those 'quick wins'. Let your spouse do all the 'ranting and raving', try to rise above it. Use your energy and emotion in a positive way to find solutions and answers.

> *"The most difficult thing in any negotiation, almost, is making sure that you strip it of the emotion and deal with the facts."*[63]
>
> *Howard Baker*

Don't waste time on vindictive acts of revenge. You will find later a judge may take a dim view of vindictive behaviour; it's important not to lose the moral high ground when you're fighting a divorce case. A case was recently heard and reported by the local press, in which a divorcee did lose the moral high ground, ending up in Reading Crown Court. The local 51-year-old

---

[63.] Brainy Quote – http://www.brainyquote.com/quotes/quotes/h/howardbake200556.html accessed 27th April 2016

divorcee threatened to release explicit porn photos of his ex-wife during a claim over child maintenance payments. The couple had been married for 20 years and had three children; the marriage broke down and ended in divorce in 2008. The threatened act of revenge has led to two charges of blackmail against the divorcee.[64.]

Try to hold back on engaging divorce lawyers in the very early days – this will buy you time to think, plan, research and establish your position; it will also give time to gather resources such as the finances to fund your divorce in the future. During this time, identify the marital assets, which could appreciate in value in the post-divorce years. If possible, try to plan and research your DMBO strategy at least six months before taking legal action. Taking this time will also allow you to identify and build free-cash to fund your legal costs, this is an area we will cover and discuss at length a little later in the book. Also, taking time-out before heading off to the family law firm allows a period of 'cooling off', which gives both yourself and your spouse some time to see and think rationally as the emotional dust begins to settle; avoid letting your 'heart rule your head'.

In this time, it may cross your mind to hide your assets – don't do this also don't move assets offshore or into trust. Don't attempt to edit or change documents such as financial statements. You must obtain full and honest independent valuations of all your assets such as the marital home, pensions, endowments, company accounts and investments. You must disclose their up-to-date and current value, right up to the final financial settlement; remember keep the moral and legal high ground and protect your integrity. Avoid running off and spending on the family credit card as if there is no tomorrow or immediately emptying the joint bank account. Ask your bank and building society to either freeze all joint accounts including ATM cash withdrawals or request any payment from the joint account requires joint signatures. In a premeditated act of revenge, do not destroy or damage any of your spouse's prize processions or expensive marital assets. Don't risk any of these; if a court considers you have hidden

---

[64.] Get Reading 'Crowthorne man Gerald McCarthy denies threatening to to publish revenge porn images of his ex-wife' 4 August 2015 http://www.getreading.co.uk/news/reading-berkshire-news/crowthorne-man-gerald-mccarthy-denies-9792209,

or wilfully destroyed assets in an attempt to defeat your spouse's claim, your assets could be frozen altogether. Also, the court will not look favourably on you when making judgements and court orders goven your attempts to hide the marital assets. It will also provide evidence against you, which in my view, and with no doubt will be used by your ex-spouse's lawyer. Again, keep the moral high ground at all times; the approach gives you a clear conscience and a robust defence if and when you are under cross-examination; you will sleep much better in your bed at night with a clear conscience.

A small anecdote from my local squash club when it comes to destroying your spouse's assets; a fellow squash player's wife, almost ceremonially, set fire to her husband's squash kit on the front lawn of the marital home for all their neighbours to see. She also cut the strings out of his prize-winning squash racket as an act of revenge for his affair with the captain of the ladies' squash team. During this time there were a number of other squash players at the same club who were going through a divorce. As a result, we set up the 'divorce club' where we would exchange hints and tips from our respective divorce experiences. At the time, I did think my local squash club was becoming a 'den of iniquity' for divorce and immoral behaviour, as a number of the divorcing squash players had affairs outside their marriage.

However, if you are fortunate and remain on reasonable speaking terms with your spouse and have avoided setting fire to each other's prize possessions, try to establish his or her financial expectations and settlement terms as quickly as possible. This will help when creating your DMBO strategy, and also when negotiating. Record financial expectations in writing and obtain signatures from both parties. If you make any early financial payments to your spouse to assist with living outside the marital home make such agreements in writing and again obtain dated signatures. Again, all signed financial agreements provide complete and substantiated evidence.

Make every attempt, and give a good argument, to stay in the marital home. Staying in the marital home gives you a degree of control over what is probably your most valuable marital asset. Remaining in the marital home also reduces disruption to your lifestyle; not having to find an alternative dwelling at additional cost of rental, furnishing, utilities, travel and removal.

As I saw it, my living in the marital home with minimum lifestyle disruption for nearly five years probably, I guess frustrated the other side. I did remind both my ex-spouse and her lawyer that it was my ex-spouse's independent decision to leave the marital home. Moving out of the marital home during the divorce months or years can bring high extra costs and a significant change in a lifestyle compared to what you have become accustomed to previously. It was recently reported by the *Daily Mail* that the wife of a couple who hadn't yet started their divorce proceedings ended up living in a shared house with three strangers and having to queue to use the kitchen and bathroom. Her rent was £400 per month leaving little left after other living costs to save for her own flat.[65]

Check all information provided by your ex-spouse relating to the marital finances. Divorce and custody disputes can become hostile and ugly, especially when a significant amount of marital property and parental rights are at stake. This includes forensically checking all account statements that are provided by your ex-spouse; diligently confirm with the banks and financial organisations providing the statements for authentication. A reminder to close or freeze joint bank and credit card accounts, and open new accounts in your own name. Never say anything to anyone about your case that you would not want to come up in the courtroom (except for your lawyer). Keep your mobile phone and computer locked; change the password on a regular basis. In this digital age, the evidence of a matrimonial offence can be mostly contained in a computer, laptop, mobile phone, tablet or any other computer resource. As more and more information is transmitted through email, social media and smartphones, husbands and wives are increasingly snooping on their counterparts' communications and whereabouts; sometimes illegally.[66] Do not send emails to your spouse or lawyer from your employer's email address; others will possibly be able to access your emails. Use only a secure and private email address. If you are using your smartphone or mobile tablet to send an email or read an incoming email or text, make sure this is carried out in private and not a

---

[65] Mail Online 'As divorce leaves more and more women unable to afford a home of their own…The lovelorn mid-lifers forced to live with strangers' 16 February 2014 – http://www.dailymail.co.uk/femail/article-2560828/

[66] http://usatoday30.usatoday.com/tech/news/story/2012-02-23/divorce-online-snoops/53223014/1 23 Feb. 2012

public place. Keep all financial and confidential documents under lock and key. If you are away from the marital home for any length of time, ask a trusted relative or friend to collect the daily post on your behalf and keep it in safe keeping until you return. Ask your lawyer to withhold sending any mail direct to the marital home, whilst you are away for a period of time such as holiday periods, or arrange for mail to be diverted to a safe address.

At the first opportunity, change your Will; it is likely your spouse will be the beneficiary of your Estate in the event of your death and receive 100% of all marital assets including property. Remember, you can change your Will at any time – changing your Will as soon as divorce proceedings begin will ensure that your new desires and wishes are in effect immediately. Further, think about 'Severance of Joint Tenancy'; if you currently own your matrimonial home with your spouse as 'joint tenants'. This means that in the event of your death your half share of the property will automatically pass to your spouse, irrespective of whether or not you have made a Will leaving your estate to someone else.

If you do not wish this to happen, then the Joint Tenancy must be severed to create a Tenancy in Common. The process is straightforward, and your lawyer can advise you and arrange it for you. When completed, the right of survivorship no longer applies, such that on the death of one tenant, his or her share does not automatically pass to the surviving tenant, but, is transferred according to his or her valid Will or to the rules of intestacy in the event that there is no valid Will.

One thing to be aware of when deciding whether to sever the joint tenancy – it is easy to sever the joint tenancy but much more difficult to change it back again. However, if you do choose to sever, and your spouse dies first, you could lose out, as their share would pass under the terms of their Will rather than going to you automatically as would be the case if you remained joint tenants.

I owned a new start-up company, which had no value at the time of divorce. However, if you do own a well-established, existing husband-and-wife-owned business, ensure you put contingency plans in place in case the relationship ends. If you divorce what happens to the business? Discussing the options or having an exit strategy before divorce can really help protect the future of the business and its employees. A friend of mine gained divorce agreement with her husband; her husband kept 100% of the accountancy business, whilst she kept the marital home. The risk being is that if a couple can't decide who takes responsibility for the business and it goes as far as court, the judge is likely to say the asset should be sold. A point of caution, if you do have a jointly owned husband-and-wife-business, the cost of valuation fees on the business can be high. In a case reported by the *Guardian*; a couple spent £154,000 on obtaining a multiple number of valuations.[67] In a divorce case that was referred to the Court of Appeal; the husband had his shareholding valued in a timber company at £216,000. Later in the same year and after the divorce settlement had been finalised, the timber company was sold for £3.7 million, from which the husband received £1.8 million payment. The lesson being that you should ensure the valuation of your company shareholding is up to date, true, accurate and verified. If not, this is the sort of thing, which can come back and bite you.

It is worth mentioning at this stage – don't spend hours on the phone to your lawyer; they will charge you for every unit of time taken. Every pound you spend on lawyers shrinks the marital pot you are fighting for.

Challenge your lawyer and maintain pressure on him or her to provide you with the best possible legal value. Remember you are the paying customer and it's a competitive market; law firms build their business on success and reputation and referrals. In my view, when it came to my own lawyer's cost performance, I said there was simply too much at stake; a 30-year livelihood of hard work and long hours building up assets, which are of lifetime value to me and should not be eroded away through unjustified and non-productive legal costs. It is in my own belief that some family lawyers should take the same view and attitude; I am fairly sure, if these were their own hard earned assets, they too would be concerned seeing them being eroded by continuing, unnecessary and sometimes inefficient high legal costs.

---

[67] Guardian 'Divorcing couple spent nearly £1m on divorce' on 13 November 2014 – www.theguardian.com/lifeandstyle/2014/nov/13/divorce-costs-of-nearly-1m-scandalous -says-judge

As touched on a little earlier in the chapter; divorce proceedings will require you to provide detailed documents, finances, forms, and responses to legal and court requests such as financial questionnaires and affidavits. Make sure you devote appropriate time and organisation to completing these tasks. Plan your time carefully and don't rush, request sufficient time from your lawyer and the court to complete documents and responses diligently. Don't let lawyers place unreasonable time limits and pressure on you. In my experience and personal opinion, this was a tactic used by the other side during my divorce, combined with the threat of court action, if I didn't meet certain deadlines. Actually, over time as these tactics continued, it became a bit like a 'broken record' saying to myself 'here we go again'. I felt I could almost predict that nearly every letter of demand would end with proposed court action if the demands or a particular deadline was not met. In 2009, I recollect the request of a copy of my original birth certificate to be sent to my pension provider. Following five decades of moving house at least eight times, and with my mum having recently passed away, I was genuinely unable to immediately locate my birth certificate. Hence, a request demanded that I provide my birth certificate within seven days. If I failed, I was threatened with court action for which I would be charged for costs, all of which I personally felt was completely out of context and unreasonable. Fortunately, with a bit of time searching through cupboards and filing cabinets, I did manage to find my birth certificate, tucked away in a file.

Divorce won't be fun – under stress, some divorcees can 'crash and burn'; you will be on a rollercoaster of highs and lows for some considerable time. When on the rollercoaster and under pressure, keep objective and focused on your long-term goals and divorce strategy. Maintain a structured, composed and controlled perspective; remember divorce is just one small part of your whole life. You will have a complete new life of opportunity waiting for you once divorce and final settlement is complete; visualise and remind yourself of your future new life. Critically, maintain the all-important sense of humour; keep everything in perspective and remain positive.

"Success is how high you bounce when you hit bottom"[68.]

George S Patton

[68.] Brainy Quote http://www.brainyquote.com/quotes/quotes/g/georgespa161896.html accessed 27th April 2016

You will make mistakes and experience failures, from which you will learn so much. One of my biggest mistakes was initially selecting the wrong lawyer, who I ended up 'dismissing' after six months and referring to the Legal Complaints Service. We will be discussing my learning and selecting the right lawyer in a later chapter.

Be mindful of further potential mistakes and failings, which can be:

- Don't let your family and friends have too strong of an influence over you, keep their opinions and advice in context; be your own person and make your own decisions.
- Don't let your lawyer make divorce decisions for you, listen and take advice; remember it's your future life and your hard-earned money at stake.
- Don't get distracted by 'red herrings' issues that are designed to act as a decoy; do not let your heart rule your head.
- Get verbal agreements; failing to obtain signed and dated written agreements from your ex-spouse leads to problems.
- Don't put your 'head in the sand' hoping matters will go away or resolve themselves; be prepared you will be hit with a wave of legal, family and financial issues.
- Be proactive and deal with issues immediately, they will mount up very quickly, if you don't deal with them straight away.
- Don't fail to make your children unconditionally the number one priority.
- Never ever, use your children as divorce negotiation collateral.
- Don't ignore any tax consequences; as Benjamin Franklin said 'there were only two things certain in life: death and taxes'.
- Don't assume everything will be split 50/50.
- Don't get into a new relationship too soon; use online dating sites with caution, some propositions are just too good to be true.
- Watch out for online dating scams. Later in my book, I will describe how I uncovered a Russian online dating fraud, fronted by a very attractive Russian lady called 'Veronica'.
- Don't let mistakes and failings distract you from achieving your objectives and wishes.
- Don't delay and organise yourself – get all your ducks in a row.

"Don't fear failure so much that you refuse to try new things. The saddest summary of a life that contains three descriptions: could have, might have, and should have."[69]

Louis E. Boone

The Divorce Management Buy-Out Model (DMBO)

As touched on during the introduction to my book; the principles of an MBO have laid the foundation to create the blueprint for the 'DMBO Model'. Without doubt, in the very beginning this idea was just a theoretical plan, a hypothesis, a bit of innovative thinking. I learnt, and spread my wings along the divorce journey; hence saying to myself in the early days 'divorce is similar to a management buy-out'. The model grew and evolved during the five years of divorce proceedings. The end result and final DMBO model provides a structured and methodical framework, which I found gave me control over my divorce and, more importantly, my future. It also provided me with a path to a good quality financial settlement.

A reminder of Einstein's quote:

"Innovation is not the product of logical thought, even though the final product is tied to a logical structure."[70]

A quick reminder of the 4 key platforms of the model; each numbered platform correlates to the following model (Diagram 4), each stage is a logical step by step process:

1. Divorce research and information
2. Free-cash-flow to finance your legal costs
3. Cost control to finance living costs
4. Your family and children, unconditionally must come first

---

[69] Brainy Quote – http://www.brainyquote.com/quotes/quotes/l/louiseboo170206.html accessed 27th April 2016
[70] Think Exist http://thinkexist.com/quotation/innovation_is_not_the_product_of_logical _thought/145948.html

We will be discussing and explaining in much more detail each of the 4 key platforms and process a little later in the chapter. Each platform will be supported by research, my own personal and third-party experiences.

Diagram 4

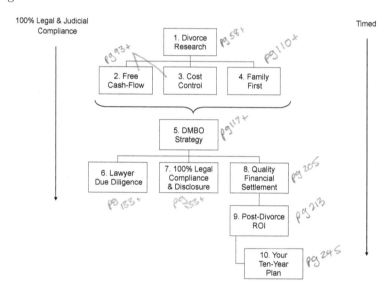

On completing the above 4 platforms; the next step of model is to construct the 'DMBO Strategy' (stage 5) The strategy, again, is a structured process, which provides you with objectivity, personal and competitive advantage; further the DMBO strategy provides control and direction of your divorce. You will have far more chance of success and achievement of a good quality financial settlement, if you create, build and implement an effective and robust strategy.

Again, the pursuing 5 strategic platforms are numbered to correlate with the above model:

6. Lawyer due-diligence
7. Legal compliance and disclosure
8. Quality financial settlement
9. Post-divorce return on investment
10. Your 10-year Plan

Likewise, we will be discussing in detail each of the 5 strategies a little later in the chapter.

The 'DMBO Model' is delivered over time and governed by three key factors;

1. First, the divorce procedures and timetable to be followed are governed by the legal and judicial system, rules and regulation, with which you must without question fully and wholeheartedly, comply; it's the law. I quickly discovered the key stages of the DMBO complemented the legal process. Particularly, divorce research and preparation, finding free-cash to help fund your legal costs, the divorce strategy and the resulting financial settlement.

2. The time and speed is dictated by the respective lawyer's ability to expedite the divorce process, also their ability to collaborate and work with each other.

3. How to use the time available, which can be several months or several years to negotiate your financial settlement; 'keep your powder dry'; know when in the time process to best use your negotiating collateral.

The complete process and structure can take, as in my own circumstances up to 15 years; nearly five years to complete my divorce and financial settlement followed by my 10-year plan after the divorce settlement.

It was Confucius who said:

"A man who does not plan long ahead will find trouble at his door."[71.]

We will now take the first and detailed step of the long plan ahead.

[71.] Famous Quotes by Confucius http://www.famous-quotes.com/author.php?aid=1645

① Divorce Research – Step One

Diagram 5

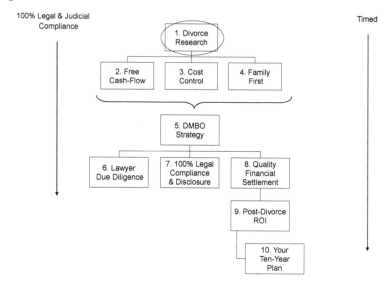

The first part of the research stage is to establish and prioritise what information you need, and how it will make a difference to the divorce financial settlement. Further, research the facts, which will win the legal arguments against the other side and, more importantly, will win your arguments, if and when in court and in front of the judge. Build a library of evidence, which will enable you to select key information to support your strategy and legal arguments. Having a library of evidence further enables you to provide compelling answers to the questions and issues that the other side will inevitably raise. As touched on earlier, add to the library of evidence signed written agreements between yourself and your ex-spouse, such as money paid after separation, transfer of company shares, prenuptial agreement and so on.

The next stage of research is to quantify the current financial value of your marital assets. Obtain at least three independent professional valuations of the five most valuable marital assets. Assess the likely value of each asset in ten years' time; this will help prioritise which assets are worth fighting for.

In my case the top five marital assets were:

1.   Marital home.
2.   Pension fund.
3.   High interest investments.
4.   Marital home contents.
5.   Inheritance.

To help forecast the likely future value of your marital assets; there are many external sources available to assist you. Most leading building societies provide long-term property forecasts; your pension provider will be able to forecast the future value of your pension. Depending on the investments you hold, whether it is stocks and shares, gold, fine art or other investments, evaluate past performance and trends and identify if these trends are likely to continue. Obtain advice from expert specialists in the particular area of investment – much advice can be found online and at no cost.

The outcome of my research and strategy led to prioritising the top five assets and identifying where to focus my energy, time and efforts. The research and strategy resulted in my retaining the marital home; four years after the final financial settlement the property through personal investment and market growth after settlement is valued at £1.3 million. Through legally compliant and legitimate negotiation, I retained 100% of the marital home contents including works of art and family heir looms. I further retained 43% of the high-interest investments and 50% of all our pension funds; all of which had long-term opportunity to appreciate in value. Little of this would not have been achieved, without the support of a research and knowledge of which assets would have real long term value.

Without doubt, the highest valued marital asset was the marital home, not only for monetary reasons – it was an asset I had worked very hard for over the years and was immensely proud of. We had purchased our first marital home in 1980 for £19,975, although interest rates in the 80s peaked at a scary 16% in order to tackle high inflation; fortunately, both interest rates and inflation declined in the following years. Between 1980 and 2001 we moved house on three occasions, each time trading-up in size and value. Knowing how hard I had worked for the marital home, and following the correct legal processes, research and my well-planned strategy I was determined not to give up the most valued marital asset as a result of divorce.

Zsa Zsa Gabor was married nine times, described herself as a good housekeeper on the basis that:

"I always get to keep the house."

The next step is to research wider external economic factors, which could make a difference to the long-term value of the marital assets you are fighting for. In my own case the following external factors that would make a difference, both positive and negative, were:

1. Current and forecast interest rates.
2. Forecast property values and the rental market.
3. Forecast pension value at retirement.
4. Current and forecast inflation.
5. Stock market performance.
6. Government pension policies and regulation.
7. Foreign currency rates.
8. Government policies, which could affect the future UK property and rental market.
9. Government policies on taxation and investment.
10. Future growth of the international arts market.

To confirm, the above prevailing market factors were unique to myself; individual circumstances will vary and market conditions change very quickly. You must decide which economic and market factors will impact on your own divorce and future plans; everyone's situation is unique and differs. A business acquaintance of mine has a collection of classic cars. Each classic car has a varying future value – for example the classic Aston Martin will increase in value faster than the Triumph Stag. My business acquaintance was intrigued by my divorce strategy. If he was ever thinking of divorce, and part of the divorce settlement were be to share his classic car collection with his spouse, he would be best advised to negotiate the retention of the Aston Martin, considering its future value. In the summer of 2015, a 1935 classic Aston Martin sold at auction for

£2.91 million and a 1963 Aston Martin DB4 sold for £964,700 at the Goodwood Festival of Speed.[72.]

To stay with researching the future 'classics and culture' market – my research discovered that arts investment had performed well over the past 25 years and the trend was forecast to continue. The research further unveiled a trend of using art investment as a means to supplement future pension returns – and I knew that I would probably be sharing at least 50% of my hard-earned pension with my ex-spouse. Experts were saying "you do not have to spend lavishly to get yourself a good art investment. Many people assume that you need to buy a Van Gogh, a Cezanne or a Renoir which sell for many millions, but this is not the case. You can invest in good quality art such as limited edition prints, new artists or even ceramics for less than £1000". The research further reported that investing in new and young artists provided a good investment opportunity. In 1994, a painting by Damien Hirst would cost around £12,000 – at the time of the research report the same painting could sell for around £200,000.[73.] Knowing that it was inevitable there would be a pension sharing order as part of my divorce settlement; investing in the arts market could be a post-divorce strategy that would recover a part of my pension losses. I guess the only compromise by investing in art is the investment does not provide a regular monthly income in retirement; you only realise the financial gain when you come to sell the piece of art. Nevertheless it is a profitable strategy to have, in order to compensate for any pension losses.

A personal saying, which I have used throughout my business career is:

"Successful strategies take advantage of changing market forces."

With hindsight, the most advantageous market force to me was the historically low interest rates, which made it affordable for me to re-mortgage the marital home at an extremely advantageous and competitive fixed medium-term interest rate. Referring to the following diagram, demonstrating how

---

[72.] Sports Car Digest 'Bonhams Goodwood Festival of Speed; Auction Result' 2015 – http://www.sportscardigest.com/bonhams-goodwood-festival-of-speed-2015-auction-results/
[73.] Sipps Pension Guide 'Investing in art with a Sipps Pension' www.sippsguide.com

the cost of borrowing fell significantly in 2008, to 0.5%, at the beginning of the economic recession. Interest rates remained at a record low from 2008 to 2014. I took full advantage of the low interest rates to raise the capital to facilitate the divorce buy-out in early 2011.

Diagram 6

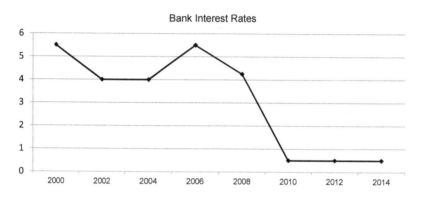

Source: Bank of England

Quickly comparing the divorce research principles to a company MBO; a company MBO team researches the value of the assets that they were proposing to purchase. The company MBO team would know their market and prepare a market researched growth strategy to be implemented after the MBO is completed. The MBO team would finally place a forecast on the future value of the assets bought as a result of the MBO; effectively the 'DMBO' and the associated research is doing exactly the same.

To briefly recap, the key principles of a successful company MBO are:[74]

1. A vendor who is willing to explore a sale of their assets.
2. A vendor who will accept a realistic price and a fundable deal structure.
3. A committed team of people.
4. Good future prospects of a return on investment; without high risks.

Source: Managementbuyout.co.uk

---

[74] Strategic Corporate Finance Transactions Limited – www.managementbuyout.co.uk – http://www.managementbuyout.co.uk/is-an-mbo-feasible

As a further part of your research, it is useful to familiarise yourself with the legal terms of divorce law. I discovered that this became very helpful information, which not only assisted my understanding of the legal side of matters, but came in very useful when later representing myself as a 'litigant in person'. It is valuable to get to know the standard divorce procedures, statutory laws and terminology. Legal terms and jargon do become very common as you progress along the divorce conveyor belt of procedures.

Here are some of the terms that I most frequently came across – knowing them not only helped the understanding of their meanings, but also the role and at what stage they played in both the divorce and financial settlement procedures:

- Divorce Petitioner: the spouse who filed the divorce petition with the court.
- Divorce Petition: the form used to apply to the court for a divorce. It contains details of both parties, when they married and the grounds and facts for divorce.
- Respondent: the other spouse upon whom the divorce dissolution proceedings are served.
- Decree Nisi: the provisional order indicating that the court is satisfied that the grounds for divorce have been established.
- Decree Absolute: the final order of the court, which brings the marriage to a final end. Both parties are then free to remarry.
- Lump Sum: capital payment, usually made to a spouse.
- Spousal Support: one spouse's payment to the other for financial support; the same as alimony or maintenance.
- Notice: the formal legal process of informing one spouse about a legal action or proceeding involving that spouse.
- Costs: the Petitioner may ask that the Respondent pay all or a percentage of the Petitioner's costs of the divorce proceedings.
- Maintenance: one spouse's payment to the other for financial support; the same as alimony or spousal support.
- Order: a court's ruling or decision on a certain matter or legal issue, usually a decision on a motion filed by one spouse.
- Marital property: includes all property acquired during the period of marriage.

- Judgement: a court's decision.
- Acknowledgement of Service: the form sent to the Respondent by the court together with the Divorce Petition. The Respondent acknowledges receipt of the proceedings, confirms whether or not he/she will defend the divorce and whether he/she agrees to contribute to the Petitioner's costs.
- Custody: When used in the context of child custody, this refers to the person who will have responsibility for the child.
- Affidavit: a sworn statement in writing.
- Retainer: a fee paid in advance for services provided by a legal professional.
- Pension Sharing Order: an order that a pension fund should be divided in percentages stipulated by the court creating a new pension fund in favour of the recipient.
- Clean Break: a financial arrangement where it is agreed or ordered that the husband and wife will make no further financial claims against each other for capital or maintenance.
- Disclosure: whether or not an agreement about Financial Provision has been reached. All the income, assets and liabilities of both parties must be disclosed and values agreed or proved.
- Application for a Financial Order: if there is a failure by one party to make full disclosure, or it is not possible to reach sensible agreement, an application to the court can be made at any time with a view to resolving the financial claims between the respective spouses. This process will involve the completion of certain legal documents procedures and court hearings.
- Form A: the form which begins the application for a Financial Order and which results in the court setting the timetable.
- Form E: formal disclosure of the assets, income etc. of each party in the standard form required by the court.
- First Directions Appointment (FDA): the lawyers must identify the issues and deal with the need for any further questions to be raised or valuations to be obtained. The court will then make the appropriate orders at the First Directions Appointment (FDA).
- Financial Dispute Resolution (FDR): the court lists the matter for a court-assisted mediation known as a Financial Dispute Resolution (FDR) hearing. The District Judge listens to each

party's case and gives an indication as to an appropriate division. The parties are given time to talk at court to see if the matter can be agreed on that day. If agreement is reached it can be recorded by way of a Consent Order at the court. If no agreement is reached, then the judge lists the matter for a final hearing.

- **Final Hearing:** A different District Judge to the one who heard the Financial Dispute Resolution (FDR) will hear the case in full and listen to the evidence of the parties, which includes the disclosure previously submitted, and the Judge will then decide on the division of the assets between the parties, making an Order on that day.

To recap, this is just a selection of the legal divorce terms and jargon, which I most commonly came across during my divorce years. Ask your lawyer to explain their meaning, when the terms are used, and in particularly the context of the terms use.

The majority of these terms fall into the following two procedures:

1. Divorce Procedure.
2. Financial Settlement.

However – be prepared. In my own view, I found the procedures onerous, expensive and time-consuming. The procedures require you to search through files, PCs, cupboards, storage boxes, the loft, the garage and even the garden shed; you will be surprised where you put things over the years, particularly if you've moved house a few times. It is important and very helpful to have all the facts and figures to hand; this is where your earlier research and library of evidence helps. In your own interest, it is well worth carrying out a detailed, almost forensic, fact-finding mission as part of your early preparation and research, this may not only give you a competitive advantage over the other side, it also saves you scurrying around at the last minute to meet legal deadlines. Preparing and planning ahead not only provides you with control and confidence, it also reduces the risk of overlooking or omitting important information, which may be used in court at a later date; meticulously, check and double check your facts and figures.

Throughout the process of creating, developing and implementing the divorce strategy it again goes without saying that full compliance with legal rules and the judicial system must be followed. The following two legal procedures provide a guide to the legal processes and framework, which must be complied with under the clear guidance of your lawyer and the courts. Again, ensure that your lawyer explains each stage of the procedure, which forms to complete and how to do so, also what you can and cannot do. Personally – as touched on a little earlier – I discovered the DMBO process did complement and was helpful when progressing through both the divorce and financial settlement procedures. My legal team did describe my financial arrangements as 'complex'; however they further described me as being organised and competent in court, which I took as an endorsement of the DMBO process. I found the DMBO particularly helpful to the divorce and financial procedures in the following areas:

1.   Having to hand the relevant information to support my reasons for divorce and counter the arguments made by the other side.
2.   Being able to pay for the two procedures from the free-cash generated through household savings and tight cost control.
3.   Setting objectives, direction and managing financial expectations.
4.   Organisation and preparation provided confidence, control and improved chance of success.
5.   Top priority and consideration for my daughter.

The particulars of the divorce process will vary from case to case, but these following charts should give you a good idea of the divorce procedure in England and Wales. On balance, I found the Divorce Procedure a much quicker and simpler process from start to finish than the Financial Settlement Procedure; despite my serving a divorce cross-petition. The overall Divorce Procedure took around three months to complete. You will know when you are nearing the completion of the Divorce Procedure when the decree nisi is pronounced in court. It wasn't necessary for myself or my ex-spouse to attend court when the decree nisi was pronounced. Six weeks after the decree nisi was pronounced the petitioner (my ex-spouse) applied for the decree to be made absolute. Our marriage was now over; the next step was the Financial Settlement, which took nearly five years to complete.

Referring to the previous paragraph and my earlier point; divorce processes and procedures can be onerous, costly and time-consuming. In my opinion, this is one area that could be improved and modernised by making the procedure much more efficient, with the use of digital technology. The processes and systems could become far more streamlined to reduce cost and time. In my view, I would imagine the procedures have been in place for many years, and over the passage of time new and relevant technologies could have been introduced to help improve the divorce processes. On many occasions it felt like it was a conveyor belt moving at a snail's pace. One example – the system is largely paper and post driven, which could be replaced by the online completion of forms and communication; access to online documents could only be gained through a unique and safe username and password. Further, it did cross my mind, what if there was a postal dispute or regularly happens important documents and information become delayed or lost in the post? The unscrupulous spouse could blame their failure to complete or send an important document by saying "it must have been lost in the post"; I've heard that excuse before.

Sending confidential documents by traditional post is potentially a security risk. I have experienced circumstances, where the law firm packed (sorry, shoe-horned) a bundle of divorce documents into a standard small envelope, which, due to lack of care in the postal system, burst open in postal transit, arriving at my home address with the confidential documents almost hanging out of the envelope. On a further occasion a law firm posted a large bundle of documents in a large envelope, which was too big to post through a standard letter box; hence the postman left the large bundle of confidential documents on my doorstep, exposed to climate elements, also – more of a concern – open to the risk of theft from my doorstep.

During the procedures, some lawyers can set unrealistic deadlines of days rather than weeks in an attempt to pressure on you, without consideration for postal time and possible delays. To overcome all of these problems; replacing traditional postal systems with online completion of correspondence, forms and communication would be more secure, through a unique and safe username and password. Further, online communication would be quicker than traditional post and avoid the risk of loss of documents or postal disputes. One day the divorce process may become completely paperless.

A further procedural area that I genuinely struggled with was the duplication of some work and cost between lawyers and barristers. If both were attending a joint counsel meeting with me, in advance, I would agree to pay one set of fees or a reduced combined fixed fee. Prior to any joint meetings with your own lawyer and barrister; ask your lawyer to explain their respective roles. This helps your understanding and avoids any complications or surprises when the legal bill arrives.

It was Confucius who said:

> *"Life is really simple, but we insist on making it complicated."*[75]

---

[75] Brainy Quote http://www.brainyquote.com/quotes/quotes/c/confucius104563.html accessed 27th April 2016

1. The Divorce Procedure

Diagram 7

Step 1 • 'Divorce Petition' issued by the petitioner

2 • Court sends the matrimonial order application to the respondent

3 • Court sends copy of the acknowledgement of service to the petitioner

4 • District judge considers the 'Divorce Petition'. If grounds are accepted, the petition gets listed in the judge's list for pronouncement of the 'Decree Nisi'

5 • The 'Decree Nisi' is pronounced

6 • The petitioner can apply for the 'Decree Absolute' after a minimum wait of six weeks

7 • The petitioner applies for the 'Decree Absolute'

8 • Application granted

9 • The 'Decree Absolute' is issued

2. The Financial Settlement Procedure

Diagram 8

Step 1 • 'Form A' completed by both parties, filed and served to start the court process

2 • The court sets the date for the first directions appointment called the 'FDA'
• It also sets dates for the filing and exchange of 'Form E'

3 • File and exchange 'Form E'

4 • FDA documents completed by both parties filed and served ; including a concise statement of issues along with a chronology of key facts, dates and questionnaire

5 • 'Form H ' provides an estimate of costs, which is filed by both parties before the court hearing

6 • The FDA at court can be combined with FDR ,if both parties agree. The court directs which questions should be answered also what expert valuations and evidence should be taken

7 • Preparation for the FDR hearing by answering questionnaires ; obtain valuation/expert evidence and file proposals for a financial settlement

8 • FDR hearing ; this is a without prejudice hearing at which the judge will try to assist a financial settlement

9 • Preparation for final hearing. If there is no settlement at the FDR, the judge will give directions and set the case down for a final hearing

10 • Final hearing ; the court will listen to evidence from all parties, grant final orders and give reasons

To reiterate, the above procedures are a widely available 'layman's guide' to steps to both divorce and financial settlements; each individual divorce case is different and may follow an alternative route, depending changing circumstances.

There is plenty of free divorce procedural information out there; an increasing amount of help is available online. It is important to filter out and prioritise the information, to identify which is relevant to your individual divorce case and what will help and make a difference to your financial settlement. At the end of my book, I have drawn up a list of organisation names, contact details and websites of people who I found most useful during my divorce years. In addition, there are dozens of law firms who provide plenty of preliminary online advice 'free of charge'. Take time to research them, this is also a useful starting point when beginning due-diligence on law firms, and selecting the right law firm and lawyer that meets your needs; more about selecting your lawyer in a later chapter.

Returning to research undertaken online; the *Daily Mail* reports flirting online is breaking up marriages even though two people chatting online may never meet. According to counselling organisations in the United States, chat rooms are the fastest-rising cause of relationship breakdowns.[76] A similar trend can be seen in Britain, where increasing numbers of people are seeking help to save their marriages by refraining from the use of chat rooms and social media. However, and as touched on earlier, social media can be a helpful research tool. Social media platforms have become important sources of data and information in divorce cases. Search through historic Twitter feeds and Facebook postings, you could find some valuable pieces of information, which could provide compelling evidence. The most common reason given seemed to be people having inappropriate sexual chats with people they were not supposed to.

The *Telegraph* reported Facebook is being cited in almost one in five of online divorce petitions.[77] The social networking site, which connects old

---

[76] Mail Online 'Chat room cheats breaking up marriages' publication data NA
http://www.dailymail.co.uk/news/article-189198
[77] The Telegraph online 21 December 2009 www.telegraph.co.uk/technology/facebook/6857918

friends and allows users to make new ones online, is being blamed for an increasing number of marital breakdowns. The infidelity websites ashley-madison.com, illicitencounters.com and affairsexconnect.com have all been launched and designed for people looking to have an extramarital affair; these three websites have a staggering combined membership of 55 million people; potentially, an awful lot of divorce cases in waiting. Flirty emails and messages found on Facebook pages are increasingly being cited as evidence of unreasonable behaviour. Probably one of the most surprising discoveries on Facebook was a couple who had separated, however they were not divorced. One of their children, whilst using Facebook came across wedding pictures of her father marrying another woman posted on the social media site, before their divorce had been completed. The offending bigamist was convicted and ordered to carry out a 200-hour community order.[78.]

Facebook has more than 800 million active users, on average they upload 250 million pictures a day to the site.[79.] There are no estimates on how many of those pictures people regret uploading, but you can be sure it's more than a few. Quick photos or 'selfies' taken on a smartphone after a few too many drinks, showing people engaged in dangerous or even illegal behaviour – anyone who's been on Facebook for a while has seen those images. But it's not just the pictures that can get you in trouble; maybe you've testified in court you were in one place at a particular day and time, but your Facebook page shows you checked in to a hotel elsewhere.

However, not to miss a commercial opportunity, computer firms have already cashed in by developing software allowing suspicious spouses to electronically spy on someone's online activities; although legality and use of such software has come under legal scrutiny. I would suggest you check the legal position first, prior to pursuing such routes of investigation.

[78.] The Mirror 'I found out my husband was married to another woman when I saw pictures on Facebook' 13 February 2015 – http://www.mirror.co.uk/news/real-life-stories/found-out-husband-married-another-5157899

[79.] Data provided by Statista portal – note data quoted at the time of writing; statistics will change. Visit http://www.statista.com/statistics/264810/number-of-monthly-active-facebook-users-worldwide for latest data

Interestingly *The Telegraph* further reports that a study has found that couples who met online are three times more likely to divorce than those who met face-to-face.[80.] Online daters are also 28% more likely to split from their partners within the first year, new figures from Michigan State University in the US suggest. A study of more than 4,000 couples found that relationships were far more stable if couples met in traditional ways such as introductions by friends or through work, hobbies or socialising. Couples who meet online are also less likely to get married and generally have a poorer relationship quality that those who met offline.

Internet revenge, the risk of being online late at night full of emotion after a couple of glasses of wine – you maybe a little worse for wear and decide to air personal marital grievances to all of your social media connections, peers and followers. If you are seeking 'big time' vengeance by informing your spouse's friends, acquaintances and even work colleagues and superiors of your grievances, you may regret it the following morning when the effects of the alcohol have worn off.

Returning to offline information and research; dig out and dust off the cobwebs from personal documents dating back to your marriage, particularly documents which relate to financial matters such as mortgage, investments, employment, pensions even criminal records. Such documents may well provide useful collateral and legal evidence at a later date. Make copies of all documents (tax returns, bank statements, credit card bills, mortgage statements, loan agreements, etc.) Your spouse's tax returns are probably the most valuable piece of financial information you will need, especially if he or she is the major breadwinner in the relationship. Make sure you have a copy of this document and preferably the last three years if possible, prior to taking action. In addition, keep copies of all correspondence including text messages sent to and from your spouse. Make notes, dates and times of telephone conversations and face to face meetings, better still, record all conversations. Create and organise a filing system, where you are able to quickly locate and refer to relevant documents. However, ensure your filing system is kept under lock and key.

[80.] The Telegraph online 26 September 2014 'Couples who met online are three times more likely to divorce' www.telegraph.co.uk/news/science/science-news/11124140

Forensically track down and document marital assets. You need to know where every penny is, including bank accounts, stocks, bonds, jewellery, etc. An important point to again make at this early stage – do not try to hide your assets or use 'dirty tricks', it's naïve and will cost you in the long-run. A judge will not look on such moves favourably, and it could tarnish your character in front of him or her; you could even end up in prison. It is my understanding that documents obtained illegally cannot be read or used by your lawyer; penalties or even custodial proceedings can be imposed. Remember, keep the moral high ground and ensure nothing comes back 'to haunt you' at a later date.

Contact the Inland Revenue or a tax adviser to check on any tax implications of your divorce, also the possible tax considerations of your DMBO. One of the key areas to obtain advice would be regarding Capital Gains Tax, particularly where this involves the transfer of assets either between the parties ie. transfer of property, shares etc., or financial transfers to third parties to raise funds to possibly pay lump sum orders. Tax liabilities may arise and capital gains tax could be payable on the transfer of assets. It is also wise to obtain tax advice after the divorce, particularly when filing your tax returns.

Decide who to trust and confide in; during this early stage, keep your discussions limited to one or two people you can trust and who have no relationship or communication with your ex-spouse. Be mindful and vigilant in you are meeting a trusted friend in a public place, such as the local pub or coffee shop, you never know who maybe within listening distance of your conversation. Likewise, if you are using your mobile phone in a public place you can be easily overheard by people around you. Friends and relatives will offer advice, which you are always grateful for. However, you must be your own person with a clear vision and set of goals and direction in your heart – it's your future life.

> *"Your vision will become clear only when you look into your own heart… Who looks outside, dreams. Who looks inside, awakens."*[81]
>
> Carl Jung

[81.] Carl Jung and in 'Attract your Dreams' by Amber Dayva

You may carry out your own private investigations; there are organisations that can carry out private investigations on your behalf, however they can be expensive. A survey carried out by Grant Thornton of 100 leading law firms found 49% of divorces in 2006 came after one partner had hired a private detective to look for evidence of adultery by the other. The survey found that more women than men hired private investigators.[82] Rather than run the expense of hiring a private investigator, I once carried out my own undercover investigations to obtain divorce related information. I made a clandestine telephone call, masquerading as a company carrying out a survey on proposed new bus routes in the city area. The 'telephone survey' lasted around ten minutes, which was authenticated with a list of carefully prepared and worded questions, which would provide me with the required informa-tion. I guess I must have been convincing as the person whom I was phoning didn't recognise my voice, and answered the complete list of questions without any suspicion.

If you are going to undertake your own investigative work, again, be sure you know what is legal and not and what is admissible in court. On another occasion, I did find myself at risk of a court injunction following my personal investigation. Therefore, check how far your investigations can go – you could end up on the wrong side of the law. A recent, high profile legal case has currently highlighted the dos and don'ts of carrying out your own financial detective work once divorce proceedings have been initiated. If you are not careful, you could end up hindering, not helping, your case.

In the US, ABA Journal reported that a former California divorce lawyer who admitted bugging a car was sentenced to two years in prison for illegal eavesdropping on her former and estranged husband. The former divorce lawyer was also among the defendants caught up in the so-called 'dirty DUI' scandal which a private investigator hired alluring women to drink with the husbands of divorce clients at bars. The women would then invite the men to follow them in their cars; the police were subsequently called to investigate the DUI scandal.[83]

---

[82] Infidelity Central 'Adultery is the primary reason for divorce' 25 April 2007 – http://infidelitycentral.com/infidelity-insights.php/archive-14/

[83] ABA Journal posted 4 February 2014 'Divorce lawyer admitted bugging car is sentenced for illegal eaves dropping' www.abajournal.com/news/article/divorce_lawyer_who_admitted_bugging_car_is_sentenced_for_illegal_eavesdropp

It is my understanding that generally in divorce cases, a spouse has the right to take documents which are easily accessible for example, not under lock and key and make a copy of them providing they return the originals to their owner before appearing in court. A spouse is not allowed to use force to obtain any information or hack into another's computer. There was a case in the US, where the husband used a piece of software to intercept his spouse's emails; the court deemed this as a violation of local law and he was fined a total of $20,000. It is understood that in the UK there is software available which can monitor your spouse's movements, text and email messages and phone calls. It was also recently revealed that members using the Ashley Madison website had fallen victim to 'hackers' with a million email addresses revealed by the 'hackers'; Ashley Madison have nearly 44 million members in total and their tag line is "Life is Short. Have an Affair".[84.] Laws vary by country so check what is legal and what is not. I guess the simple rule was resist using any evidence which could be deemed as illegally accessed or even hacked from an infidelity website.

To refresh on the earlier and more scrupulous point: throughout your research and investigations make detailed and copious notes, dates, and times – you will need to refer to them throughout the coming months and possibly years of the divorce process. Make sure you are prepared, with as much relevant evidence as possible. Even if you think your case will eventually be uncontested, do not under estimate your ex-spouse's potential to make things difficult. As I personally found, what starts out amicable may easily end in a courtroom battle, so make sure you are prepared with relevant and compelling evidence.

Although we will discuss financial planning and budgeting in a later chapter; begin to research additional income streams to earn you extra money; allowing you to supplement your early legal costs. Maybe consider a part-time job or weekend work; if you are living in the marital home it is possible to rent a spare bedroom and take in a lodger. Try to accumulate as much cash reserve as possible before taking legal action and engaging a lawyer. Law firms may require advance payment on account, which can amount to several thousand pounds, they can also require payment at the

---

[84.] The Ashley Madison website www.ashleymadison.com accessed 27 April 2016

end of each month. Remember, you need to cover your day to day living costs, mortgage, child costs and now find extra cash to pay your lawyer. In some instances, where there were two salaries coming into the marital home, instantly that becomes only one, but the same bills still need to be paid.

Any research or divorce plans should be kept in a very secure environment, particularly if your spouse has access to the marital home. Better still, keep all divorce-related documents, research and plans at a safe and secure location well away from the marital home. During the early years of my divorce, my ex-spouse did legitimately have free access to the marital home and could make random visits when she knew I wouldn't be at the home for a period of time. First, when absent from the marital home, I would ensure all divorce-related documents were removed; second, knowing my ex-spouse legitimately had free access to all parts of the home I placed thin pieces of discretely hidden cotton inside each internal door, including cupboard doors. This enabled me to check on my return home, if any doors had been opened in my absence. I did think of placing false documents and information at the marital home, which would act as a decoy – however, I maintained my policy of keeping the moral high ground.

The very early stages of a divorce and certainly the future months and years can be stressful. There are, again, many websites providing advice and counselling; friends and relatives offer advice, which you are always grateful for. However, we are individuals and have differing and preferred ways of dealing with stress and anxiety. One stress management programme doesn't fit all; if needed, create your own stress management plan that suits you, your lifestyle and your needs; your own GP maybe able to provide guidance and help. My own stress management plan was to focus on my desires and ambitions post-divorce and play lots of squash, regular visits to the gym and to travel. To further help with managing stress; I had a 5-point, 10-year plan of opportunity – we will be able to discuss the 10-year plan in much more detail in the final chapters.

My 5-point, 10-year plan was:

1. Build a successful business.
2. Continue to travel the world.
3. Write two books.
4. Maintain a high level of personal fitness.
5. Own an international holiday home.

> *"When written in Chinese, the word 'crisis' is composed of two characters. One represents danger and the other represents opportunity."*[85.]
>
> *John F. Kennedy*

In summary, my key learning from carrying out divorce research was:

- Research allows you to remain rational, targeted and objective throughout the divorce months and years.
- Research provides you with compelling and factual evidence; it gives you a competitive advantage.
- It begins to identify and focus on what will make a difference to your financial settlement; helping you to achieve the best possible outcome.
- Research provides the foundation for the direction you wish to follow.
- Research provides you with control and assurance.
- Research provides collateral and confidence when negotiating your financial settlement.
- Research is ongoing and seamless throughout your divorce; new information will continually surface and be helpful to make your case even more compelling and secure a quality financial settlement.
- From research; it is paramount to keep records and notes of documents, findings, conversations and correspondence.
- Set priorities, which again allows you to focus on achieving a favourable financial settlement.

[85.] Brainy Quote – http://www.brainyquote.com/quotes/quotes/j/johnfkenn103820.html accessed 27th April 2016

- Research should include ways to enhance your income, to not only cover your legal expenses, but also improve your long-term financial returns post-divorce.
- Research will help you find solutions, new ideas and even innovation.

It was Albert Einstein who said:

> *"Imagination is the highest form of research."*

And:

> *"If we knew what we were doing, it would not be called research, would it?"*

From my research, I did discover a few more interesting findings:

- One in eight separated women (12%) said they have no pension/savings plans as they were relying on their partner to fund their retirement.[86]
- One in ten respondents (10%) said they would be significantly worse off in their retirement as a result of their break up.[87]
- More than a third (36%) of respondents said they would prefer to remain single following their break-up, but 25% would marry (again).[88]
- Two thirds (66%) of separating couples had joint finances: four in ten of these shared all finances, while the remaining six in ten had some shared and some separate.[89]

---

[86] Aviva "Cost of divorce reaches £44,000 for couples" 19 August 2014 – http://www.aviva.co.uk/media-centre/story/17337/cost-of-divorce-reaches-44000-for-uk-couples/

[87] Aviva "Cost of divorce reaches £44,000 for couples" 19 August 2014 http://www.aviva.co.uk/media-centre/story/17337/cost-of-divorce-reaches-44000-for-uk-couples/

[88] Aviva "Cost of divorce reaches £44,000 for couples" 19 August 2014 http://www.aviva.co.uk/media-centre/story/17337/cost-of-divorce-reaches-44000-for-uk-couples/

[89] Aviva "Cost of divorce reaches £44,000 for couples" 19 August 2014 http://www.aviva.co.uk/media-centre/story/17337/cost-of-divorce-reaches-44000-for-uk-couples/

- One in five women took out protection insurance (e.g. life cover) after separating, compared to one in ten men, but a quarter of respondents said they didn't have life cover following the split (25%).[90]

Source: Aviva

Preparing your divorce plan

It was Benjamin Franklin who said:

"By failing to prepare, you are preparing to fail."[91]

Having completed the divorce research, we should now have a foundation of true facts and evidence on which to build the divorce plan.

The first step of the divorce plan is to set a positive vision of how you want your new and changed life to be after divorce. Take plenty of time to think it through and write it down in a single sentence; it may need several attempts. Your vision should set personal goals and inspire you to achieve them; it should be simple and memorable, representing not only what you are setting to achieve, but as a passionate statement of how people see you, and to know your values and beliefs. Your vision needs to be inspiring, motivating and different.

---

[90] Data source provided by Aviva "Cost of divorce reaches £44,000 for couples" 19 August 2014 http://www.aviva.co.uk/media-centre/story/17337/cost-of-divorce-reaches-44000-for-uk-couples/

[91] Brainy Quote http://www.brainyquote.com/quotes/quotes/b/benjaminfr138217.html accessed 27th April 2016

My own vision is:

"To achieve wealth, success and fulfilment, which I can share and spend passionately with my loved ones."

Once you have set your personal vision of the future; the next step is to conduct the 'divorce position assessment'. This is to establish where you are right now; think of it as putting a stake in the ground, a starting point for the future ahead. However, first scrutinise your ex-spouse's current position; assessing the circumstances, which are likely to have an impact on the outcome of the divorce financial settlement.

As part of your position assessment of your ex-spouse, consider the following:

1. Employment.
2. Cash in the bank.
3. Access to credit.
4. Access to finance i.e., overdraft, bank loans, credit cards.
5. Mortgage and debts.
6. Personal assets i.e., cars, jewellery.
7. Pensions.
8. Property net equity.
9. Length in marriage.
10. Time until retirement.
11. Current and future income.
12. Children's educational needs and fees.
13. Financial needs, responsibilities and obligations.
14. Typical monthly expenditure, during and after marriage.
15. Lifestyle needs i.e., holidays and house style, standard of living.
16. Family needs.
17. Age.
18. Earning capacity.
19. Co-habitation after separation.
20. Contribution to the home and who's the breadwinner.
21. Matrimonial vs. non matrimonial assets i.e., inheritance after separation.

Second step, now carry out the same 'position assessment' on yourself. Use the same, like for like, 21 key considerations as for your spouse. And the third step, using the information from steps one and two, create a master matrix or excel spreadsheet, which compares your own position vs. your spouse. See diagram 9:

Position Assessment Matrix – Strengths vs. Weaknesses

Diagram 9

	My Spouse	Strength	Weakness	Myself	Strength	Weakness
Employment						
Cash in the bank						
Access to credit						
Access to finance ie.overdraft, bank loans, credit cards						
Mortgage and debts						
Personal assets ie cars, jewellery						
Pensions						
Property net equity						
Length in marriage						
Time to retirement						
Current income						
Children's educational needs and fees						
Financial needs, responsibilities and obligations						
Typical monthly expenditure during marriage						
Lifestyle needs ie. holidays and house style, standard of living						
Age						
Earning capacity						
Co-habitation after separation						
Contribution to the home and who's the breadwinner						
Matrimonial vs. non matrimonial assets ie. inheritance after separation						

The penultimate step, is to use the position assessment to identify each of your top five respective strengths and weaknesses, which would most likely impact on the divorce financial settlement – prioritising your top five strengths and weaknesses may uncover a major flaw, an 'achilles heel', which may have a major impact on the outcome of your divorce. Finally, the fifth step; using your own position assessment set five key divorce financial settlement objectives that you wish to achieve as an outcome. As I touched on earlier, if you are able to establish your spouse's divorce objectives or at least his or her expectations it will serve as a very useful comparison to confirm your respective desires and wishes. In addition, the comparison serves as a useful analysis and provides information when it comes to negotiation and possible trade-offs and incentives.

As a result of my own and ex-spouse's 'divorce position assessment'; my five financial settlement objectives were:

1. Retain the marital home.
2. Retain all contents of the marital home.
3. Secure 50% of all pension funds.
4. Achieve a 'clean break' settlement.
5. Retain 50% of financial investments (high interest accounts, endowments, stocks and shares).

As a footnote; these were my own objectives, your own objectives may very well differ by choice and circumstances.

> *"It's a funny thing about life; if you refuse to accept anything but the best, you very often get it."[92]*
>
> Somerset Maugham

My rationales and priorities for each settlement objective were:

1. Keep the marital home – priority number one

I assessed the historical increase in value of the marital home since purchase in 2001, which was 118%. Therefore, there was substantial equity in the property. If I needed to re-mortgage the property, the net equity combined with prevailing low interest rates could provide me with a lump sum buy-out to offer my ex-spouse as a financial settlement, placing me in a strong position to keep the property. My next step was to be comfortable that the marital home would be a good future investment and continue to appreciate in value. At the time, property prices were forecast to increase on average 8% per year over the next 10 years 2010–2020. On this basis, allowing for inflation, I was assured that future property would continue to be a good investment. Further, at the time of my divorce, house prices had actually dropped the previous years, following the 2008 recession. It was a financially beneficial moment

---

[92] Brainy Quote – http://www.brainyquote.com/quotes/quotes/w/wsomerset110037.html accessed 27th April 2016

in time to make a lump sum buy-out offer to my ex-spouse to acquire her share in the marital home. My decision was underpinned by the following data published by the Office for National Statistics 'Index Values and % House Price Index';[93] considering the two sets of trends and forecasts, overall and looking at the 'big picture' indicators were positive. An important caveat at this point; although it was forecast that the UK property market would be a good investment – I was fully aware that economic conditions can and will change. We will be discussing later how volatile market conditions can cause risk and uncertainty; for example the UK's exit from the European Union and how this may impact on your divorce strategy and final financial settlement.

Diagram 10

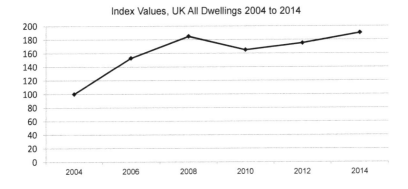

Index Values, UK All Dwellings 2004 to 2014

Source: ONS

---

[93] Office for National Statistics 'House price index statistical bulletins. 12 April 2016 www.ons.gov.uk/economy/inflationandpriceindices/bulletins/housepriceindex/previous Releases

Diagram 11

% House Price Index

Proposed timing of the lump sum
buy-out offer late 2010, when house
prices were relatively low.

Source: ONS

In 2014, after the buy-out, the ONS reported the following:

- UK house prices increased by 9.1% in the year to February 2014, up from 6.8% in the year to January 2014.
- House price annual inflation grew by 9.7% in England, 5.3% in Wales, 2.4% in Scotland and 2.8% in Northern Ireland.
- House price growth is increasing strongly across most parts of the UK, with prices in London again showing the highest growth.
- In February 2014, prices paid by first-time buyers were 10.5% higher on average than in February 2013. For owner-occupiers (existing owners), prices increased by 8.6% for the same period.[94]

---

[94] The Office for National Statistics 'House price index Statical bulletins. 12 April 2016 www.ons.gov.uk/economy/inflationandpriceindices/bulletins/housepriceindex/previous Releases

In addition to the positive figures produced by the ONS; the UK government had introduced various schemes to help first-time property buyers, which would stimulate further growth in the property market.

With the Help to Buy Equity Loan Scheme; [95.] the government provided £9.7 billion of additional investment to help people into home ownership. The Help to Buy Equity Loan was available to all those who wished to own a new build home that had a 5% deposit.

The Help to Buy Mortgage Guarantee Scheme:

The UK government report that "The scheme was designed to help people to buy a newly built home or an existing property with a deposit of only 5% of the purchase price. The scheme was open for loans to existing home-owners, as well as first-time buyers. The loans were available on new and existing houses with a value of up to £600,000. The Help to Buy Mortgage Guarantee Scheme[96.] would increase the supply of high loan-to-value mortgages by offering a government guarantee to lenders who provide mortgages to people with a deposit of between 5% and 20%."

At the time, the combination of positive property forecasts, and regional trends published by the ONS and leading estate agent Savills, plus government financial assistance for the housing market has without doubt confirmed my number one priority to retain the marital home had been the right decision. In addition, the economics of supply and demand would further support the growth in the UK property market. Demand refers to how much of a product or service is desired by buyers; in the case of the UK property market it was clear for some time that housing supply is not keeping up with demand. Reasons for rising demand include improved life-expectancy rates and a growing number of one-person households. Supply represents how much the market can offer; the UK property market was being under-supplied by approximately 100,000 new houses every year.

[95.] Data source provided the UK government 'Affordable Homes Scheme' 7 October 2015 www.gov.uk/affordable-home-ownership-schemes/help-to-buy-equity-loans
[96.] The UK government 'Affordable Homes Scheme' 7 October 2015
www.gov.uk/affordable-home-ownership-schemes/help-to-buy-mortgage-guarantees

The quantity supplied refers to the amount of a certain good producers are willing and able to supply when receiving a certain price. The correlation between price and how much of goods or services is supplied to the market is known as the supply relationship. Price, therefore, is a reflection of supply and demand. Again, in the case of the UK property market; in 2007 the government set a target of increasing the supply of housing to 240,000 additional homes per year by 2016 to meet demand. This target has not been met; hence in the current UK market demand continues to outstrip supply, which contributes to increasing house prices.

A report relating to property supply and demand by House Ladder in early 2016 said:

"Demand by buyers and landlords to buy property is outstripping the supply which is now at a 14-year low. There has also been a massive increase in registered buyers with 435 registered per branch and increase of 21% since December 2015. With lack of property supply and increased demand from buyers, house prices are continuing to rise."[97]

More recently, the UK government has introduced major pension reforms, which allows easier access to your pension and the ability to withdraw your pension as a lump sum. Latest research indicates that some pension holders are taking advantage of the government reforms by withdrawing their pensions to invest in the UK property market, which is a further factor that will help and support future investment and growth. In the first ten weeks since the pension reforms were implemented around 60,000 people have taken part of their pension as cash, the government announced. The Chancellor of the Exchequer told the House of Commons that more than £1 billion has been withdrawn from pension funds in the first ten weeks since introduction on the 6th April 2015. The government offer free and impartial advice to anyone considering withdrawing their pensions, including a 45-minute face to face or telephone meeting.[98]

---

[97] Houseladder.co.uk news ' Demand by landlords to buy properties surges' 12 January 2016 http://news.houseladder.co.uk/news

[98] Government pension advice website and helpline – 'Pensionwise' https://www.pension wise.gov.uk/

Regional UK House Price Forecasts 2015–2020

Diagram 12

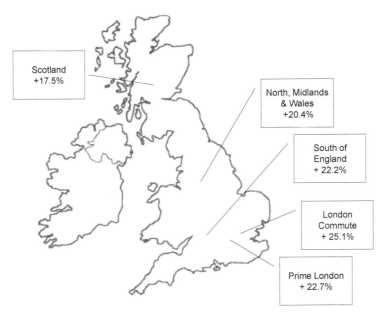

Scotland
+17.5%

North, Midlands
& Wales
+20.4%

South of
England
+ 22.2%

London
Commute
+ 25.1%

Prime London
+ 22.7%

Source: Savills

Savills reports that UK house price growth will be 4% in 2015 and 25.7% overall in the five years to the end of 2018.[99]

There are significant cost savings when buying your spouse's share of the marital home, namely no estate agents fees, removal fees, legal and conveyancing fees, which saved both myself and ex-spouse sale costs of just under £20,000, which is a massive benefit of the DMBO. In addition, there would be further savings on the purchase of a new property namely stamp duty, legal and conveyancing fees, property survey, combined saved an estimated £35,000. In total, by retaining the marital home saved an estimated £55,000, which is a significant amount of money as a result of

---

[99.] Savills UK 'Mainstream Capital Values' November 2015 http://www.savills.co.uk/research/uk/residential-research/forecast-pages/mainstream-capital-values.aspx

the DMBO. Further, I managed to remain in the marital home during what became a protracted divorce process, which in my view placed additional cost pressure on my ex-spouse. My ex-spouse had to find additional finance to rent alternative accommodation, plus utility costs, taxes, insurance and furnishings. These are good reasons to make every attempt to stay in the marital home during the divorce process. Another financial benefit of retaining the marital home – at the time of writing my book, if and when I decided to sell the property, I do not have to pay Capital Gains Tax on the sale value as it is my only home, which I've lived in since the time of purchase in 2001. Retaining the marital home as an investment is one of personal choice; some divorcing couples may choose to sell their home as part of the divorce settlement or sell soon after the settlement.

Retain 100% contents of the marital home – priority number two

As part of the DMBO negotiation, there was a significant cost saving by my not having to replace furniture, electrical items etc. A reasonable pro-portion of the home contents, such as pieces of art had a relative high value and would financially appreciate over the course of time; well worth hanging onto as an investment. Finally, I had a number of inherited heirlooms, which had belonged to my family; these had sentimental value over and above financial value.

Secure 50% of all pension funds – priority number three

Having worked hard and paid into my company pension scheme including AVCs (Additional Voluntary Contributions) for over 20 years my 'pension pot' had a relatively high value. Thinking about retirement years ahead, ask your pension provider to give you an estimate as to what your pension will be worth at retirement age. Also, find out how your pension has been performing over the previous ten years; all useful information to assess the relative value of your pension now and in the future vs. the other assets you are attempting to secure as part of the financial settlement. It is well worth obtaining expert advice in this area. Most pension organisations will provide advice on your pension during the divorce process. Further, and as touched on a little earlier; consider new pension reforms introduced by the UK government. Assess the new options available to you by contacting the government pension helpline called 'Pensionwise'.[100.] The pension changes give you more flexibility and control over your pension savings from the age of 55 years old onwards. Again, it is important to obtain expert advice from your pension provider or an independent pension expert. It is almost certain your pension on retirement will be reduced as a result of divorce. Therefore, it is beneficial to think about ways to supplement your hard earned pension in later years; more about how you are able to achieve this in a later chapter by investing wisely the tax free lump sum element of your pension.

Achieve a 'clean break' settlement – priority number four

The meaning of the term 'clean break': once the 'clean break' has occurred, via a court order neither party has any continuing financial claim on the other. Once a 'clean break' is made the court will not hear any further claims that the spouses have for the duration of the parties' lives and even after death of one or other of the ex-spouses. This type of financial settlement will only put in order the finances of the spouses; your lawyer will be able to offer specific advice here.

Considering my strategy of retaining 100% ownership of the marital home through a negotiated buy-out agreement and retaining 100% ownership of my new 'fledgling' company; it was critical to achieve a 'clean break' agreement. Throughout my divorce process, achieving a 'clean break' agreement was probably one of the few areas which all parties were able to agree on.

[100.] Pensionwise helpline telephone 0800 1383944 – https://www.pensionwise.gov.uk/

Recently, a case was brought before the Supreme Court[101.], reported by a variety of media channels and the courts. A woman won a landmark bid to claim cash from her millionaire ex-husband, 20 years after they divorced. The ex-spouse first took legal action against a successful businessman and founder of a windpower firm. The businessman had previously appealed against his ex-wife on the basis she had lodged the claim too late. But five Supreme Court justices unanimously ruled his ex-wife's case should go before the family court.

The couple separated in the mid-1980s and divorced in 1992. The BBC and other news channels reported, in the mid-1990s the entrepreneur began a business career and went on to become a green energy tycoon after launching his renewable energy company, said to be worth at least £57 million. The ex-wife lodged a claim for 'financial remedy' in 2011, but it was blocked by the Court of Appeal in 2013 before the latest Supreme Court ruling. The entrepreneur's legal costs for the case have left him with a further bill of over £500,000; he also has to pay his ex-wife's legal costs. The total cost of the case is likely to be in excess of £1 million. The judgment is a reminder that divorcing couples who want protection from such claims, even if they have no money at all, should obtain an order from the court at the time of the divorce, in which they both agree that there will be no further financial claims. The *Telegraph* reported divorce lawyers described the ruling in favour of the ex-spouse as 'unprecedented' and said it meant spouses could keep their options open 'indefinitely' before staking a claim. But while some said it could 'open the floodgates' to 'many thousands' of divorces in which financial orders were never finalised being revisited, others said the 'extraordinary circumstances' of the case meant it would have only limited implications.[102.]

The same case further demonstrates of retaining in a safe place all court and legal documents into perpetuity. In the same case no written records of the divorce proceedings were found. The Supreme Court judgement published and released online the following:

[101.] Supreme Court 'Wyatt (Appellant) vs Vince (Respondent)' – judgement date 11 March 2015 https://www.supremecourt.uk/cases/uksc-2013-0186.html
[102.] The Telegraph 'Delayed divorce battle' 11 March 2015 – www.telegraph.co.uk/news/uknews/law-and-order/11463632

"The suit for divorce proceeded in the Sunderland County Court and, within weeks of the grant of the decree absolute on 26 October 1992, the court file was transferred to the Gloucester and Cheltenham County Court. But that court has either destroyed or mislaid the file. The current internal instruction to courts is to retain divorce files for 100 years but to allow them to strip them of most documents (including, oddly, the petition) after 18 years from the date of the final order. The fact that not even a stripped file has been found suggests that the whole file has been mislaid. Furthermore, neither party presently holds any document relating to the divorce proceedings other than the decree absolute."[103]

In 2009, a further case was reported by several media channels and in the public domain involving a husband who became a millionaire after their divorce. The case was successfully referred to the Court of Appeal; however, the judge ruled that the husband was not required to give his ex-spouse any more money. In October 2005; the husband owned 45% of the shares in a private timber company. Early in 2006, the timber company was approached by an international investment company, contemplating a prospective acquisition. However, management accounts demonstrated a pre-tax loss in the timber company. Negotiations came to an end in May 2006. Approximately three months after the divorce settlement was finalised the timber company was sold for more than £3.7 million. The husband's ex-spouse was given permission by the County Court to appeal and return to court to obtain an improved settlement on the basis the company had been sold; termed as a 'new event'. The judgement upheld the husband's case and he was not required to make any further payment to his ex-spouse.

Returning to my divorce settlement objectives;

---

[103] Supreme Court 'Wyatt (Appellant) vs Vince (Respondent)' – judgement date 11 March 2015 https://www.supremecourt.uk/decided-cases/docs/UKSC_2013_0186_Judgment.pdf

My fifth and final priority was to retain 50% of financial investments

Our remaining marital investments were sat in either high interest building society accounts or stocks and shares. Interest rates were at an all-time low and returning very little after taking into account prevailing inflation at that moment in time. Stocks and shares, were linked to endowment policies, again, relatively, the policies had not performed particularly well over the previous ten years. In terms of negotiation collateral, the long-term investment opportunity of money sat in building society accounts and endowments offered relatively small returns compared to higher returns from the property and arts market. Since my financial settlement was reached, bank base rates have remained to date at 0.5%; the best building society savings rates have been around 3%.

A key concern was ensuring that our daughter's university education continued to be financially supported. Achieving her degree would provide the platform for a successful and rewarding career in her years ahead. Our building society investments had been 'ring-fenced' to financially support our daughter through her three years at university.

In summary; my learning from preparing a divorce plan:

- Use your divorce research and legally compliant fact-base as the foundation to build your divorce plan.
- Research and assess the present and future external market conditions, which will impact and make a difference on your divorce financial settlement.
- Market and economic conditions will and can change, which create uncertainty and risk.
- It is important to set a future vision of what you want to achieve post-divorce; this is inspirational and motivates you to accomplish clear goals.
- Analyse yours and your spouse's position through the 'divorce position assessment', the process will help identify respective strengths and weaknesses.

- Set five objectives, which each have a rationale to achieve a quality financial settlement. Setting objectives will provide direction and what you wish to achieve.
- A divorce plan will help keep you on strategy; providing control, confidence and ability to manage your divorce costs and cash-flow.
- The plan will set priorities, which will focus your mind and energy on the best long-term financial returns.
- Divorce proceedings are sometimes like war zones. You need to be prepared for each battle to enable you to win the war. The following quotation from Viscount Montgomery does have certain similarities to the battle of divorce.

"The commander must decide how he will fight the battle before it begins.
He must then decide who he will use the military effort at his disposal to
force the battle to swing the way he wishes it to go; he must make the
enemy dance to his tune from the beginning and not vice versa."[104.]

Viscount Montgomery of Alamein

Freeing Cash-flow and Cost Control – Steps Two to Three

Once you have completed the research part of the model and prepared a divorce plan, the next step is to find free-cash to fund your legal costs, whilst keeping a tight control on day to day living costs. You may be surprised as to how resourceful you can be when legitimately discovering and accumulating free-cash, without heading into debt or borrowing money from friends and family to pay for your divorce.

[104.] Leadership Thoughts – http://www.leadershipnow.com/preparationquotes.html

Diagram 13

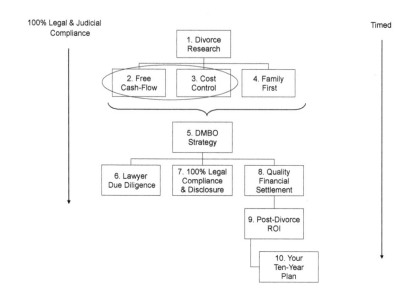

From my own experience, the direct legal cost of divorce can be between £15,000 and £20,000; legal firms can then add VAT, disbursements, expert assessments, court fees, and general expenses i.e., travel, photocopying. Further, add the in-direct costs, such as the loss of a spouse's salary, non-legal costs such as property and asset valuations; and the real cost of divorce can be in excess of £40,000.

The challenge, when having to pay your legal costs at the end of each month, is to find free-cash over and above your day to day living costs. The current mortgage has to be paid, utilities, insurance, food, travel, child costs etc. all have to be paid. Legal costs will be on top of day-to-day living re-quirements; keeping a roof over your head and food on the table. Ideally at this initial stage, avoid borrowing money or extending an overdraft, as this attracts further cost in the way of interest payments.

First, prepare a financial plan which will free up cash to help pay for your divorce. Identify your top five living costs and what percentage proportion of the top five costs make up the total household budget.

Typically, the top five costs can make up to 80% of total outgoing household bills. Analysing your top five costs; there is every chance the number one cost is your current monthly mortgage repayment. There are a number of options to consider here, which could reduce your monthly mortgage re-payments and save several hundreds of pounds a month. The options could be: move to a low-cost fixed rate mortgage scheme with your current lender, or switch to a different but cheaper mortgage provider altogether; you could take a mortgage payment holiday as many mortgage lenders can provide a three-month payment holiday; enquire about the possibilities of switching to an interest only mortgage as oppose to repaying a proportion of the capital each month; call your mortgage adviser to ascertain what is available as a means to reduce your monthly repayments.

Be aware, if you have a joint mortgage with your spouse, you will require his or her agreement to make any changes to your mortgage. The result depends who is paying the monthly mortgage premium; if it is being paid equally between yourself and your spouse any saving that is made would probably need to be shared between you and your spouse. In my own case, I continued to solely pay the monthly mortgage, hence the savings made by switching to an improved low-cost fixed rate mortgage were 100% retained. The savings contributed to my monthly legal costs. The actual savings were significant as it was at a time the Bank of England had reduced and maintained the base interest rate to 0.5%.

A further way of saving cash is to bundle your utility services and get two or more from the same provider, for example utility providers or telecoms and internet providers. It is a very competitive market, where providers want your custom, and offer cash incentives to encourage you to take more than one product from them. We often stick with the same bank, mobile phone network or utilities provider for years. Shop around for the best deal; I estimated by switching providers can save you up to £500 a year. In addition, search online for internet anti-virus providers; some offer basic anti-virus protection free of charge.

Paperless billing may not provide a huge saving, but you could cut your bills by hundreds of pounds by choosing an online-only deal, especially with energy providers. I estimated, you could save on average around £300 a year on your energy bills.

It's worth reviewing all of your insurance policies to see if any changes could be made that could save you money. Contact your incumbent insurer and tell them you are thinking of switching to save money; most insurers will find you savings, if they think they are going to lose your business. If you decide to switch, there are several insurance comparison websites you can use; also check out the insurance companies who do not use the price comparison websites, they prefer to deal direct with customers and not pay a commission to the price comparison site. If you do find an alternative cheaper insurance; first check the level of cover meets your needs, further check the level of excess; some insurance companies offer reduced insurance premium costs, however charge a higher excess if you make a claim. Finally, if you decide to switch insurance providers make the change and open your account online, which many insurers offer a discount by opening online.

Get rid of products you don't need. Review your satellite TV agreement, are you paying for channels you don't need? Mobile phone insurance can also be pointless, as most people are already covered by their home insurance; so don't double up but ditch your cover instead. By cancelling it you can save around £100 a year. Check extended warranties you may have bought on electrical goods, computers etc. cancelling unnecessary warranties can save money. Run a check on any agreements that are now out of contract such as internet broadband or utility suppliers; call the provider and re-negotiate fixed terms at the lowest possible price, for the longest possible period of time.

Switching to a 0% interest on your credit card, depending on your credit card balance could save you a significant amount of money in interest charges. Some credit card companies offer 0% interest deferred payment schemes of up to 18 months, providing you pay the minimum balance each month and you don't exceed your credit limit. Use cash-back credit cards, if you pay off your credit bill in full each month, a cash-back credit card could save money. These offer you money back on purchases in certain shops or on goods such as petrol and food. You can earn even more money from shopping online. Cash-back websites will automatically pay you every time you buy a product or a service from selected retailers, from your weekly groceries to switching your utility provider.

From experience, I estimated by switching to using a water meter, un-metered households can pay up to £60 more per year. If you switch to a meter but then find it doesn't save you money, you can come back off it again; as long as you do so within a year. Install a smart meter, most utility company's supply them free of charge. You will be able to see instantly when you're using the most energy and how much it costs. This means you can adapt your energy use in line with the smart meter information and cut down on waste to provide and make financial savings. Many of us can be throwing money down the drain by not considering how we use the appliances in our home. Simple ways to cut energy bills include not leaving devices on standby and always turning off lights when you leave a room; draught-proofing windows, doors and floorboards, and fixing dripping taps. Other tips include switching to energy-efficient light bulbs and avoiding using high-energy tumble dryers in favour of line-drying your clothes. I use my smart meter to save on energy costs, also to tell me when my daughter was using her TV and hairdryer at the same time; the meter reading would jump up. I would tell my daughter to turn one of the appliances off; making the point how you can dry your hair with a noisy hairdryer and listen to her TV at the same time.

By changing to paying as many bills by direct debit, typically you can save up to £100 per utility bill a year; I now receive a 4% discount when paying a fixed charge monthly direct debit to my electricity supplier. Further, paying by direct debit is one less thing to think about, whilst you are completing copious amounts of forms and paperwork during your divorce.

Shop smarter at the supermarket, consider switching to discount stores, shop around for the best prices and promotions and look to reduce food waste. Use your loyalty card such as Nectar or Clubcard; buying weekly groceries and petrol can accrue to a reasonable amount of points by the end of the year to maybe buy goodies for Christmas. Vouchers and coupons are more valuable than ever: whether it's a discount on the weekly grocery shop, a two-for-one deal at a restaurant or a few quid off at the petrol pump, it's really worth the effort. Scour magazines and newspapers and check out websites; even better, buy some seeds, invest in a few gardening tools and grow your own fruit and vegetables.

If you employ a gardener, window cleaner or dog walker, or use a car wash, consider whether you're paying for a service you don't need; it's a sure-fire way to make some savings. If you live near your colleagues, suggest starting a car pool where you take it in turns to drive each other to work to save on petrol costs.

The expense of gym membership and exercise classes is an easy area to cut back on, by incorporating exercise into your daily routine instead. Go for a run each morning or evening, cycle to work or at home, borrow exercise DVDs from the library.[105.]

As touched on a little earlier, take in a lodger. At the time of writing my book, under the government's 'rent a room' scheme, you don't need to pay tax on the first £4,250 you receive either, which means you could charge up to £354.16 a month without being lumbered with a tax bill. In the Chancellor's 2015 summer budget, he announced that the amount that householders can earn by renting out a room will rise to £7,500 a year tax-free. Remaining with property rental; rent your home to film makers, if you live in an interesting property, you could bag upwards of £1,000 a day renting your home to film and TV companies. The BBC recently completed the filming of a three-part drama called *The Casual Vacancy* – a neighbour of ours rented out his home for filming of the drama. A further opportunity, a business acquaintance rented out excess storage capacity at his warehouse to the same filmmakers to enable them to store their cameras, lighting and rigging during several months of filming.

If you live close to a city centre, train station or football stadium and don't use your parking space or garage, you're sitting on an untapped income. Renting an empty parking place to a commuter or football fan could see you rake in the pounds. Alternatively, some of my local friends rent out their spare bedroom during the Cheltenham Festival; they charge £100 per night per person, including traditional English breakfast and transport to Cheltenham racecourse.

[105.] Moneywise – http://www.moneywise.co.uk/

Sell unwanted items on eBay, who estimate the average British house has about £450 worth of unwanted items that could be sold on the site. If you have old mobile phones, the re-sale price can vary so shop around recently an old iPhone 5 (16Gb) sold for £105.04. Alternatively, after you have cleared out the garage, cupboard and loft storage space; book a pitch at your local car boot sale. The best ones tend to be between April and September, when the weather is fine (worth checking the local forecast first). Typically clothes, tools, CDs and vinyl records, books, perfumes and cosmetics, small electrical items and bric-a-brac all sell well at car boot sales. Sales of vinyl records have increased significantly, recently hitting an 18 year high; sales have leapt from 6.1 million to 9.2 million between 2013 and 2014.[106.] My collection of 1970s and 80s Northern Soul and Tamla Motown vinyl records are collecting dust in the loft at the moment, perhaps they will be finding their way onto eBay shortly.

As gold had increased significantly in price; I paid a visit to my local jeweller, who valued my gold wedding ring at several hundred pounds. I clearly had no use for the ring, therefore after some negotiation with the jeweller we agreed a purchase price. Well-known celebrities have had to sell prize possessions to pay or recover financially from the high cost of divorce. The expense of divorce has already forced the actor John Cleese to sell many of the TV and film props and signed photos. The items he had to sell include a helmet used in the film Monty Python and The Holy Grail, with a sale tag of £999. A 1970 photo which shows the Monty Python stars doing silly walks, sale price of £29.99, and a signed photo of the legendary Fawlty Towers scene in which he plays Basil Fawlty, the hotel owner – the scene shows Cleese thrashing his broken down red Austin car with a tree branch. The British actor even sold his 1987 Bentley Eight, which was bought for £17,100.

When it comes to obtaining valuations on the marital home and assets; shop around and negotiate best prices with valuers. It is a competitive market and valuers will want your business. I recollect receiving my first property valuation cost at £587.50 inc. VAT, which I rejected, eventually, we reduced the cost to £235 inc. VAT; a saving of £352.

[106.] Nielsen 'Thanks to strong sales, vinyl albums are off and spinning' http://www.nielsen.com/us/en/insights/news/2015/thanks-to-strong-sales-vinyl-albums-are-off-and-spinning.html 16th April 2015

Sell your skills, we all have skills and talents why not use these to raise free-cash. If you spent years of your life learning different musical instruments or a foreign language, why not put these skills to better use and offer local lessons at home or at nearby educational establishments. A friend of mine and fellow squash player teaches school children to play the drums; probably not always to the complete acceptance of their parents as he encourages his drumming pupils to practice at home. In addition, and to earn more cash, he plays drums in a local band at pubs and clubs at the weekend.

There are many ways to generate income outside the 9–5 job, which will contribute to paying your legal costs. Utilise your own personal and career skills; consider part-time work at weekends or evenings. Become a mystery shopper – you drop in unannounced in shops and restaurants and rate the experience. After you send in your feedback, you'll be paid for your time and reimbursed for any purchases you made. If you're physically fit and committed enough to sign up, the Army Reserves is always looking for recruits.

Another option to build new income in your spare time is to become an independent utilities distributor. Many discount utility companies seek local independent representatives to win new customers, whether that is your friends, family, neighbours, work colleagues or a personal network of residential and business customers. Distributors are paid a commission for each new customer they win. You can earn around £50 for every new customer, and a regular monthly income based on how much your customers spend on the services the utility company provide to them. You can also receive ongoing training and marketing support. This was an opportunity I took in 2008; representing a London utility company who not only offered energy service, also insurance, telecoms and merchant services. The service and opportunity to create new income was a bit of a 'no-brainer' for me; I had several hundred small business clients who I could immediately offer the utility and telecom services to and subsequently make considerable financial savings, some reduced their utility and telecoms cost by several thousands of pounds. A number of my business clients used the savings to pay my consultancy fees; a definite win-win business deal.

As with my fellow squash player come drummer, use your hobbies to generate extra income. If you are a photographer, selling your work to stock

100

imagery sites can be a fairly painless and financially rewarding experience. If you enjoy gardening, planting, potting or just mowing the lawn, you could help out those less able and make a little money too by offering your services, particularly in the spring and summer. You may be a culinary expert – you could offer your catering or baking skills; local people are willing to pay for a buffet, maybe for a family anniversary or for a show stopping birthday cake. Make sure you're charging enough to cover the cost of the ingredients. Alternatively, if you do not have any immediate hobbies that can earn extra cash, simply offer to tend to local neighbours' pets while they're away. Alternatively, if you're at home during regular working hours, people pay good money to have someone come round to look after their pets while they're out at work. If you are a driver, you could provide transport by becoming an 'Uber' driver – they claim you can earn up to £565 per week extra cash[107].

Once you have established where you are able to free up cash; draw up a financial matrix of savings and extra income and forecast a financial value against each. You may be surprised how much cash could be 'sitting on the table' to help pay your legal expenses. See Diagram 14

Example Savings and Extra Income Analysis

Diagram 14

New Savings	Annual Savings in £	New Income	Annual Income in £
Switch utility suppliers	350	Take in a lodger	4250
Low-interest mortgage	1500	Part-time work	3500
Car insurance	175		
Cancelled warranties	100		
Cancelled satellite TV	460		
Install water/smart meter	140		
Switch to direct debits	125		
Cancel gym membership	500		
Cancel window cleaner	120		
Sell old mobile phones	50		
Sell old DVDs	65		
Food shopping vouchers, promotions, discounts	1300		
	4885		7750
Grand Total – Free Cash	12635		

[107.] Uber 'Make great money driving with Uber' 29 April 2016 https://get.uber.com/cl/uk/

Once you have identified savings and free-cash, create your own personal cash-flow forecast. There are many benefits of doing this; it provides a road map, ensuring that you are able to finance both day to day living costs and your legal bills. It can also pinpoint additional savings in the months ahead. Further, it provides advance warning of potential financial problems during the divorce months or possibly years ahead; giving you enough time to work out solutions to address such financial challenges. See Diagram 15

Example Personal Cash-flow Forecast

Diagram 15

	Jan	Feb	March	April	May	June	July	Aug	Sept	Oct	Nov	Dec
Balance	500	570	515	460	505	550	595	640	685	730	775	820
Salary	2500	2500	2500	2500	2500	2500	2500	2500	2500	2500	2500	2500
Lodger	350	350	350	350	350	350	350	350	350	350	350	350
Part-time Salary	292	292	292	292	292	292	292	292	292	292	292	292
Sale of DVDs	75											
Sale of Cell Phone	50											
Total	3767	3712	3657	3602	3647	3692	3737	3782	3827	3872	3917	3962
Mortgage	640	640	640	640	640	640	640	640	640	640	640	640
Utilities + Fuel	300	300	300	200	200	200	200	200	200	200	200	200
Council Tax	157	157	157	157	157	157	157	157	157	157	157	157
Credit Card	350	350	350	350	350	350	350	350	350	350	350	350
Clothing	100	100	100	100	100	100	100	100	100	100	100	100
Insurance	100	100	100	100	100	100	100	100	100	100	100	100
Food	300	300	300	300	300	300	300	300	300	300	300	300
Miscellaneous	150	150	150	150	150	150	150	150	150	150	150	150
Legal	1100	1100	1100	1100	1100	1100	1100	1100	1100	1100	1100	1100
Total	3197	3197	3197	3097	3097	3097	3097	3097	3097	3097	3097	3097
Balance	570	515	460	505	550	595	640	685	730	775	820	865

The above financial analyses are examples only.

Remaining on the subject of finances a quick reminder; if you haven't already done so, close any joint accounts as soon as possible, such as bank, investment and credit accounts. You do not want to be held responsible for your ex-spouse's purchases or new charges, especially considering that they may be for legal fees for their own lawyer. Be mindful when closing any accounts; usually a creditor will require the account be paid off before it can be closed. It is a good idea when closing joint bank accounts that you keep good records of any money taken from them. If any proceeds are removed, keep a careful account of where the money is placed or how the proceeds are spent. Accurate records will be a big help in court later.

Interestingly, there has been the surge in women's earnings of late; women's careers have now become crucial to household finances. As a result, an increasing number of women will choose to keep their finances independent from their partners. Recent reports and estimates from This is Money.com claim that 7.2 million women are now financially independent.[108] In only 20 years, the proportion of women in relationships who earn more than their partners has soared from seven per cent to 23%. The pay gap still exists, but it is narrowing; as the gap has closed, more women have assumed financial responsibility in their households. Twenty years ago, fewer than 10% of mortgages were taken out by women alone; today, that figure is 23%.

Studies have found that couples with a high-flying wife are more likely to split up; women who become the chief breadwinners in their domestic partnerships are more likely to pay the price with divorce. Researchers admit that the reason is unclear, but it may be that male pride is wounded by not being the biggest earner in the household. Successful women, for their part, may grow to resent a husband who doesn't appear to be pulling his weight. The finding, the result of a 25-year study of more than 2,500 marriages, comes hot on the heels of other research showing that househusbands are prone to affairs.[109]

American researchers studied the marriages and income of more than 2,500 women who married for the first time between 1979 and 2002. They found that those women who consistently made more money than their husbands were up to 38% more likely to divorce than others.

Returning to finding your own free-cash, as touched on a little earlier, the more you and your spouse save on legal fees the more you will be awarded

---

[108] This is Money.co.uk 'Love is a cash divorce' 12 July 2005 www.thisismoney.co.uk/money/saving/article-1591905
[109] This is Money.co.uk 'High earning wives more likely to divorce' 9 September 2010 www.thisismoney.co.uk/money/news/article-1703752

when the divorce is finalised. I carried out an approximate calculation; in my estimated opinion, my ex-spouse's net share of our agreed final financial settlement had been reduced by 22% in order to pay her legal costs. Using the principles of the DMBO and creating a divorce strategy of disciplined cost control and negotiating terms with my lawyer; my net share of the final settlement had only been reduced by just 7.5% after paying my legal costs.

The further benefit of freeing up cash through savings and cost control is that it sets a good habit once the divorce and financial settlement is agreed and complete; you are able to continue to enjoy the benefits of the savings well into the years after your divorce.

A reminder, when negotiating payment terms with your lawyer, propose that your legal fees are interest free and paid when the financial settlement has been agreed and you have received your share of the marital assets. This agreement will help your personal cash-flow by not having to find thousands of pounds at the end of each month to pay your lawyer. Further, keep the pressure on your lawyer to keep costs down. It is pointless generating free-cash through your cost savings and new income, if your lawyer spends your hard earned free-cash in a non-productive way. A good analogy is 'the leaking bucket'; it's no good topping up the bucket with extra cash, if money is leaking through the holes in the bottom of the bucket through non-productive legal costs – the holes need plugging. I was regularly reminding my lawyer to reduce spending and find more efficient methods of saving my money.

See extract from one of the several reminders sent to my lawyer:

> "The matter of costs remains a concern to me, my opinion being, key matters could be negotiated and resolved with a telephone conversation with the other side, which I have suggested in the past, rather than the ping-pong faxes and correspondence we experience and are charged for, which is very frustrating and brings an onerous cost burden! Could I propose that charges are based on issues resolved and results, rather than the number of faxes, telephone calls and letters?"

The financial impact of divorce is also clear from people's behaviour when a relationship breaks down. The insurance company Aviva report that almost a third of couples (29%) said they tried to reach an amicable settlement to save on legal fees. Whilst, one in ten said they effectively separated but continued living together for several months because they couldn't afford to live apart immediately. A further 6% initially put off getting a divorce because of the costs involved.

Interestingly, the research finds that women are more likely to make financial adjustments after separation; women were more likely than men to make lifestyle changes to supplement their income following a separation. One in eight women (13%) said they worked longer hours or took a second job following a break-up, while one in ten who didn't work before the split got a job. Women were also more likely to use short-term fixes to make ends meet after a separation: 27% of newly-single women dipped into savings compared to 16% of men, while 23% relied on credit cards, compared to 14% of men.

The Aviva research also found, four out of ten couples said they were financially worse off following their separation and more than half of couples (53%) took longer than six months to settle financial matters. The typical time to settle was 11.5 months, but one in ten couples (11%) said the process took more than two years. With this in mind, it's perhaps no surprise that 36% of people surveyed said they'd prefer to stay single in the future!

Allowing yourself an affordable treat: the research suggests that four out of ten newly-separated people splash out on items to treat themselves. The research found one in eight people (13%) took a holiday to celebrate their newly-single status at a typical cost of £1,925, while the same (13%) treated themselves to new technology, shelling out an average of £1,292 on gadgets and gizmos.[110.]

[110.] Aviva report 'Cost of divorce reaches £44,000 for UK couples' 19 August 2014 – http://www.aviva.co.uk/media-centre/story/17337

I understand there is a further way in which to reduce your legal costs, and that is to run off and sleep with your divorce lawyer. This would certainly give you an advantage at significantly reduced legal costs; it has been known to happen.

During the five years of my divorce, I took the view that I should ask myself, is this an affordable treat? I had accumulated a significant number of air miles, following my years of corporate international travel. Due to my frequency of long-haul travel, I became a valued customer of British Airways, who rewarded me with a BA Executive Gold Card; this brought many travel benefits, including being able to regularly 'blag' an upgrade to BA first class travel. Fortunately, I was not required to relinquish a share of my BA Air Miles as part of the divorce financial settlement. The exemption, as I saw it, was a small bonus, and caused some annoyance and frustration to the other side, my ex-spouse having enjoyed extensive world travel during our marriage. The other side once described our past lifestyle as 'lavish'. I decided to use the saved air miles for holidays in Hawaii, Paris, San Francisco and Barbados; these well-earned holidays gave me an opportunity to relax, keep my morale up and most importantly gave me some quality thinking and planning time. As touched on a little earlier, the other side did attempt to raise my expenditure over these holidays. My truthful and perfectly legitimate response being the holidays were paid for using British Airways air miles, and at this point the line of questioning came to a swift end.

There was one further small treat I managed to afford myself after separation. Despite my countless attempts to iron my own shirts, I failed miserably having more creases in my shirts after ironing than before. The only answer was to use the services of my local dry cleaner to iron my weekly quota of shirts. However, and on a more productive note, I did manage to master the washing machine, eventually working out how much detergent to use without turning the kitchen into a giant bubble bath, and never to mix coloured and white clothes in the washing machine, unless you want to turn your underpants pink. In addition, and after some practice, I became a champion of bachelor cooking and microwave ready meals. I soon abandoned the traditional oven; I was forever placing a dish in the oven to return a couple of hours later to find it completely cremated – the microwave was much more reliable, safer and quicker. On a number of occasions and in the middle of a game of squash, I would think 'oh shit, I've left the chicken in the oven for over 2 hours'; I'd return home to a blackened and smoking piece of poultry that was only fit for the bin. My little sister did buy me a large red alarm bell to set when cooking; needless to say it was of little use when on the squash court. On a further occasion during my new found bachelorhood I actually managed to poison my date, unintentionally of course. I had invited my new acquaintance for dinner to celebrate New Year in 2008. I prepared a candle-lit dinner for two; first course was oysters and champagne followed by a main course of lamb shank, and to add to the romance I lit an open log fire. The evening was a perfect success; the oysters lived up to their aphrodisiac powers. Until the following morning; we were both struck with a bout of food poisoning, spending most of New Years' Day in the bathroom with a bottle of Imodium. My perfect alibi being the oysters must have been suspect, needless to say for health reasons and medical grounds, I abandoned home entertaining; it was much safer to eat out or stick to ready meals.

On a more positive note, I quickly established the art of supermarket shopping and navigating the checkouts. In the early days of supermarket shopping, I used to tell the female checkout assistant that I was an apprentice shopper and new to the weekly food shop; some offered sympathy, understanding and helped with the technique of opening and apparent science of packing supermarket carrier bags, learning to put the heavy items at the bottom of the bag and packing fresh items, meat and toiletries separately. The next challenge was to work on my technique at the self-serve checkout; the mystery voice telling me 'assistance required, unidentified item in bagging area' or a human assistant would be called by the same mystery voice to confirm that I was over 18 and able to buy a bottle of wine; on the odd occasion and worryingly, I would hear a fellow shopper talking back to the mystery voice. I am still to be convinced whether self-serve checkouts actually speed up shopping or they are another shopping irritation when the mystery voice behind the checkout is constantly saying 'assistance required'.

A somewhat related story; an Egyptian member of the local squash club had recently moved to the UK with his family, he was a sociable guy and a good squash player, for some reason Egypt seems able to turn out good squash players. He would tell the story, whilst back home in Egypt that it was customary to barter for every purchase, including food. Now, on his first visit to his local Tesco store, he arrived at the checkout with a trolley full of food for his family; passing the family shop through the checkout scanner, the assistant presented the bill to which my fellow Egyptian squash player offered cash payment in return for a discount off the total. Suffice to say his attempts at negotiating a discounted bill with the checkout assistant failed miserably and probably narrowly avoided being escorted from the supermarket by a member of store security.

Returning to placing the relative costs of affordable treats in to a UK national context; the *Daily Mail* reports the cost of family breakdown to the country has shot up by more than £10 billion a year since 2009, a government study has found. It put the price to taxpayers in 2015 of clearing up the damage after families fail and looking after the separated adults and children at £47.31 billion. The bill takes in the cost of benefits, health and social care, housing, policing and the courts, and the price of failure in the education system of children hurt by divorce or the parting of their parents.[111.]

Remaining with paying for the cost of divorce; following the UK recession divorce loans have now become a rarity. ThisisMoney.com reports that many banks have scrapped short-term divorce loans since the financial squeeze hit in 2008,[112.] while others are using stringent lending criteria to turn away even wealthy clientele, or charging extraordinarily high interest rates between 11 and 17% a month. Even in London, which has a reputation for being the world's 'divorce capital' it has become very difficult to borrow to cover divorce costs. One divorce law firm has reported a threefold increase in cases of women, who statistically are the lower earners in most marriages, turning to friends and family to fund their divorce as a result. Even women with wealthy partners are being forced to seek handouts just to pay living costs during separation. Other

---

[111.] Mail Online "The £50 billion price of failed families' 13 February 2015 – http://www.dailymail.co.uk/news/article-2953053

[112.] This is Money.co.uk 20 September 2011 – http://www.thisismoney.co.uk/money/cardsloans/article-2039618

borrowers are being forced to sign a contract agreeing to let the bank manage the assets arising from a divorce settlement. Others will only agree to a loan if there is the prospect of cash being split between a couple as well as, or instead of, property; this is to make sure the debt is cleared immediately.

A divorce lawyer, Liz Cowell, a partner at Pannone, said: "Women looking to meet the costs of divorce have been successively squeezed. They have been hardest hit by the withdrawal of litigation loans because they had predominantly relied on them, often having no income or assets of their own. Many find themselves caught in a grey area where they might not be able to persuade their spouses to pay their costs too, don't qualify for legal aid and haven't got the means to afford legal fees themselves. Other family members and friends are increasingly the only sources of money left to turn to." Cowell further said "Even in relatively wealthy couples, a wife may have devoted herself to building a home and been provided with house-keeping by her husband but had little or no income herself."

'No win no fee' arrangements maybe available in certain areas of law; however, they are illegal in family law. As touched on earlier in my book; legal aid has been cut as a means to financially support your legal costs.

It may cross your mind to use a Payday loan; seriously think twice about using these loan companies, who charge in my opinion an unjustified and immoral rate of interest. Taking out such a loan can cause yet further financial problems in the future. Such situations, further underpin the need for a divorce plan, which frees up cash; also the importance of a personal cash-flow forecast, which enables you to manage your finances through the divorce months and years. Also, be aware of loan mis-selling and hidden costs such as financial penalties; the media has recently broadcast several cases of mis-selling, penalties and high-handed tactics used by loan companies. Having such a plan to free up cash, will put you in control and avoid having to take out financial loans at high interest rates or borrow money from family and friends. In addition, having a financial plan and cash-flow forecast avoids your funds drying-up and finding yourself in the dilemma and risk of your lawyer refusing to carry on representing you, until you settle their bill. Although lawyers could use this tactic, it is in both parties' interests to identify any potential financial problems ahead and re-negotiate payment terms. If you do hit cash problems, don't be an ostrich and 'bury your head in the sand' – the problem won't go away and will only end up biting you in the arse.

> *"He behaved like an ostrich and put his head in the sand, thereby exposing his thinking parts."* [113.]
>
> George Carman QC

Family and Children Must Come First – Step Four

The next stage of the process is ensuring your family, and particularly your children's, interests are categorically and unconditionally put first. Divorce can be stressful, sad, and confusing; at any age, your children may feel uncertain or angry at the prospect of parent's divorce.

Diagram 16

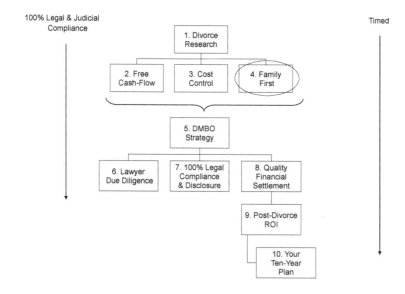

[113.] Brainy Quotes – http://www.brainyquote.com/quotes/quotes/g/georgecarm185927.html accessed 27th April 2016

Family Justice Review Interim Report March 2011

"Every year 500,000 children and adults are involved in the family justice system. They turn to it at times of great stress and conflict. The issues faced by the system are hugely difficult, emotional and important. It deals with the failure of families, of parenting and of relationships. It cannot heal those failures. But it must ensure it promotes the most positive or the least detrimental outcomes possible for all the children and families who need to use it, because the repercussions can have wide-ranging and continuing effects not just for them, but for society more generally." [114.]

Research reported by the *Daily Mail* has found there is no such thing as a good divorce when children are involved.[115.] The analysis of almost 1,000 families found that children suffer when their parents' marriage ends; no matter how amicable the split. The researchers said their finding contradicts the widely-held belief that it is possible to have a 'good divorce' in which the children and adults emerge relatively unscathed.

There are many lines of help and guidance, which can be useful when it comes to family, children and divorce. However, I discovered when divorce arrives we are very much in uncharted waters. Every family situation is unique, requiring a one-to-one bond, deep understanding and chemistry between you and your children during the divorce months and years. My thoughts are that no one is likely to know their children and their emotional needs better than their mum and dad. In my own case, my daughter had just taken her A-levels and was about to head for a new life at university; she was now a young adult. However, and without any doubt and uncon- ditionally, my daughter's interests were always put first; it was important that I made her and my lawyer aware of this from the very beginning; I also made every possible attempt to make the other side aware of the same.

[114.] The Family Justice Review's interim report ; : March 2011 – https://www.gov.uk/ government/uploads/system/uploads/attachment_data/file/217357
[115.] Report by the Mail Online 'A divorce can never be good for children' 2 February 2012 – http://www.dailymail.co.uk/news/article-2095181

Extracts from one of my initial emails; placing my daughter's interests first:

> *"Further to our conversation last week, it has been suggested that we arrange to meet to discuss the most amicable way to proceed."*

> *"It remains my hope along with our daughter that we are able to agree deferring divorce until she completes her university education"*

> *"The protection of my daughter remains my priority. Ensuring that she progresses through her final years of university with minimum distraction and emotional stress"*

A UK report commissioned by Resolution claimed divorce can lead to the children of divided couples achieving poor exam results and turning to drugs to ease their stress.[116.] Almost two thirds of children whose parents divorced said that the break-up affected their GCSEs, while one in eight turned to drugs or alcohol. In the UK around 100,000 children under 16 have to contend with their parents' divorce each year; the report found 25% struggled with homework and 12% skipped lessons either at school, college or university.

During the divorce years, I would regularly visit my daughter, while she was at university; remaining positive and optimistic at all times discussing her future plans and her career after graduation. I would reassure her that her interests came first and she would always receive my 100% support. I would also share and discuss with her my own future plans, how my new company was developing and talk about travel to places like Hawaii and the west coast of the US. Using my remaining British Airways air miles, we both shared travel together; on my daughter's 21st birthday we travelled to San Francisco and Los Angeles, visiting places like Alcatraz, Hollywood and Universal Studios. We also took a holiday together to Sri Lanka. During the times together we kept the old humour and jokes alive, which were a big part of her life when growing up before divorce. We would share past stories from her school days and our travels together to different countries.

[116.] The Telegraph 'Divorce: the devastating cost for children' 24 November 2014 – http://www.telegraph.co.uk/women/sex/divorce/11249446

When telephoning home, whilst I was away on international business; my daughter, who was still in her school days would regularly ask where I was in the world, what the time was and which movies I had watched in-flight, whilst travelling. On return home, using little orange stickers we would plot on a world map, the places where we had visited and share stories from the visit. During her pre-teens, my daughter and her school friends would have regular sleep over at weekends; her school friends would say "I like sleeping over at your house, because your dad tells great stories". Thinking back, I would never read traditional stories to them from a book; I tended to make the storyline up as I went along, commonly known as 'winging it'; if I'm honest, I would never really know how the story would end – hey, isn't life like that anyway.

It was important to remain open, honest and transparent with my daughter about the divorce. Also, keep the family spirit and values as much as possible; our travelling together and wider family events such as Christmas, birthdays and social occasions were very important. Talking about the fond memories held with my mum and step-father as my daughter was growing up in her school years. She would love listening to stories about my childhood and my mischievous nature, the practical jokes and pranks I would play on my younger sisters. It was equally important to listen to her experiences in student life, talking about her friends and how she was feeling. It was important to give and respect my daughter's own personal time and space to adjust and deal with her parents' divorce. I had found over the prior years it was best to ask teenagers what they wanted to do and help them do it. In support, many of her friend's parents had been through divorce, which allowed my daughter to listen to their experiences and gain new friendship and help.

When my daughter came home from university during the holiday period or the occasional weekend, she would meet up with her old high school friends, sometimes she would bring new university friends home. On a Saturday night they would head into town or go clubbing, enjoying a girls' night out together; the inevitable question would be "dad would you mind being the taxi service and drop us off in town at around 8pm", which of course I always obliged. *En route*, there was plenty of banter between us, particularly after the girls had consumed a couple of glasses of Chardonnay.

As referred to earlier in my book, call it serendipity, I discovered a new relationship and bond with my daughter through entering the unknown and uncharted waters of divorce.

> *"Sometimes serendipity is just intention unmasked."*[117]
>
> *Elizabeth Berg*

There were family occasions during the years of divorce such as my mum's funeral and my daughter's graduation, where both myself and ex-spouse attended. When it came to graduation day, I gave my 100% assurance and guarantee that this was my daughter's day and both parents were grown up and mature adults, we were both there to celebrate and enjoy her graduation and the effort, study and success she had achieved during difficult family years. I guess, the only slightly awkward moment was when it came to the graduation family photograph; the photographer kept referring to my ex-spouse, myself and daughter as 'the happy family', obviously he was not to know that we were in the middle of acrimonious divorce proceedings. Again, another important point for family lawyers to show 'emotional intelligence' to their clients; divorcing parents will inevitably meet at family occasions such as school events, funerals, family weddings or graduation ceremonies. This is another good reason why there is a responsibility to the respective lawyers to make every effort using 'emotional intelligence' to keep relationships as amicable and respectful as possible.

A personal discovery when selecting your lawyer; ask if they have children. I found with my lawyer, who had a family, I genuinely felt that there was a further dimension of understanding and support when it came to discussing the needs and choices of your children.

---

[117] Goodreads http://www.goodreads.com/quotes/233714-sometimes-serendipity-is-just-intention-unmasked

In summary there are very strong reasons to unconditionally put your family first:

- Divorce takes you and your children into uncharted waters; every family situation is unique requiring a one to one bond and chemistry between you and your children.
- Uncharted waters will take you to new discoveries and relationships with your children – call it serendipity.
- From the very beginning make your lawyer and your spouse's lawyer aware in no uncertain terms that your family comes first.
- Discuss with your children the positive aspects of the future and share holidays, family occasions; share humour and positive family memories.
- Keep reminding and showing 100% support for your children.
- Remain open, honest and transparent with your children.
- Keep the family spirit and culture alive.
- Provide and respect your children with their own space; I found that they find their own individual ways and mechanisms when dealing with family traumas such as divorce and bereavement.
- Allow their friends to give support and share experiences.

My daughter was over 18 years old and had just begun a new life at university. I look back and think that over just 2 years of her life, she had left school to begin university, her beloved grandmother had passed away and her parents were going through a divorce. She adapted and coped reasonably well; I guess it also prepared and taught her that life ahead will always present uncertainty and the unexpected.

Chapter Two
The Divorce Management Buy-out
(DMBO) Strategy – Step Five

Diagram 17

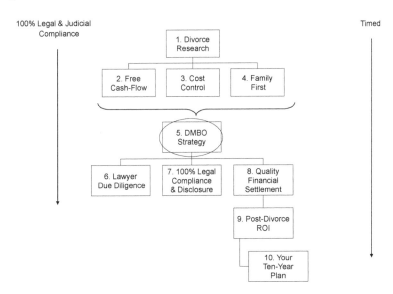

The 'DMBO Strategy' is the plan to direct and achieve your five divorce objectives. The success of your strategy will shape and affect the rest of your life; the strategic decisions and actions taken will be pivotal, defining and will guide your future years. Remember, it is critical to remain focused, positive and determined in order to achieve your objectives. Remind yourself that each objective is a long-term investment, which will not only deliver a healthy financial return but also impact on your future lifestyle and enjoyment; this is motivational and keeps your spirits up.

Taking each objective in turn, create at least two strategic options to achieve the objective. The reason for creating two options? You may discover certain strategies do not provide an acceptable level of financial return or that unforeseen circumstances occur, which impact on your strategy, particularly if matters become hostile between you and your spouse or there maybe a change in external economic conditions, which will impact on your divorce strategy. Therefore, having a second option (Plan B) ready not only provides a contingency and mitigates risk; it also maintains control over your divorce, with a far better chance of achieving your objective and financial goals.

Using your divorce research, prioritise the information and data that will financially support your strategy. For instance, in my own case, the forecast value of the marital home in ten years would have increased by an estimated 60%. Interest rates are forecast to remain at a historical low for the next two years. My arts collection remains a good future investment, which could potentially compensate for my pension loss. These three pieces of research would not only have a major impact on my ability to achieve my divorce objectives, also the information would have a significant influence on my investments well beyond the completion and financial settlement of the divorce itself. Remember, this was the divorce research for my own DMBO; no doubt your individual research will differ and will be bespoke to your DMBO.

Once you have prioritised the research to support and financially justify your strategy, the next step is develop the strategy itself. Remember each strategy must deliver an acceptable financial return after your divorce. If you discover the strategy does not deliver an acceptable financial return, do not pursue it and find an alternative. This shows the importance of having two strategic options, so you can select the best option to meet your objectives.

My strategies to achieve the 5 final objectives:

Objective 1 – Retain the marital home

Strategy A
Leverage the equity in the marital home and propose a realistic financial 'buy-out lump sum' to purchase my ex-spouse's share of the marital home.

Estimated £55,000 saving on estate agent, surveyor, stamp duty, removal, sale and legal fees by retaining the marital home. Re-invest the savings in future property development.

Strategy B
Place the marital home on the open market. Obtain a 'preliminary purchase offer' from a prospective buyer; match the 'preliminary offer' to justify a legitimate and acceptable 'buy-out lump sum' paid as final settlement to my ex-spouse.

As with strategy A; an estimated £55,000 saving on estate agent, sale and legal fees by retaining the marital home. Re-invest the savings in future property development.

Objective 2 – Retain 100% contents of the marital home

Strategy A
Retention of all marital home contents as a negotiated part of the total 'buy-out lump sum'.

Strategy B
Make a separate cash offer for all marital home contents, to be funded from free-cash generated through savings.

Objective 3 – Secure at least 50% share of all pension funds; improve long-term pension investment return

Strategy A
Re-invest retained pension share tax-free element in future property development. Rent a room in the retained marital property to enhance pension return on investment.

Strategy B
Retain works of art and family heirlooms. Invest in the arts market after the financial settlement to help recover pension loss.

Objective 4 – Prevent any future claims against me, after the financial settlement

Strategy A
Obtain a 'clean break' court order to remove the risk of my ex-spouse from making any future financial claims against me, after the settlement is legally finalised and binding.

Strategy B
Obtain a 'clean break' court order to remove the risk of any future legal costs against me, after the financial settlement is legally finalised and binding.

Objective 5 – Retain 50% of financial investments

Strategy A
Invest retained investments in high-growth property development and rental market; possibly overseas. Invest in high-yield markets that return at least 3% above the best bank or building society investment rates.

Strategy B
Invest in my daughter's university education, providing an opportunity for her to pursue a career in business marketing and assist within my new company, where appropriate.

A further benefit by preparing two strategic options; you are either able to apply a combination of the strategies or apply them independently. For instance, interlinking my daughter's university education with my new company has without any doubt further strengthened our relationship. After her graduation, my daughter has undertaken part-time key research projects and prepared digital plans. She also proofreads business proposals prior to sending them to company clients.

A further example of justifying combined strategies; investing my pension share lump sum and remaining financial investments in property development and the rental market was supported by further new research. As touched on a little earlier, research findings stated property values were forecast to rise at an average 8% per year, in addition the rental market was set grow at 4 to 5% per year. A point to note – continue researching the markets in which you have placed your investment; market conditions can change either way enabling you to act accordingly. A current example of continuing investment research would be as follows:

Savill's reported in January 2015:

"We are forecasting that the number of households in the private rented sector will rise by 1.2 million over the next five years."

> "... *relatively buoyant mainstream sales market has limited stock availability in the rental market. This has maintained positive rental expectations across the country.* "[118.]

My divorce strategy was further underpinned by a piece of more macro research carried out by Professor Stephen Jenkins, a director of the Institute for Social and Economic Research and chair of the Council of the International Association for Research on Income and Wealth. The research was reported by the *Guardian*.[119.]

"Men become richer after divorce. Male incomes rise by a third after a split, while women are worse off and can struggle for years."

Jenkins's research found that the incomes of "separating husbands" rise "immediately and continuously" in the years following a marital split. "The differences between the sexes are stark," he said. "But this is not so much a gender thing as a parent thing. The key differences are not between men and women, but between fathers and mothers."

He found that, when a man leaves a childless marriage, his income immediately rises by 25%. Women, however, suffer a sharp fall in income. Their financial position rarely reaches pre-split levels.

[118.] Savills UK – Rental growth in mainstream market' 8 January 2015 http://www.savills.co.uk/research_articles/186866/185225-0

[119.] Guardian 'Men become richer after divorce' 25 January 2009 – www.theguardian.com/lifeandstyle/2009/jan/25/divorce-women-research

Maintenance paid by former partners also has little impact, said Jenkins, as just 31% of separated mothers receive payment from the father of their children.

"There are only two factors that have an impact on women's financial position, post relationship breakdown," said Jenkins. "The percentage change in income is less if they have worked beforehand and continue working afterwards. The impact is also reduced if they start working after the relationship breakdown. There is also a potential positive impact if she remarries," he added, "although the impact is a small one".

The position can be reversed if a separated man has more children with a new partner while paying maintenance to his first family. The only way to level the playing field is to make men and women more alike in terms of roles in the family and in the labour market. "Until these fundamental issues change, these realities will remain essentially unchanged," he said.

Professor John Ermisch, author of *An Economic Analysis of the Family and Lone Parenthood: An Economic Analysis*, agreed that women are disproportionately penalised following relationship breakdowns, but said that the margin of unfairness is gradually reducing.

"Employment transition rates reveal that the proportion of women with dependent children who stop working after a marital split has almost halved between the late 1990s and early 2000s, from 16% to 9%," he said.

According to Labour Force Survey data, the proportion of all separating wives in paid work has increased over the 1990s from around 66% in 1993 to 74% in 2002. The proportion of separating women with children who have remained in work has increased from 41% to 58% over the same period, increasing this group's employment rate by 16%.

"The most likely explanations of these trends are increases in women's attachment to paid work, and increases in government rewards to paid work, relative to not working, both of which are associated with the various changes in the late 1990s to the system of in-work support," said Ermisch.

Returning to the DMBO strategy, at this stage it is worth carrying out a quick check list and review on what has been completed so far:

1. Carried out divorce research; including preparation for the divorce procedures, strengths and weaknesses analysis and market economic conditions
2. Established your future vision; defining the years after divorce
3. Set 5 key divorce objectives; each objective must achieve an acceptable long-term financial return
4. Created free-cash to finance your divorce
5. Built a cash-flow forecast to manage day-to-day and legal costs
6. Developed 2 strategic options to achieve each objective; select the best option to deliver the best financial return

The next step when creating your strategy is to financially evaluate what each strategy is likely to return over a 10-year period, once your divorce is complete, and the financial settlement is agreed and ratified by the court. This analysis will confirm (or not) that your strategies are projected to deliver an acceptable level of return on investment.

By example only, the following 10-year Divorce Valuation Projection (DVP) lists a selected example of the top five investments as a result of the divorce strategy, making a value forecast for each investment based on credible research, trends and future projections. It is important to regularly review your DVP as circumstances and market trends change rapidly. Don't be afraid to change your strategy or investment if financial performances change or you are blown off track for any reason.

10-year Divorce Valuation Projection (DVP)

Diagram 18

Value £	2017	2018	2019	2020	2021	2022	2023	2024	2025	2026
Existing Property	850000	918000	991440	1070755	1156415	1248928	1348843	1456750	1573290	1699153
New Property			100000	108000	116640	125971	136048	146932	158687	171382
Property Rental			13030	13410	13813	14227	14654	15093	15546	16013
Stocks Shares			23370	25707	28277	31105	34216	37637	41401	41401
Fine Art	2500	2625	2765	2894	3038	3190	3350	3517	3693	3878
Total	852500	920625	1130605	1220766	1318183	1423421	1537111	1659929	1792617	1931827

NB: The values in the above diagram are purely used for demonstration and forecasting only; the figures are not actual values.

It is interesting to note the most common age at divorce is between 40-44 years of age.[120] Potentially, this is at a time and age where there is a reasonable level of equity in the marital home and financial investments; meaning there is possibly more being at financial stake now and looking forward in ten years' time. As discussed earlier, official figures have shown a marked increase in divorce among couples around retirement age in recent years. It is likely marital asset equity; particularly property equity will be even higher, along with a high value pension pot, resulting in even more at stake during the financial settlement. With stakes being much higher in your later years of marriage; the need for a robust divorce plan and a good quality financial settlement is even greater.

This is further underpinned by changing social attitudes, the prospect of a longer retirement as people increasingly live longer and the fact that many marry later in the first place. This has resulted in a boom in 'silver separations'; pensioners are the only age group where the divorce rate is rising. On reaching retirement, and without the routine of work to fill the day, many realise they can no longer stand their husband or wife. Some discover

---

[120] Office for National Statistics 'Divorce in England and Wales 2012' 6 February 2014 http://www.ons.gov.uk/peoplepopulationandcommunity/birthsdeathsandmarriages/divorce/bulletins/divorcesinenglandandwales/2014-02-06#age-at-divorce

they have nothing in common with each other once their children fly the nest. Somewhat déjà vu here; although my divorce was pre-retirement years, the same symptoms of little or nothing in common anymore combined with my daughter leaving home to study at university were the contributory factors to my 25-year marriage coming to an end.

Picking up on the earlier figures; the *Daily Mail* reported in 2011 that more than 11,500 over-60s were granted a divorce in 2009,[121.] this is up 4% in a matter of two years. The over 60s lead an active lifestyle and continue to enjoy activities from their 40s and 50s such as outdoor pursuits, sport, holidays and adventure to all corners of the world. What is the cliché – 'age is but a number'?

Reinventing yourself in your later years includes re-evaluating relationships and deciding to start again after divorce. The 'baby boomers' realise there is still time for new adventures and new relationships. Again déjà vu; as I enter into my twilight years, my approach is the 'glass is only ever half-full'.

Projected UK Age Population 2012 to 2036

Diagram 19

millions

Ages	2012	2017	2022	2027	2032	2037
0-14	11.2	11.7	12.2	12.3	12.2	12.2
15-29	12.6	12.4	12.1	12.3	12.9	13.3
30-44	12.8	12.7	13.3	13.6	13.5	13.2
45-59	12.6	13.3	13.0	12.6	12.4	13.0
60-74	9.4	10.1	10.7	11.6	12.3	12.1
75 and over	5.0	5.5	6.6	7.7	8.5	9.5
75-84	3.6	3.8	4.6	5.3	5.4	5.9
85 and over	1.4	1.7	2.0	2.4	3.1	3.6
All ages	63.7	65.8	68.0	70.0	71.7	73.3

Source: Government Actuary's Department/ONS

[121.] Mail Online 'Rise of the "silver separations": Divorce rate for over-60s surges' 18 November 2011 – www.dailymail.co.uk/news/article-2063430

Government and ONS figures tell us that ten million people in the UK are over 65 years old. The latest projections are for 5½ million more elderly people in 20 years' time and the number will have nearly doubled to around 19 million by 2050.[122] Within this total, the number of very old people grows even faster. There are currently three million people aged more than 80 years and this is projected to almost double by 2030, reaching eight million by 2050. While one-in-six of the UK population is currently aged 65 and over, by 2050 one in-four will be.

I'm sure family law firms have seen the trend of older couples divorcing, particularly among families in which the husband had a well-paid job while his wife stayed at home, possibly to look after young children. Again, this was the same in my own case, after 25 years of marriage, raising a family and both of us getting ever closer to our twilight years. *The Telegraph* reports, historically, the relative financial weakness of the wife in such cases had in the past often acted as a brake on divorce, with many reconsidering after realising that they would have to downsize to a much smaller property even if they got half of the joint assets.[123] However, this could now change, re-membering the recent pension reforms, there could be further possibilities of using money from the pension pot to put toward another property, either meaning that the family home might not have to be sold or that the couple could divide their assets and buy two similarly sized houses.

Despite the relative increase in the number of divorces at the age of 60 and over; by comparison and to recap from an earlier chapter, the most common age at divorce remains between 40 and 44 years old.

---

[122] Key Issues for the New Parliament 'The ageing population', Richard Cracknell www.parliament UK 2010 – http://www.parliament.uk/documents/commons/lib/research/key_issues/Key-Issues-The-ageing-population2007.pdf
[123] http://www.telegraph.co.uk/news/uknews/11301378/Osborne-pension-reforms-could-trigger-silver-splitter-divorce-boom.html 27 December 2014

Diagram 20

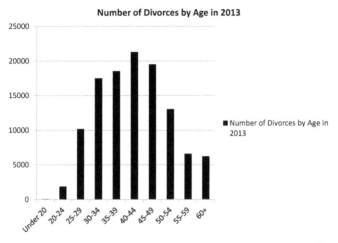

Source: ONS

A further issue that has arisen within the ageing population; when Viagra was introduced into the UK, it was hoped that its influence on middle-aged men's waning libido would help to save marriages. However, reported by the London *Evening Standard*[124.] at least one British couple found it had the opposite effect – by leading to divorce. A London housewife, who has not been named, cited her husband's irrepressible sexual appetite as 'unreasonable behaviour' in her divorce petition. She said he became 'sexually aggressive' after taking the blue pill and was insatiable in the bedroom. Although the husband, who is in his 50s, initially took Viagra because their sex life was flagging, his demands soon escalated out of control. The lawyer who dealt with the case, said: 'One complaint was that Viagra changed his behaviour and his wife found it offensive.' There were fears that the case, the first of its kind in the UK, could trigger an avalanche of similar divorce petitions. With more than 500,000 Viagra users reported in Britain, there are fears that men who rediscover their libido could cheat on their partners or become too demanding in bed. Viagra has already been cited in dozens of divorce cases in America, where more than seven million men take the

---

[124.] Evening Standard 'The Viagra Divorce' 18 April 2004 – www.standard.co.uk/news/the-viagra-divorce-6972591

prescribed pill. Reported by the *Guardian*[125.] – a leading New York divorce lawyer, who has dealt with at least 70 such cases, said: 'Older men are able to perform so they are going elsewhere. They are seeking younger, greener pastures.' In South Africa, surgeon Christian Barnard, who carried out the world's first successful heart transplant, was divorced by his wife Karin when she found Viagra in the 76-year-old's toiletry bag. She said he taunted her about wanting sexual adventures elsewhere and concluded he was having an affair.

As couples get older, men are more likely to file for and be granted divorce. In 2011, 34% of all those granted divorces were men;[126.] however, in the older age group men were just as likely as women to be granted the divorce. This suggests that it may be down to older women being more likely to lose out financially if they divorce because of lower earnings over their lifetimes and lower pensions. Although following recent government pension reforms these statistics may change in future years.

So, considering these changes in divorce trends; we are living longer, over 60s are healthier and adventurous, new pension reforms make it easier to access the pension pot and we have Viagra; wow quite a cocktail – no wonder, I'm having a blast since my divorce, but what are the risks? Seriously, within your divorce strategy, we now need to identify the potential risks to your plan; does your divorce plan have a serious flaw an 'achilles heel' that could seriously blow you off track? We have already considered where the respective party's individual strengths and weaknesses lie. Now identify where the strengths and weaknesses are in your plan itself. What could go wrong and hinder you, therefore, it is important to have a contingency plan, and hence it is wise to always have the second strategic option (Plan B) up your sleeve. Assess the level of risks and rank them high, medium and low – what level of risk will there be financially to you? Consider whether you are able to easily implement your contingency plan.

Keep a focus on the financial risks such as:

[125.] Guardian 'Ten years on; it's time to count the cost of the Viagra revolution' 24 February 2008 – www.theguardian.com/theobserver/2008/feb/24/controversiesinscience
[126.] The Office of National Statistics Archive released 2011 'Divorces in England and Wales 2012 6 Febbruary 2014 – http://webarchive.nationalarchives.gov.uk/20160105160709

1. Your divorce becomes protracted incurring higher than expected legal costs.
2. Your spouse appoints a new lawyer.
3. Your spouse starts to use 'dirty tricks'.
4. Personal cash flow dries up.
5. Loss of employment and income.
6. Engaging and cost of a barrister.
7. Your spouse raids the bank account, before you close the accounts.
8. You need to fire your lawyer and find a replacement.
9. Your spouse selects a lawyer who is confrontational and hostile.
10. Are there any hidden tax implications?
11. Changes in interest rates.
12. Changes in asset forecasts for example a decline in house prices, a stock market crash or economic downturn.

Using the above risk checks as a starting point, add further risks that maybe unique to your own divorce. Next, draw up a simple template to write the risks and what actions or contingencies, which you can put in place to mitigate such risks. This will give you a visual check and a plan to manage the risks.

There are many benefits of having a risk management plan in place:

1. It improves your chances of achieving your objectives.
2. It provides better control when matters do not go to plan.
3. It can save you money.
4. It provides reassurance that you have thought through what the risks are and how you plan to overcome them.
5. It gives you an advantage over your spouse and his or her lawyer.
6. It gives better control of your finances.
7. It helps when negotiating your financial settlement.
8. It provides damage limitation to unforeseen circumstances.
9. It helps reduce stress and sleep better at night.
10. It puts you at least one step ahead of the other side.

Example risk analysis template:

Diagram 21

Risks to be addressed	Risk causes	Actions to mitigate risk	Date of action

A quick reminder, whilst in the US in the late 1990s at an airline convention; listening to Jim Lovell the captain of the stricken Apollo 13 mission in 1970 say:

"Always expect the unexpected."

Within Jim's speech, he talked about the many risks and decisions we need to make in life. He draws appropriate parallels to the Apollo 13 mission. Remember the famous message Jim made "Houston, we have a problem". He called the Apollo 13 mission "a successful failure", in that he and his crew returned safely but never made it to the moon. Later Jim went on to say:

"There are people who make things happen, there are people who watch things happen, and there are people who wonder what happened. To be successful, you need to be a person who makes things happen".[127]

To summarise; what I learnt from having a divorce strategy:

- A divorce strategy provides you with a clear set of priorities and direction.
- It reduces your costs and provides other sources of income to contribute to your legal costs.
- Having a strategy helps manage the risks in your divorce.

---

[127] Brainy Quote http://www.brainyquote.com/quotes/quotes/j/jimlovell202153.html accessed 27th April 2016

- Your strategy tells you what and how much is at financial stake.
- It provides a structure to follow; providing organisation, control and management of your divorce.
- A strategy will provide you with confidence to achieve your goals and objectives.
- It will help prepare, control and win in your negotiations.
- It will make your divorce case and evidence more compelling.
- Having a good strategy will help to reduce divorce stress and emotion.
- A good strategy will give a competitive advantage over the other side.
- A strategy provides a road map on how you will achieve your objectives and future vision.
- "Age doesn't matter unless you're a cheese."

"Divorce is the start point for a brand new life. Don't lose the chance to redesign it upon your dreams."[128.]

Rossana Condole

[128.] Goodreads – http://www.goodreads.com/quotes/789675-divorce-is-the-start-point-for-a-brand-new-life

Chapter Three
Lawyer Due-diligence and Legal
Compliance – Steps Six to Seven ⑥ + ⑦

Select your lawyer very carefully

Diagram 22

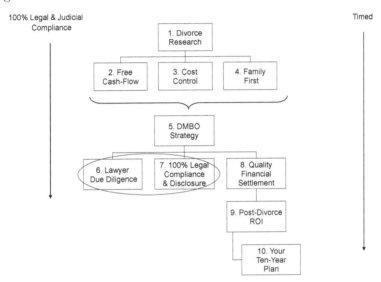

Hiring the right lawyer can pay extraordinary financial dividends well after your divorce has been completed; choosing the wrong lawyer can be very expensive, unproductive, stressful and may leave you with a financial settlement which is to your disadvantage for years to come. Finding a lawyer, who is able and committed to achieve your 5 divorce objectives can take time, requiring thorough due-diligence and a proper search, much like an executive interview process. On balance, there are many good family lawyers out there, who will provide you with good customer service and legal value for money. However, in a recent case study:

Mrs L. and her husband had been married for 20 years when they divorced. They have three children, aged 11 years, 3 years and 18 months old. The *Guardian*[129.] reported:

"My husband told me we would split everything down the middle. I got a huge shock when I realised he had hired a crack legal team who managed to hide a large proportion of his assets and write off most of his income. I didn't stand a chance. On paper I got 50% of everything. In reality, however, he walked off with enough money to buy a house in town outright and a new car, while also taking the kids on a couple of foreign holidays each year."

Personally, I made a very early mistake by selecting the wrong lawyer, which resulted, after approximately six months, in a successful complaint to the Legal Complaints Service. In my opinion, I had lost confidence in the lawyer's ability to provide legal value and good customer service.

First, do not assume you need a lawyer immediately. Before selecting your lawyer, give yourself a sufficient amount of time to research and prepare your objectives and divorce strategy. It also buys you time to think rationally and gives a 'cooling off' period, allowing a big part of the early divorce emotion to drain away, enabling you to think clearly. It's time to help put things in to personal perspective. What you are about to enter will be a period that will put at stake not only your hard earned finances and assets, built up over previous years; more importantly the shape and success of your future life. Be patient, skilful and wise, before selecting your lawyer and rushing off into the divorce ring.

> "When I found Jesus Christ, I learned to be a better athlete. I didn't have to go out there and knock them out in the first round. I've learned to be patient, skilful in the ring. At the same time, I wanted to prove to other boxers that you can take off this killer instinct stuff, you can be a great athlete, a great boxer, and love your brother."[130.]
>
> *George Foreman*

[129.] Guardian 'Men become richer after divorce' 25 January 2009 – http://www.the guardian.com/lifeandstyle/2009/jan/25/divorce-women-research

[130.] Brainy Quote – http://www.brainyquote.com/quotes/quotes/g/georgefore469506.html accessed 27th April 2016

Consider alternative options, which can save early legal costs, time and stress. A reasonable alternative to using a lawyer could be engaging the services of a mediator. However, in most cases you will still need to use a lawyer, if an agreement is reached as a result of mediation. A lawyer needs to draw up the agreement, which could then be made in to a court order. If you decide to use a mediator, it is important to obtain a legally binding court order to avoid any legal challenges at a later date.

Think carefully about the type and style of lawyer you will need to deliver your strategy. A lawyer must understand and support your strategy. Remember, you are entrusting your finances, marital assets, your past and future livelihood with your lawyer. He or she should share and support your basic philosophy or attitude toward your divorce. Use your lawyer to obtain a second opinion on your divorce strategy. Try to obtain his or her opinion on your strategy before recruiting them and directly ask them 'are you able to achieve the objectives?'; ask 'is the strategy stretching but achievable?'. I guess one of the issues when asking a lawyer these types of questions is that they could err on the side of caution. In my opinion, and based on personal experience, I have sometimes found lawyers similar to accountants; on occasion they can be non-committal and can 'sit on the fence' – not wishing to generalise, I guess that's one of the characteristics of being a lawyer or an accountant.

It was JP Morgan who said:

> *"Well, I don't know as I want a lawyer to tell me what I cannot do. I hire him to tell how to do what I want to do."*[131.]

Contact the Law Society and the Legal Ombudsman; they are able to provide help in selecting the right lawyer also provide free impartial advice, much of which can be found online. Personally, I was wary and cautious of family lawyers who advertise in the local newspaper. Good lawyers should be able to build their business and attract new clients through reputation and referral; not having to advertise in the local rag.

[131.] Brainy Quote – http://www.brainyquote.com/quotes/quotes/j/jpmorgan158095.html accessed 27 April 2016

Draw up a lawyer shortlist; research each lawyer and the law firm they work for before you meet them; do your basic homework first. Meet and interview at least three experienced family lawyers, prepare interview questions that help you decide and meet your needs. At each interview, make detailed notes of your discussion, ask the lawyer to forward a summary of the meeting and the proposed terms discussed. Always remember it is a competitive market; there are probably dozens of family law firms in your area to choose from. Seek the best legal value, without compromising your own finances or legal quality. Ask each lawyer you interview "what makes you different and better than your competitors?" You are looking for a lawyer who can 'stand out from the crowd'. Ask lawyers what technology they use to reduce costs and time, such as Skype, paperless correspondence and billing. Confirm that you would not be prepared to pay for correspondence and time that didn't add legal value; enquire about fixed fee arrangements, check what is and what is not included. In context, you are likely to be paying anything up to £350 an hour for your lawyer's advice and time, therefore productivity and efficiency are essential.

Your lawyer should be someone you trust and feel comfortable with, because you may have to reveal highly personal information about yourself, your family and your marriage.[132] Remind your lawyer that you are placing your marital assets, finances, family and children's interests and your hard earned cash in his or her hands. However, don't be tempted to treat a sympathetic-sounding lawyer as a shoulder to cry on as well as a legal adviser. As that legal meter ticks away, don't waste time and money indulging your emotional state. Your GP should be able to refer you to a specialist family counsellor to help you cope with the emotion of divorce.[133]

Many lawyers request advanced payment on account before they commence work on your case; this is a negotiable payment. When interviewing the shortlist of lawyers, propose no or minimal payment on account; this money is best sat in your bank account. Remember, you are the client in a relative strong negotiating position; the lawyer wants your business.

---

[132] Divorce for Dummies – www.dummies.com/relationships/divorce/choosing-a-divorce-attorney/

[133] Daily Mail – www.dailymail.co.uk/home/you/article-413694/How-best-divorce.html 3 November 2006

If you have children, no matter at what age; look for a lawyer who makes it clear that during your divorce he or she must put your children's needs first. Seek a lawyer who will not pursue unreasonable demands for child support or help you pursue vindictive child custody and visitation arrangements.

An extract of an email sent to my family lawyer:

> *"The protection of my daughter remains my priority. Ensuring that she progresses through her final years of university with minimum distraction and emotional stress. I have further discussed my concerns with my daughter, who completely understands and supports the reasons…"*

When selecting a lawyer, you want one with the legal skills and knowledge needed to get the job done for you and to provide the best legal value. In a recent case, Mr D instructed a law firm to oversee his divorce after an initial consultation in which the lawyer claimed to be a specialist in matrimonial law. Unfortunately, Mr D eventually discovered that the lawyer knew very little about matrimonial law, leading to a catalogue of errors and escalating costs.[134.]

If you need help negotiating your divorce and financial agreement, the ideal lawyer needs to be able to find solutions and be innovative within the realms of the law, they must work well and be able to influence and persuade people, in particular the opposing legal team. He or she should be adept at compromise, and comfortable in court. Although you and your spouse may have no intention of going to court, a lawyer's trial record and history of success in court can have some bearing on his or her ability to negotiate a settlement with your ex-spouse's lawyer. In a later chapter and in my firm opinion, I'll explain how our respective lawyers were removed from the negotiating table, following months and years of what I genuinely felt was 'going round in circles', court appearances, volumes of letters and high legal costs, without achieving a negotiated settlement. With the utmost

---

[134.] Legal Ombudsman 'The price of separation: Divorce related legal complaints and their causes' 31 December 2012- http://www.legalombudsman.org.uk/reports/divorce/mr-d-story.html

respect to them, at times in the height of frustration, I felt that I just wanted to 'bang their heads together'.

In my opinion, I believe some family lawyers need to develop new skills, particularly in the areas of collaborative negotiation. Family lawyers need the ability to remove hostility and conflict and be able to work with you your spouse and their lawyer to secure a 'win–win settlement'. Team building and leadership skills are also a critical element of success in that all the team and collaborative efforts are directed towards the same clear goals, which are in the categorical interest of the client and their children. This relies heavily on good communication in the team; having cooperative relationships between lawyers, barristers, administration staff, the court, the client and their families. In the true sense of their title they are called 'family lawyers'.

The best results do come from a team approach and the process is starting to change, albeit these are early days and client awareness is relatively low. In the collaborative law process specialised professionals such as family lawyers, coaches and financial neutrals are all part of the team. The team must have a commitment to keep your divorce 'under the radar' and out of court; the team approach further means that you will have more opportunities to come up with creative solutions; this is something that a judge could not provide. Also, negotiations will be private so that information about your family and your assets will never be disclosed in an open courtroom.

However, despite all best intentions and efforts, if you know that you're heading for a divorce trial, you want a lawyer who has considerable courtroom experience and unequivocal respect for client confidentiality; sometimes family lawyers may inadvertently overlook the need for confidentiality when in a busy court waiting room.

If your financial situation is complex, the lawyer you select should have a solid understanding of the issues and laws that pertain to your divorce. As simple as it may seem, check the lawyers' level of numeracy. During my divorce, I experienced pension discrepancies following the erroneous calculations made by the other side. In addition, there were several invoicing and valuation errors made by my lawyer, which I had to personally redress.

A point of responsibility; lawyers negotiating divorce settlements must tell the authorities if they suspect that any family assets result from tax evasion. Barristers and lawyers who fail to report any tax dodging or social security fraud to the National Criminal Intelligence Service (NCIS) risk committing a criminal offence. The ruling applies equally to the family who pay a builder or nanny partly in cash, and the millionaire with a string of offshore accounts.[135.]

A case in question, which was reported by the *Guardian*[136.]; a couple named as Mr and Mrs P. Mrs P, 52, was divorcing her 50-year-old husband after a 24-year marriage. She told her lawyers the couple's assets could be worth more than £19m. After seeing the financial details provided by Mr P and taking an accountant's advice, Mrs P's lawyers suspected tax evasion by Mr P. They made a report to the NCIS, which told them they could not tell their client, or her husband, they had made the report, for fear this would constitute the offence of 'tipping off' under the Act. But the judge ruled that unless the lawyers were acting from an improper purpose, they were entitled to tell their own client or their opponent that a report had been made.

It is also helpful if the lawyer you choose is familiar with the family law judges in your area. Knowing the courtroom style of the judge who's likely to hear your case, and how the judge has ruled on previous cases similar to yours, helps your lawyer adapt his or her legal strategy and style to that particular judge. Returning to court on six occasions; I became familiar with a selection of judges and noted the differing styles between each judge. In my personal observation, and I trust that I will be forgiven for noting that one judge in particular had a very pragmatic style and was always mindful of client's costs. I would always hope that he would be the presiding judge, each time we returned court.

The area of collaboration was touched on earlier; a recent development has been the practice of Collaborative Law, which is a process whereby you

---

[135.] This is Money www.thisismoney.co.uk/money/news/article-1519600/Divorce-lawyers-tax-brief.html 9 Oct. 2003

[136.] Guardian 'Divorce lawyers must tell of tax dodges' 9 October 2003 – www.the guardian.com/money/2003/oct/09/divorce.uknews

and your lawyers sign an agreement that commits you to trying to resolve the issues without going to court and prevents them from representing you in court if the collaborative process breaks down. Applying the collaborative process, both you and your spouse each appoint your own trained collaborative lawyer; you and your respective lawyers all meet together to work things out face to face. One of the benefits of the collaborative process, is that it is not governed by the court processes and timetable; to a large extent, you are able to agree between the respective parties a timetable and priorities, which meets yours and your family needs.[137.]

Alternative Dispute Resolution (ADR) is a further process, which should be considered. The ADR process is a means of settling disputes outside of the courtroom. ADR typically engages a further set of legal skills and practices such as neutral evaluation, negotiation, conciliation, mediation, and arbitration. Ask your shortlist of lawyers about ADR and whether they are qualified to provide this service. ADR will potentially reduce your costs and time delays; it will also help in reducing court time and pressures on courtroom staff and district judges. A further advantage of ADR is that it allows you and your ex-spouse to control the process and the solution. However, a key requirement as with any negotiated settlement and if you are considering ADR or Collaborative Law, you, your ex-spouse and respective lawyers must be 100% committed to the ADR or Collaborative Law process and finding a resolution, without referring matters to the courtroom. In my opinion, perhaps ADR should become mandatory, whereby a court will not hear a divorce case, unless it has already been preceded by the ADR route and all means of resolution have already been exhausted with 'no stone left unturned'; effectively the courtroom becomes the last resort.

When preparing and researching this book, I discovered through social media discussions with divorce professionals that awareness and availability of both ADR and Collaborative Law requires improvement; I hope my book contributes a small part in achieving higher levels awareness and availability of ADR and Collaborative Law. Remember at the shortlist interview to ask your prospective family lawyer about the options of Collaborative Law and ADR and whether they are a qualified practitioner in both areas.

[137.] Collaborative Process - http://www.resolution.org.uk/collaborative_process/

When selecting your lawyer, check whether there is any conflict of interest; confirm your lawyer or the law firm they work for has ever represented you or advised you and your spouse jointly in the past. In the very early days of my divorce proceedings, my ex-spouse selected a lawyer whose firm had provided advice to me on a completely unrelated matter several years prior to my divorce. I raised the potential conflict of interest with the law firm January 2007; my ex-spouse changed her legal representation to a new lawyer late February 2007. The change of lawyer bought me some additional time; allowing me to further research and prepare my divorce plan.

Check your lawyer has a green and black Law Society Advanced logo on their official documents such as letter heads, business cards and on their website. The accreditation informs and assures you that the law firm has reached a high standard in selected areas of family law and judged to be competent and a caring professional.

Don't let a lawyer's physical appearance or body language influence your decision; some lawyers can appear to be intimidating. You need to feel comfortable with the style, gender and personality of your lawyer; you will be working with them for several months or possibly years. Your lawyer needs to use plain English, which you are able to understand and not use legalese and jargon.[138.]

Your lawyer should be affordable and you should know precisely what and what not you will be paying for. I must admit, as soon as I became fully aware of the hourly fees family lawyers were proposing and after picking myself up off the floor, I knew that this would require favourable negotiation and strict legal cost control.

UK couples are spending a total £5.7 billion per year on divorce, a report from insurers Aviva revealed.[139.] At your lawyer interview ask him or her for full details of their charging policy; will you be charged at an hourly

---

[138.] 'Divorce for Dummies 3rd edition' www.dummies.com/relationships/divorce/divorce-for-dummies-3rd-edition/

[139.] Aviva report 'Cost of divorce reaches £44,000 for UK couples' 19 August 2014 – http://www.aviva.co.uk/media-centre/story/17337

rate or at a fixed rate? Obtain a cost quotation and the expected number of hours they will work on your divorce case.

According to the Legal Ombudsman and reported by the *Guardian*, some solicitors are failing to advise divorcees to settle courtroom battles before costs rise out of control because of the 'emotional rawness' of those involved. In a report on the costs of separation, it says during in the 2008 economic downturn there was increasing tension between lawyers' financial self-interest in prolonging legal action and their responsibility to offer clients informed advice. The report, says: "One of the reasons why costs can spiral out of control lies in the emotional rawness of many of those going through divorce proceedings. It is common for people to rely heavily on the one in-dividual who is both an expert in how to negotiate the process and who is seen to be on their side: their lawyer."[140.]

In a further reported case by the *Guardian*,[141.] in eight months a husband and wife spent what the judge described as "an eye-watering total of £920,000 from their total joint assets of almost £3m on lawyers and experts", said the presiding judge. The couple, known only as J and J spent almost a third of everything they had built up together over nearly 18 years. The husband, a market gardener aged 54, and the wife, aged 44, separated in 2011 after having been married for 15 years. They had two children of 17 and 16. The costs of their case started to rise when they were permitted by a district judge to each hire their own experts to value the husband's business. These experts charged a total of £154,000 for six reports and a joint statement setting out their disagreements. The couple eventually com-missioned so many reports that they presented the court with an archive of evidence comprising 12 files. This, said the judge, was "very wrong" and "a contemptuous disregard" of court rules limiting evidence to one "essential reading bundle".

[140.] Report posted by researchingreform.net and Guardian 'The Legal Ombudsman's Adventures: Tales of Diplomacy' 28 February 2013 – https://researchingreform.net/2013/02/28/the-legal-ombudsmans-adventures-tales-of-diplomacy – http://www.theguardian.com/law/2013/feb/28/divorce-costs-warning-issued-lawyers
[141.] Guardian 'Divorcing couple spent nearly £1m on divorce' 13 November 2014 – www.theguardian.com/lifeandstyle/2014/nov/13/divorce-costs-of-nearly-1m-scandalous-says-judge

These experiences, further confirm the importance of carefully selecting the lawyer you are intending to instruct, and of getting a clear quotation or estimate of the likely total cost of your divorce. Make sure you know whether it is a fixed cost quote or an estimate, and what it covers. You will also need to agree how the lawyer will keep you informed of the cost you have incurred as the case goes on, so that you are able to keep a strict control of your costs.

In some circumstances, and despite the cuts to legal aid, there are still some sources of funding available. If you are concerned about how you'll pay for your divorce, ask your lawyer to explain if these sources apply to you. Also, it is worth discussing with the lawyer when you are expected to pay: up front, in stages, at month-end or after the final settlement; again payment terms are negotiable – don't just accept your lawyer's first proposal. Negotiate an acceptable hourly rate. Most lawyers are prepared to negotiate; it is a competitive market and you are the customer have a choice of lawyers; you are seeking the best legal value for each pound of expenditure. Again and better still, negotiate a fixed rate; this enables you to have an even tighter control on your costs.

When you receive the lawyer's written terms and conditions; carefully check the wording and small print to ensure the terms reflect what you have agreed and there are no surprises – as the saying goes 'the devil is always in the detail'. Also, it is likely there will be a number of legal terms and jargon within the proposed terms and conditions; ask your lawyer to explain the terms and jargon in plain English. If you should need independent advice regarding the set of terms proposed by your lawyer, contact either the Law Society or the Legal Ombudsman for help and guidance.

Agree with your lawyer in advance that you will not be charged for court waiting time or travel time to the court. Divorce cases are known for running over time, leaving you and your lawyer sat in the court waiting room with the legal clock left running. A further point to note whilst we are in the court waiting room; the waiting room can become very busy with other divorcees and their lawyers. I was very surprised that some lawyers were having open discussions with their clients in the court waiting room, where some nearby could overhear what the very confidential discussions were about. Lawyers should have the utmost respect and discretion for client privacy and confidentiality, and request from the court clerk a private room where confidential discussions with their client can take place.

Task your lawyer to find efficiencies and cost saving solutions, make him or her accountable for minimising your legal costs; a reminder that, after all, it is your hard-earned money that is being spent.

When negotiating your legal costs, always negotiate inclusive of VAT. It seems common practice for some lawyers to quote a cost then add 20% VAT on top of a high legal bill which amounts to a significant extra cost for the client to carry. Lawyers charge in units of time; some may have a policy of rounding up to the nearest unit. I would challenge this notion; suggesting as an act of good faith and generosity on occasion to 'round down' to the nearest unit; ask your lawyer to confirm their policy. There was one instance which was completely unrelated to my divorce; a commercial lawyer acting on my behalf during a business case attempted to charge me for a telephone call to the lawyer's colleague. At the time the lawyer's colleague was not available to answer the call, nevertheless the lawyer argued I should be charged for the time taken to make the attempted telephone call, regardless of whether his colleague was available or not to take it. I advised the law firm in question that I would never dream of charging one of my own business clients for the time it took to make a failed phone call.

Be aware of charges such as 'Personal Attendance', which is where you are potentially charged at the full legal hourly rate by your lawyer for attending a joint meeting or court hearing with your barrister, who is leading the principal legal representation on your behalf; this would be an opportunity to propose a fixed fee arrangement, if this situation arises. With every lawyer's invoice, request a narrative, which provides a detailed breakdown and cost justification. Do not be afraid to challenge individual costs, particularly relating to non-legal activity such as photocopying, basic administration tasks, travel and court waiting time. Further, do not be reticent to question costs relating to correspondence or activity that is not adding any legal value, such as acknowledgements or simple admin-istrative confirmation. I made many challenges on my own legal costs, saving over the course of time several hundreds of pounds; I would regularly say to myself "is this cost justified and does the charge actually add legal value?"

My divorce process had a number of joint conference meetings and court hearings with both my barrister and lawyer present, which would have normally attracted the full hourly rate of the respective legal representatives. In such instances negotiate and agree a fixed fee in advance, which prevents any cost surprises and keeps your own personal legal costs under control and on budget.

Confirm with your family lawyer that they will use a proposed set of cost guidelines and principles, namely your lawyer:

1. Must make every attempt to keep your case out of court.
2. Must keep costs 'proportionate' to what you can afford.
3. Must be kept aware of your personal financial position.
4. All costs must be justified, fair and reasonable.
5. Must advise in advance what you will and will not be charged for.
6. Keep proceedings as conciliatory as possible, so that clients have a chance of behaving without animosity to one and other at family events and post-divorce occasions. This was an important personal point; my daughter's graduation ceremony was due to take place in 2008 in Oxford, also she was recently married. My ex-spouse was naturally attending the two events and both passed with decorum and in an adult grown up manner.
7. Agree early directions from the court and ask if a judge is able to meet all parties as early as possible in the proceedings. The court's directions will help expedite the process and assist in avoiding future conflict. It will also help manage expectations and keep costs down in the long run.
8. Must keep the divorce process, communication and correspondence productive and efficient; this is what I would call 'lean divorce management'.

A lawyer's hourly rate can depend on your region of the country; living in London or a major city you can expect to pay the most. If you are living in an area, where expensive lawyers reside, an option could be to select a lawyer that has a practice in the less expensive areas of the country. Today's digital communication allows you to remain in full communication with your lawyer, whether you are five miles or 500 miles from each other.

A recent study carried out by online company DivorceDepot.co.uk found the charges in London were £350 per hour[142.] paid for a top grade divorce lawyer; Cardiff's average rate was £262 per hour and Bournemouth at £252.25 per hour. Followed by:

- Birmingham at £247.50 per hour.
- Newcastle at £252 per hour.
- Manchester at £242 per hour.
- York at £228 per hour.
- Leeds at £227.50 per hour.

When negotiating the hourly rate with your lawyer; ensure and ask for confirmation that the hourly rate will be constant throughout the divorce period and there will be no price increases, also confirm the rate includes VAT. Remind your lawyer; unlike a VAT registered business you are personally unable to recover 20% VAT from HMRC. Also, ensure that your lawyer identifies any work carried out by junior or trainee lawyers confirm their respective hourly rate and you are charged accordingly with supporting invoice narrative of what the charge relates to.

A further option to be considered to significantly reduce costs is to bypass lawyers altogether and work directly with a barrister, reports *This is Money*.[143.] It can halve the cost of a divorce but you will need to do more legwork than you would perhaps undertake with a lawyer. Alternatively, you may propose that it won't be necessary for both your lawyer and barrister to attend court together, as this potentially duplicates cost. Mitigating your legal costs has a further benefit; it demonstrates to the court

---

[142.] DivorceDepot.co.uk and The Express 'Cost of divorce surges with London most expensive location for marital splits' 16 August 2013 – http://www.express.co.uk/finance/personalfinance/422608/Cost-of-divorce-surges-with-London-leading-most-expensive-location-for-marital-splits
[143.] This is Money – www.thisismoney.co.uk/money/news/article-2560103/Divorce-rise-cut-costs.html

that you are attempting to keep costs under control and acting diligently, which can be looked upon favourably by the presiding judge.

Recently the Legal Ombudsman has levelled criticism at lawyers when it comes to communication and the use of legal cost jargon; the Ombudsman stated:

"We see lawyers regularly using legal jargon, irrespective of whether these words will be understood. Terms such as 'disbursements' regularly appear in costs estimates without adequate explanation of what it means and, more importantly, whether it means additional costs. But it is not just about the language. What the complaints we see tell us is that we need to place the person at the centre of these transactions to make what's happening meaningful for them. We know from the complaints we see how hard it can be for an individual to challenge an expert – and people go to see lawyers for expert views on often complicated personal matters. We also know from research that people place their trust in lawyers. Like doctors, people trust lawyers to do what's right for them: like doctors, people use a lawyer to do something that they can't do themselves."[144.]

As touched on earlier in the chapter, London has earned the status as divorce capital of the world, particularly in the world of celebrities. Among the high-profile cases reported by many media channels to have been settled in London was that of Heather Mills, who secured £24.3m when she parted from the former Beatle Sir Paul McCartney in 2008. Orianne Cevey, the former wife of the musician Phil Collins, secured a settlement of £25m the same year.

Bernie Ecclestone is reputed to have paid out £750m in a private settlement to his ex-wife, Slavica.

When Guy Ritchie divorced Madonna, he was said to have renounced any claim on his ex-wife's fortune because he is wealthy in his own right. Legal

[144.] Legal Ombudsman 'Costs and customer service in a changing legal market' 2012 31 October 2014 http://www.legalombudsman.org.uk/downloads/documents/publications/Costs-Report.pdf

commentators suggested he could have been entitled to a significant share. I say good for Guy Ritchie and Madonna as they clearly applied family common sense and no doubt saved a small fortune in legal fees. In my view, a great celebrity example of 'an application of common sense and not an application to the courts'.

In another extraordinary case, reported in the *Evening Standard*[145], two wealthy solicitors spent five years and virtually all their money battling over the terms of their acrimonious split. Despite both being practising lawyers they spent almost all their assets in litigation' during the lengthy court battle. Tragically, they had squandered their fortune and had little more than £90,000 left between them.

Law is also a business, and lawyers are in an increasingly competitive and financially challenging market with a need to achieve financial returns. In a context where charging is usually still done on the basis of time spent rather than results achieved; corresponding with the other side soon mounts up in billable costs.[146] In my opinion, divorce cases which result in lengthy court hearings are often more profitable for lawyers than cases which settle early. To briefly recap on my earlier proposal; financial models need to be revisited with a percentage of your legal fees should be paid on the results and performance of your lawyer and barrister. The current status quo; whether you achieve a good, bad or indifferent divorce settlement the legal bill is the same.

Watch out for quotes that look a lot cheaper than others – as the saying goes, 'if it looks too good to be true, it probably is'. Some family law firms provide you with an estimate of the amount of work and their costs, rather than a quote. Personally, I feel more comfortable with a tight and accurate quote rather than an estimate; in my view, I think an estimate always provides the law firm with 'wriggle room' when the final bill arrives. Therefore, it is important that your lawyer keeps you updated throughout, particularly if there is likely to be any deviation from the quote or estimate; this avoids any nasty surprises when the final bill drops through the letter box. Don't forget

---

[145] Evening Standard 'Lawyers squandered their £1m fortune and sell their £3.2m home in divorce battle' 19 September 2012 – http://www.standard.co.uk/news/london/lawyers-squander-their-1m-fortune-and-sell-32m-home-in-divorce-battle-8156859.html
[146] Legal Ombudsman www.legalombudsman.org.uk/reports/divorce/on-the-meter.html

to ask your lawyer whether you will be requiring the services of barrister, and at what cost. Barrister's costs are normally higher than the cost of a family law lawyer. Ironically, I actually found barristers or their clerks were more prepared to negotiate rates than some divorce lawyers.

Keep the pressure on costs from start to finish, it shows your lawyer that you are 'on the ball'. I challenged my first lawyer regarding charges for their ten-minute travelling time on foot from the law firm's office to the local court. My first lawyer also attempted to charge me at her full legal hourly rate for her personal delivery (plus waiting time) of legal documents to the local court. My redress was this was probably the most expensive hand postal service in the country and should have been hand delivered by my lawyer's secretary or the office manager; the charge was credited.

When it comes to your lawyer negotiating on your behalf make sure you set objectives for him or her to achieve. I recollect challenging my legal team prior to a court hearing, telling them that they were aiming too low when it came to negotiating my percentage share of the marital assets. I don't think this went down too well, however, I did remind them that they were negotiating with my hard-earned money and assets built up over several decades.

However, and in context, the study by Aviva reports[147] the true cost of divorce. The study found that on top of essential costs, such as legal fees and housing, separating couples regularly spend up to £13,000 on the hidden extras they feel they need to launch their new single lives. For many the divorce process involves re-branding or in some cases even re-inventing themselves. Some buy a complete new wardrobe or get in shape by joining a gym, while others give themselves a psychological boost with a post-divorce holiday or make a break with the past by learning a new skill or taking up a new hobby.

The study by Aviva and further reports by the *Telegraph*[148] state that newly divorced couples are collectively spending tens of millions of pounds a year

---

[147] Aviva report 'Cost of divorce reaches £44,000 for UK couples' 19 August 2014 – http://www.aviva.co.uk/media-centre/story/17337
[148] The Telegraph 'The hidden cost of divorce' 19 August 2014 – http://www.telegraph. co.uk/women/sex/divorce

on the less obvious costs associated with divorce. The study states that "a typical divorcing couple spends a total of £43,958 on the divorce process. The survey also highlighted further unexpected costs; couples could add an average of £12,840 to the cost of the divorce. They include an average of £1,277 on dating in the search for a new partner and the £1,370 the partners who remain in the family home typically spend redecorating the place to erase memories of their former life together. One in seven treat themselves to a post-divorce holiday at an average cost of £1,925, a similar proportion bought expensive new gadgets and technology averaging £1,292, and just over one in ten took up a new hobby or skill, at an average cost of £2,105. An increasing number of divorcing couples are treating themselves to cosmetic surgery of some description such as liposuction, rhinoplasties, botox and breast enhancements. Such treatments can be deemed to increase self-esteem and confidence, also spending large amounts of money on cosmetic enhancements can reduce the joint marital finances and deemed as an act of revenge."

The research went on to say "around one in twenty bought themselves new clothes or jewellery or even underwent a makeover, at a cost of £1,483 on average. Men spent more on the extras than women, with those who took a post-divorce holiday paying out an average of £2,352; almost twice what women in the same position spent and £1,599 on clothes and jewellery, £275 more than women. Just over one in twenty spent money on therapy or a life coach to help them embark on a new life and a small number took out gym membership or hired a personal trainer to help them get in shape for the dating market at a cost of £1,535 on average."

The Aviva research splits divorce hidden costs into several categories:

- Post-separation holiday – £1,925
- Gadgets/technology – £1,292
- New skill/hobby – £2,105
- Redecorating – £1,370
- Dating – £1,277
- Life coach/therapy – £1,853
- New clothes/makeover – £1,483
- Gym/personal trainer – £1,535

My personal complaint against my lawyer

As referred to a little earlier, the largest area for divorce complaints against lawyers is cost;[149.] around one quarter of the divorce complaints the Legal Ombudsman deals with relate to this.

It is essential that the lawyer keeps the client regularly updated as costs mount. An example publicly reported by the Legal Ombudsman stated,[150.] "Mrs C's case: for her divorce and the associated ancillary relief work, her lawyer estimated costs of around £10,000. However, by the end of the case she was asked to pay more than double this amount. The firm had provided no updates about her escalating costs since the initial estimate and no warning that the final bill would be so much higher than quoted. An ombudsman therefore decided the firm should reduce its final bill by around £15,000."

The BBC further reported[151.] "changes to legal aid mean that an estimated 200,000 fewer cases each year will be eligible for publicly funded legal representation. People who previously were able to fall back on state help to fund their divorces will now have to fund them themselves; many low to middle income earners will have to manage their legal budgets carefully. There will also be an increasing onus on lawyers to help them do so."

[149.] The Legal Ombudsman report 'The price of separation: Divorce related legal complaints and their causes' 2012 – http://www.legalombudsman.org.uk/downloads/documents/publications/The-price-of-separation-LeO-report.pdf

[150.] The Legal Ombudsman 'The price of separation: Divorce related legal complaints and their causes' 2012 – http://www.legalombudsman.org.uk/reports/divorce/mrs-c-story.html

[151.] BBC News 9 April 2013 and the Telegraph 4 July 2013 – http://www.telegraph.co.uk/news/politics/10160022/Legal-aid-overhaul-may-lead-to-lack-of-legal-representation.html

The Legal Ombudsman reports:[152.]

"An instance of this type of issue can be seen in the case of Miss A., where she, unlike her relatively wealthy husband, was unemployed and funding her divorce by borrowing money from friends and using credit cards. Her law firm knew her financial position; unfortunately, despite agreeing a budget with the firm at the start of the process, she was told to pay costs of £15,000 over what was agreed. Given her limited means, she was unable to meet the firm's demands that she borrowed the outstanding sum."

In my opinion and as touched on a number of occasions already; lawyers need new financial models to take into account changing market conditions, legislation, government cuts and most importantly client needs. Many other professional service industries have had to forensically look at their cost and financial models and adapt to changing market and competitive conditions. Likewise, businesses in the private sector are under relentless cost scrutiny by their customers and shareholders; all demanding the very best service and value for money.

A reminder of the statement made by PricewaterhouseCoopers in their recent Wealth Management Report:

"The industry also needs new pricing models. Clients want to know exactly what they are paying for, and regulators want clients to have the ability to compare prices across the industry. Transparency is the name of the game."

"… [the] approach starts by articulating a clear and compelling cost agenda from the front line to the back office; continues with building lean and resilient processes, systems, operations, and organization structures; and culminates in the institutionalization of capabilities that keep resources flowing to 'good' costs and away from 'bad' costs."[153.]

[152.] The Legal Ombudsman 'The price of separation: Divorce related legal complaints and their causes' 2012 – http://www.legalombudsman.org.uk/reports/divorce/mrs-c-story.html

[153.] Price Waterhouse (PwC) report 'Global Wealth Management' – 'New strategies for a changing industry' 2014 http://www.strategyand.pwc.com/media/file/Strategyand_Global-Wealth-Management-Outlook-2014-15.pdf This report was originally by Booz & Company in 2014

In my opinion, maybe family lawyers could follow some of the principles and best practices from the wealth management industry; arguably and in my experience divorce does have similarities and parallels with the wealth management industry.

If there is a problem with your family lawyer's service, you should tell them immediately. If you are unhappy with your lawyer, remember that you are entitled to complain. If you do complain, be clear and objective about what you think has gone wrong and what you want done. Hold your ground, you are the client and it is your divorce case and your money. If things do go wrong, and you can't resolve the complaint with your lawyer directly, you can refer your complaint to the Legal Complaints Service, which is what I did.

In 2007, I had genuinely lost confidence in the legal management of my divorce, considering the ability to best represent my financial interests. I was entrusting my 30-year livelihood, which I had worked so hard and diligently for over the previous decades. I further trusted the legal management with my all-important financial future. After a series of problems, I raised the following concerns and issues:

In preparation for a court hearing scheduled late 2007; in my judgement my lawyer had made notable inaccuracies and omissions, which would have placed us at a financial disadvantage in court. We requested that the court hearing scheduled in November 2007 be adjourned, which was not agreed.

In my own assessment, errors had been made within key financial documents, which amounted to a significant amount of money. There were invoicing discrepancies, which resulted in overcharging and inaccurate fee charges. Charges were made for walking time from the lawyer's office to the County Court. The time to walk from the office to the court was only ten minutes; I argued the charge for such a short walk was unreasonable.

The Legal Complaints Service investigated and upheld parts of my complaint; awarding compensation of £1175.00.

My complaint was accepted by the law firm, I respected them for admitting I had genuine grounds for certain complaints. I was primarily concerned with the quality of legal diligence and lack of attention to detail within the work being carried out. I needed to meticulously check all correspondence including invoice charges in fine detail, which was an onerous task. In my view, this shouldn't have been necessary, considering the level of trust, faith and reliability you should have in a lawyer; not to mention the high fees they charge. As stated at the time "I am placing my hard earned assets, trust and livelihood in the hands of a legal professional, the least should be an acceptable level of diligence and quality of service in return".

I recollect at a meeting with the investigating law firm partner. At the meeting it was said that I was "efficient and meticulous with a keen eye for detail" – no, this was not the case. I was the client, as any other client 'off the street', expecting the best possible legal value and confidence in any lawyer and should be acting in my best interests at a fair and reasonable price.

Recently the Legal Ombudsman published into the public domain a full report[154.] and supporting case studies regarding complaints against lawyers; a key and comprehensive part of the report said:

"Traditional views of lawyers as experts, separated from other businesses by this notion of professionalism, still dominate not just the legal sector but also general perception about legal services provision. And nowhere is the battle between the traditional view of client and customer more marked than in the notion of cost and pricing. The term 'client' embodies the traditional view of the relationship between lawyers and those they represent."

The ombudsman added:

"The notion of a consumer turns this relationship on its head. In most businesses, the consumer has the power and can choose which services to buy from which provider. The traditions of the law are different, though, and many lawyers have historically been able to treat the notion of customer service as somehow lesser than their professional obligations. What we are

---

[154.] The Legal Ombudsman ' Costs and customer service in a changing legal market' March 2012 – http://www.legalombudsman.org.uk/downloads/documents/publications/Costs-Report.pdf

seeing now though are market changes forcing lawyers to face the possibility that their traditional view of how they go about their daily work may have to undergo a fundamental change. Those who adapt to the market, it appears, will survive: those who cannot, may be doomed to disappear.

The collision between what lawyers are used to providing and what the modern users of professional services are increasingly accustomed to expect is at the root of the 80,000 to 90,000 contacts from disgruntled customers we receive every year and, as we have already said in this report, cost complaints represent by far the largest portion of our workload."

To again confirm, do not be afraid to challenge your lawyer, if you feel that you are receiving poor service or being over-charged. If matters do not improve do not hesitate in referring your complaint to the Legal Ombudsman, as many do.

Mrs S's complaint to the Legal Ombudsman:[155.]

"Mrs S used a firm of solicitors to take care of her divorce. The firm told her that she wasn't eligible for legal aid so she would need to pay them privately. Mrs S paid the firm £6,000 but thought that things were moving too slowly. She spoke to another lawyer, who told her that she had, in fact, been eligible for legal aid all along. This was particularly distressing because she had wanted the lawyer to apply to the court for a non-molestation order to stop her husband from bothering and harassing her but had thought she wouldn't be able to afford it.

The firm agreed that they had made a mistake and refunded Mrs S the difference between what she had paid and what she would have paid if the work had been done under legal aid. Mrs S was still unhappy, though, because although she had her money back the refund didn't do anything to compensate her for the lawyer's bad advice.

[155.] The Legal Ombudsman 'Costs and customer service in a changing legal market' March 2012 – http://www.legalombudsman.org.uk/downloads/documents/publications/Costs-Report.pdf

What the investigation found the firm had provided a poor service: their failure to tell her that she was eligible for legal aid had had a direct and adverse impact on the case by preventing her from applying for the non-molestation order. Mrs S had wanted the order because she was worried about what her husband might do to her. If the lawyer hadn't given her the wrong information she would have been able to apply for the order and set her mind at rest.

The ombudsman ordered the firm to pay Mrs S £2,000 compensation to reflect the gravity of the poor service they had provided. When the ombudsman ordered this, he intended to put Mrs S back into the position she had been in before. The refund and compensation both helped but Mrs S remained upset about the way things had happened."

Following my complaint, I made the decision to change my lawyer. Honestly, my confidence and faith had completely disappeared; there was not only the complaint I had made against my lawyer, my further worry being, in my heart-felt opinion, there was the risk that my best interests would not be represented at the forthcoming court appearance.

In my view, lawyers rely on their reputation to build their business and referrals; unconditionally a lawyer has a responsibility to deliver a quality service to their client. In a recent study by the Legal Ombudsman, 62% of legal service users said that reputation was key; making it the biggest single driver for choosing a lawyer. And reputation is influenced most heavily by the standard of service being provided. Despite this, there are numerous cases in which service levels simply aren't good enough.[156]

To a client, lawyers can appear to be intimidating when complaining, if you can justify a complaint with sustainable facts; first seek advice from the Law Society or the Legal Ombudsman. If justified; do not be afraid to complain and change your lawyer.

---

[156] The Legal Ombudsman 'The price of separation' 2012 – http://www.legal ombudsman.org.uk/downloads/documents/publications/The-price-of-separation-LeO-report.pdf

A further report published by the Legal Ombudsman in the public domain; the ombudsman's report made the following findings:

"Every day I see cases like these that illustrate the effect that poor service and a lack of a customer service ethos can have on individuals, sometimes with drastic consequences. All of these stories are about costs, but they are also about poor communication. This is a pressing issue for consumers and legal services providers alike."[157.]

Further the ombudsman stated "The legal services market is dynamic, innovating – especially in the area of costs and charging and how legal business models operate. And what we are seeing from complaints is that there are challenges for us all to ensure that consumers do not experience significant detriment as a result of these changes. In each of those cases where we found that there was poor service, the problem would not have arisen had the lawyer done, at least, a better of job of explaining their costs".

"I hope that putting this information in the public domain will help people to make informed decisions about how to choose a legal service and, if they need to, where to take their complaints," the ombudsman said within the report. A further recent piece of YouGov research reported by the *Guardian*[158.] states that lawyers have been very slow to adapt their practice to modern customer demands. There is a sense of powerlessness and fear which lawyers engender in their clients. The YouGov research showed that the biggest brake on complaints was customer fear. In some cases, that was merely fear of looking a fool. Using the Legal Services Act the Law Society set up the Legal Ombudsman, an independent, statutory complaints scheme, which opened for business in October 2010. Critically, the scheme put an end to the unedifying spectacle of lawyers judging complaints about lawyers.

[157.] The Legal Ombudsman ' Costs and customer service in a changing legal market' March 2012 – http://www.legalombudsman.org.uk/downloads/documents/publications/Costs-Report.pdf

[158.] YouGov and quotation from the Guardian 'Don't be afraid to complain about your lawyer says the Legal Ombudsman' 15 October 2012 – www.theguardian.com/law/2012/oct/15/legal-ombudsman-complaints-lawyer

The statutory powers given to the ombudsman – the ombudsman has the ability to command co-operation of lawyers and remedies including compensation of up £30,000. But whereas in other areas of professional life the introduction of a genuinely independent ombudsman scheme led to a significant rise in the number of customers complaining, there was no such increase with lawyers.

In my opinion, there should be much more accessible information and transparency regarding lawyer's performance and complaints (if any) made against them. Perhaps the Legal Ombudsman should consider publishing all of their complaint decisions against lawyers. For instance, you should be able to search a lawyer's name to see if successful complaints had been brought against them. This information would be very helpful when carrying out due-diligence and selecting your lawyer; it would also expose lawyers who need to improve their services. However, this must be balanced with the many family lawyers who provide a good level of service to their clients.

A detailed report by YouGov further stated "an increase in the number of DIY divorces". The report finds, the government's recent elimination of legal aid for all but a limited number of divorce cases is likely to spark a rise in so-called 'DIY divorces'. YouGov found, less than a third (30%) of those arranging a divorce themselves used DIY divorce websites; of these the largest percentage (67%) used them to find free information and advice. Almost as many (65%) downloaded divorce-related documents. Just 11% used these sites for some free legal consultation and advice. Amongst those using web divorce sites, Divorce-Online has been used by 30% and Quickie Divorce by 25%. Over 80% of those arranging their own divorce were 'satisfied' or 'very satisfied' with the way they were able to deal with the divorce proceedings, and with the final outcome of the process. A friend of mine recently completed his own successful DIY divorce in order to save costs. His comment was that "he and his ex-spouse had to be in amicable and balanced agreement when it came to the sharing of the marital assets and care of their children for the DIY divorce to be a success".[159.]

[159.] Divorceonline.co.uk and YouGov 'DIY divorce set to rocket' 27 June 2013 – http://www.divorce-online.co.uk/blog/diy-divorce-set-to-rocket-according-to-yougov-report/

There is a now an opportunity to obtain an 'over the counter' divorce from a new network of regional divorce centres around the UK; officials at the centres aim to process uncontested divorce applications on the day, or within 48 hours at the latest. There are 11 divorce centres located throughout the UK, at which a legal adviser will be based to provide guidance. Advisers will be supervised by a district judge; the judge will handle contested applications, annulments and judicial separation applications. Legal advisers will not handle any financial remedy cases, again such cases will be dealt with by the district judge, who could refer the case to a hearing at the county court. Returning to the more traditional divorce procedures and a refresher of the earlier research; YouGov report just over half (53%) received a bill covering the legal fee they were expecting at the end of the process, while the other 47% were not expecting the bill they eventually got. For the vast majority (90%) of those surprised by the bill, the charge was higher than they expected.[160.]

In my opinion, and as touched on in the introduction to my book; I believe each divorce case could be evaluated on a cost vs. benefit basis, which informs the divorcing client the financial benefit of each stage of the divorce procedure vs. the maximum financial cost of each respective stage. Perhaps an entrepreneurial and innovative technology company could develop a new piece of software to undertake such a cost vs. benefit algorithm.

Possibly new software could be developed to reduce client legal and court room costs, which would be less of the £47 billion burden on the UK taxpayer. There is a considerable cost vs. benefit model here; the cost of software development could be offset and funded from taxpayer and direct client savings.

[160.] YouGov posted 25 June 2013 'Potential surge in DIY divorces' – https://yougov.co.uk/news/2013/06/25/potential-surge-diy-divorces/

It is just not in the UK, in Canada there are similar challenges with the high cost and adversarial court system. A family lawyer and president of the Ontario Collaborative Law Federation said "Putting families in crisis through the adversarial court system has been likened to pouring gasoline on a fire, but while many agree change is needed ideas about how to achieve that vary wildly... the adversarial system, which is our traditional court system, it inflames a lot of these emotions that people have when they separate... It really isn't working, period. And it hasn't been working for some time."[161.]

My own thought and idea to make the UK divorce system less adversarial and to further reduce cost to the client and taxpayer could be the proposed principle of a 'tribunal style' procedure; similar to that of employment legal cases. A tribunal style could be less stressful and emotional for spouses and their families, also, hopefully removing some of the confrontation, onerous paperwork, lawyer's letters, form filling and litigious administration.

As touched on a little earlier, and before leaving the topic of legal complaints; before writing and researching this book, I was under the impression that my personal experience of divorce hostility and legal complaint was in the minority, even unique. You know, once my research began; I was surprised at the level and sheer number of complaints made relating to divorce cases, in particular cost and customer service complaints. Such information and insight has provided me with yet further confidence in not only writing this book, but also 'there has to be another way' – in part, perhaps new technology is the answer.

Divorce and technology

We live in a fast-moving global world of digital technology and change; there will be a time in the not too distant future where private clients and organisations large and small will, amongst other considerations, select their legal professionals based on their digital and technological capabil-

---

[161.] CTV News 'Canada's adversarial divorce system targeted' 16 March 2011 – http://www.ctvnews.ca/canada-s-adversarial-family-law-system-targeted-1.619387

ities. The scope, scale and economic impact of technology continuously changes our lives; the sheer ubiquity of technology makes it part of our everyday existence. It took more than 50 years after the telephone was invented until half of our homes had one. It took radio 38 years to attract 50 million listeners. But Facebook attracted 6 million users in its first year and that number multiplied 100 times over the next five. In 2009, two years after the iPhone's launch, developers had created around 150,000 applications. By 2014, that number had hit 1.2 million, and users had downloaded more than 75 billion total apps, more than ten for every person on the planet.[162] By the time you read this book, I bet your bottom dollar that digital growth and number of users would have significantly increased further.

Global research carried out by McKinsey across all industries states "70 percent of the senior executives in a survey we recently conducted say that technology innovation will be at least one of the top three drivers of growth for their companies in the next three to five years." It is estimated that technology has the potential to grow from $3.9 trillion in 2015 to $11.1 trillion a year by 2025, globally.[163]

Can the next generation of family lawyers innovate and change?

It may require a new generation of law firms, possibly new start-up legal practices, to disrupt the market and bring latest leading-edge technologies to the forefront of family law and divorce in order to create a truly consumer-centric industry. The market is competitive; I am sure family law firms seek points of differentiation, which would provide them with a competitive advantage and commercial growth.

---

[162] McKinsey ' The four global forces breaking all the trends' April 2015 – Authors Richard Dobbs, James Manyika, and Jonathan Woetzelhttp://www.mckinsey.com/business-functions/strategy-and-corporate-finance/our-insights/the-four-global-forces-breaking-all-the-trends

[163] McKinsey "Leadership and innovation" January 2008 – Joanna Barsh, Marla M. Capozzi, and Jonathan Davidson http://www.mckinsey.com/business-functions/strategy-and-corporate-finance/our-insights/leadership-and-innovation

Globally, social technology communities had grown to over 1.5 billion by 2012, with 90% of businesses that use social technologies reporting benefits;[164] again, and with no doubt, these figures will have grown considerably by the time you read this book. IT growth has brought speed, efficiency, scale and economic value to businesses. Without any question whatsoever, social technologies have radically changed the way we live, behave and do business.

It can't have gone without notice that the legal industry relies heavily on data analysis, interactions and collaborations with their clients and professional colleagues, incorporating intellectual capital, research, knowledge, information, efficient communication, professional litigation, confidentiality, recruitment and marketing; all are characteristics that point to significant value and benefits from social and digital technologies. In my view, it appears little of this value is being captured by family law firms because social technologies are not being used to the extent that they might. Slow adoption by law firms reflects the pace of cultural and organisational change. A report from McKinsey said that 85% of law firms view social media as important. However, 29% said they would not engage in social media due to their risk policies. Further resistance is due to a history of difficult technology implementations. In addition, lawyers must generate 'billable hours' – to learn new systems means lawyers taking time away from revenue generation, even though it would make them more productive, cost efficient and improve their client service.[165]

---

[164] McKinsey 'The social economy; unlocking value and productivity through social technologies' July 2012 – Authors Michael Chui James Manyika Jacques Bughin Richard Dobbs Charles Roxburgh Hugh Sarrazin Geoffrey Sands Magdelena Westergren www.mckinsey.com/.../The%20social%20economy/MGI

[165] McKinsey 'The social economy'; unlocking value and productivity through social technologies' July 2012 – – Authors Michael Chui James Manyika Jacques Bughin Richard Dobbs Charles Roxburgh Hugh Sarrazin Geoffrey Sands Magdelena Westergren www.mckinsey.com/.../The%20social%20economy/MGI

Innovation Curve – how companies can transform markets

Diagram 23

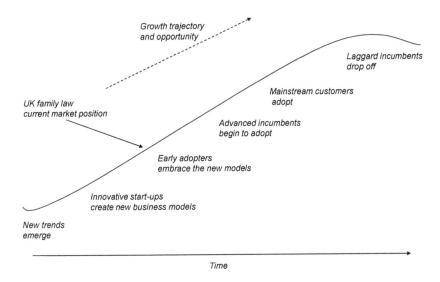

The position of industries on the 'Innovation Curve' depends on the degree that companies have embraced innovation and technology change. My educated judgement would place family-law companies who embrace innovation and in particular digital technology at the beginning of the curve. From this starting position, the curve represents scale, scope and opportunity to commercially grow by embracing digital innovation and new business models. Within any industry, including family-law this requires leadership and aspiration; regarding innovation-led strategies as critical to their future profit and growth – to invest time, resources and effort into innovation, to discover new and differentiated business models, providing law firms with a competitive advantage. To use innovation to target new market segments and meet changing customer needs, to motivate, recognise and reward lawyers who innovate and create new ideas. In my view, perhaps this may mean too much of a cultural change for many traditional family law practices; it would be left to the next generation of family lawyers to expedite the much needed technology change.

Remember it was the Legal Ombudsman who said:

"The legal services market is dynamic, innovating – especially in the area of costs and charging and how legal business models operate."

The ombudsman further states:

"We look here at the challenges facing the legal profession to adopt a customer service culture to meet modern consumer demands. We regularly are met with statements that people should have access to greater information to make them more effective consumers; possibly an easier challenge to meet in the context of swapping energy companies than in comparing costs for a bespoke legal service."[166.]

By comparison, there are now a growing number of digital businesses operating within traditional industries such as business support, consultancy and advice, marketing and PR, finance, insurance and consumer markets. These digital businesses, which are operating in traditional industries, are delivering double digit growth each year, not only in London but across the UK. Again, there are relevant best practices from such traditional industries, which could transfer to the family-law market to improve efficiency, productivity, customer service and profitability.

I have personally spent a big part of my corporate career and more recently running my own company innovating, creating new ideas and products in emerging markets; many of which have become globally successful and sustained their commercial performance for many decades. I hope one day to write a further book on my 30-year career, which has covered all corners of the globe. For now, I have applied some quick analysis and 'low hanging fruit' ideas to the family law market.

An idea when thinking specifically about family lawyers; it crossed my mind for a lawyer to have an online portal, where each client had a secure unique

---

[166.] Legal Ombudsman report 'Costs and customer service in a changing legal services market' March 2012 – http://www.legalombudsman.org.uk/downloads/documents/publications/Costs-Report.pdf

username and password to obtain updates and progress on their case, this would save client time and cost through telephone calls, written correspondence and postage. Rather than holding legal meetings and court hearings, where lawyers, barristers and clients need to travel, why not hold a video conference via Skype or a cloud based web-conference; this would save time and cost. Where possible send correspondence, invoices (e-billing) and administration electronically rather than by traditional post. Social media allows customers to post their experiences and opinions through sites such as Facebook and Twitter; law firms can monitor such customer feedback to make improvements to their service and better meet customer needs. In 2014, 31.4 million people in the UK used Facebook; Twitter boasted 15 million UK users at the end of 2013.[167.] When researching and writing this book, I used social media platforms to obtain topical views, opinions and discussion from lawyers, family professionals and divorcing couples; this provided me with real-time feedback and opinion on divorce matters, which were relevant and important.

The following diagram produced by Statista shows the number of Facebook users in the United Kingdom. There were 28.3 million Facebook users in 2012 and it is forecast that the number of users will rise to 33.6 million by 2017.[168.]

Globally, the number of social network users worldwide by 2018 will be 2.44 billion a growth from 1.79 billion in 2014. There will be an additional 1 billion smartphone users by 2020.[169.] All of these technology shifts will be game-changers, which surely family lawyers cannot afford to ignore.

[167.] Statista 'The Statistics Portal' Number of Facebook users in the United Kingdom (UK) – http://www.statista.com/statistics/271349/facebook-users-in-the-united-kingdom-uk/
[168.] Statista 'The Statistics Portal' Number of Facebook users in the United Kingdom (UK) – http://www.statista.com/statistics/271349/facebook-users-in-the-united-kingdom-uk/
[169.] Statista 'The Statistics Portal' Number of social network users worldwide from 2010 to 2019 (in billions) – http://www.statista.com/statistics/278414/number-of-worldwide-social-network-users/

Number of forecast UK Facebook users 2012 to 2017

Diagram 24

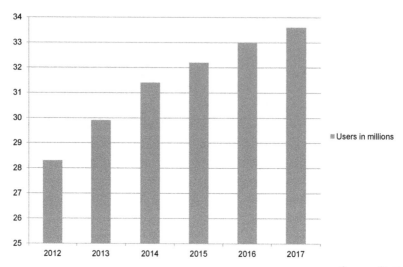

Source: Statista

In a landmark ruling reported by ABC News, a New York judge recently directed the service of a summons with notice for an action of divorce via Facebook. It was reported "The divorcing couple had not lived together since 2009; their only communication was through occasional phone calls and communication via Facebook. New York has relatively strict laws stipulating how a party must serve divorce proceedings personally. However, the law does allow the court flexibility to deem what is appropriate to effectuate the appropriate service in a matrimonial matter. The ruling may herald the beginning of a trend to give divorcing couples alternative ways to serve divorce notice; in this case via Facebook."[170.]

Returning to opportunities for UK family lawyers; social media can also help lawyers keep up to date with latest market trends and practices; it can

---

[170.] ABC News 'New York Woman Allowed to Serve Divorce Papers Via Facebook' 6 April 2015 – http://abcnews.go.com/Business/york-woman-allowed-serve-divorce-papers-facebook/story?id=30119759

also be a useful tool to obtain competitor information. Social media can provide a wealth of information and research, which should be playing an important part of a law firm's overall business strategy and provide a competitive advantage and growth. Social platforms such as LinkedIn provide opportunity to network with other legal professionals. There are several LinkedIn family-law discussion groups such as UK Divorce Network, Marketing for Divorce Professionals and Alternative Dispute Resolution, where legal and family professionals create bespoke social communities, and where each community posts divorce related stories, opinions and discussions. Writing a regular blog on industry experience on topical subjects provides further opportunity to network and build business. I note some early adopter lawyers are beginning to write regular blogs on industry related topics; the blog provides legal opinion on high profile divorce cases.

Legal apps are a technology tool that is showing some relative growth in the US. An app has a number of platforms, which can be used by a client to obtain information about a law firm, basic legal information, customer service information, key contacts, legal fees, newsletters, topical information and stories in the news, helpline and the list of opportunities goes on. The great characteristic of an app is its flexibility; an app can be designed and implemented to specifically meet a lawyers and their client's needs for use on their smartphone, tablet or laptop computer. An app has a further use for the lawyer; it can be used whilst working remotely in the courtroom as file sharing system that allows users to share files (photos, documents, videos, etc.) from one device to another, a document manager to access PDFs, MS Office documents (Word, Excel, and PowerPoint), a law library and legal research system, a legal notepad. Instead of taking notes with pen and paper, lawyers can use a stylus or even just a fingertip to write notes on the tablet or smartphone by hand, a digital tool for organizing case presentations for the courtroom. In fact, an app can allow a lawyer to be completely paperless and operate a virtual law practice. Perhaps operating a virtual family law practice is the market entry point for the next generation of start-up family lawyers. Starting a virtual business does not require high start-up capital costs such as office buildings, staff, administration and expensive equipment; the market barriers to entry are considerably lower. In the industries, where I have provided consultancy advice and new strategies; start-up companies regularly use the 'virtual model' to avoid high capital costs; many start-ups launch their new business from home. Steve Jobs the founder of Apple started his business from the garage of his home in Los Altos, California.

Returning to the non-virtual world of divorce; as touched on in an earlier chapter, some family lawyers seem to churn out letter after letter, all of which are chargeable to the client. I question the level of productivity from using a paper-driven system. Particularly as so much paper made little or no progress in reaching my final divorce solution. There are many examples from other industries, which have reduced the mountains of paper used to a minimum – some are even completely paperless; surely there can be some technology 'best practices' transferred from other industries to reduce the sheer volume of letters received during a divorce case. I hold no less than a library of 15 files of divorce letters and legally related paperwork.

Reducing the amount of paper during divorce proceedings can further help the environment and save many a rainforest. Reducing the amount of paper throughout the divorce would further decrease cost and postage; such savings could be passed onto the client. On average, I would receive two letters by post each week from my lawyer and or my ex-spouse's lawyer; calculated at a cost per letter including post, paper and envelope at £1.50 per letter; rounding up over the near five years of my divorce equated to around £780. To a lawyer £780 in the grand scheme of things may not sound much; however, to a client £780 saving is a relative high cost saving.

Almost three billion people, that is around 40% of the world's population, used the internet in 2014. Nearly one in three people living in developing countries is online.[171] Microsoft forecasts that internet users will increase worldwide to four billion by 2020.[172] The growth in worldwide internet access has implications for family lawyers. Referring to the earlier research conducted by YouGov; there is a growing number of DIY divorces particular within the younger generation who are downloading free advice

---

[171] ITU World Telecommunications and Internet Live Stats – http://www.internet livestats.com/internet-users/
[172] Neowin – http://www.neowin.net/news/microsoft-internet-users-will-double-to-4-billion-worldwide-by-2020

and information online, with 30% of couples arranging DIY divorces using divorce websites such as Divorce-Online and Quickie Divorce.[173.] Perhaps the more innovative and entrepreneurial family lawyers may extend their business and divorce offering in this online sector of the market.

Individuals using the Internet 2005–2016

Diagram 25

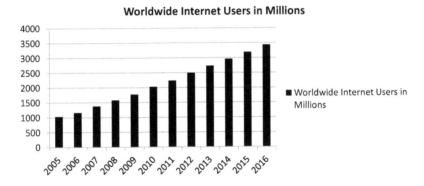

Worldwide Internet Users in Millions

Source: ITU World Telecommunications/ICT Indicators database

Broadly, research in the US has found four benefits to the legal sector through the use of digital technology:[174.]

1. Digital innovation fuels efficiency; innovative technology allows us to be more efficient and productive. It allows us to accomplish a job with a minimum expenditure of time and effort.
2. Digital innovation creates opportunity; more and more clients these days are looking for legal teams who are not afraid to use technology in their casework.

[173.] YouGov 'Potential surge in DIY divorces' 25 June 2013 – https://yougov.co.uk/news/2013/06/25/potential-surge-diy-divorces/

[174.] Live Deposition Redefining Legal Technology '4 Reasons why attorneys need to to embrace digital innovation in the litigation process' – posted by Evolvelawnow.com http://evolvelawnow.com/wp-content/uploads/2016/04/4-Reasons-Attorneys-Need-to-Embrace-Digital-Innovation-in-the-Litigation-Process.pdf

3.   Digital innovation cuts costs; embracing digital innovation allows lawyers to reduce operating expenses, which in turn allows them to provide services to their clients that fit within the client's budget.

4.   Digital innovation improves accuracy; in the legal industry there is no room for error. Manually reviewing documents and exhibits leaves room for human error. Innovation in electronic discovery, more commonly known to the legal industry as 'e-discovery', has given lawyers tools which allow them to be more accurate, more thorough and more informed.

The research further states:

"Digital innovation is part of our past, it is part of our present and it will be an even larger part of our future. As a new generation enters the workforce, a generation accustomed to using technology in all aspects of their life, embracing innovation and new ideas is more important now than ever if one wishes to stay relevant and competitive in the legal industry."

As touched on a little earlier; perhaps the next generation of family lawyers will think differently. There is without any doubt a high capacity and opportunity to improve client service, create a competitive advantage and grow their business.

A survey conducted by Accenture[175] across a comprehensive portfolio of different business sectors and executives reports on the top five outcomes of multiple digital technologies. I am sure there are the same 'best practice' opportunities for family law firms and their divorce lawyers.

---

[175] Accenture 'Growing the digital business; Accenture mobility research 2015' – https://www.accenture.com/us-en/_acnmedia/Accenture/Conversion-Assets/Microsites/Documents14/Accenture-Growing-The-Digital-Business-Acn-Mobility-Research-2015.pdf

Diagram 26

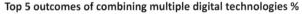

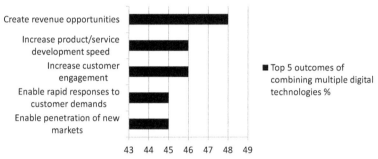

Source: Accenture

The research concludes that there are numerous positive benefits executives expect from digital's use. The surprisingly high number of chief digital officers in place reflects considerable optimism that digital can help improve business performance across all functions, including back-office and customer-facing. The correlation found between digital platforms and profitability further underscores that relationship.

An interesting challenge has arisen in the US; how to calculate accurately, after divorce, what is needed to achieve living standard equality or a fair differential that both spouses agree is reasonable and acceptable. New software is now being introduced, which accurately calculates the post-divorce living standard requirements for both spouses, considering all relevant factors including income, taxes, government benefits, outgoings etc. As touched on earlier in the chapter, perhaps the software principle could be further developed to produce divorce cost vs. benefit analysis; helping each client better understand the cost of each stage of divorce and the likely financial outcome for them.

A further cautionary note; remember to be mindful of what is legal and what is illegal when it comes to using technology to obtain information. There was a case heard in 2010 in which a successful businessman claimed the brothers of his estranged wife obtained personal and private information without his authority from a shared computer. Selected information was used by his wife's lawyers and given to the court after divorce proceedings had commenced.[176.]

Using best practice from other industries can travel well. McKinsey reports that a Chicago based law firm has been assessing its practices and processes, which has resulted in applying 'lean management' principles to improve client service and value.[177.] "Lean Management is a widely practiced and a successful strategy used in manufacturing, distribution and operations. The law firm has expanded the scope of its advice beyond the resolution of legal problems, and now includes improving workflows with clients, internal law departments and providing training for employees and partners." Over the past four years, the firm's revenues have grown more than 20%, and profits are up more than 25%. To continue the evolution within the law firm, new recruits combine the practice of law with the business of law; the firm hires law-school graduates into project management and technology roles, which provides and develops a much wider set of skills and capabilities. One of the firm's clients says "that he doesn't buy legal services so much as he buys business solutions delivered by lawyers". To change the 'mind set' of the more traditional lawyers, the law firm asked the lawyers to 'stand in the client's shoes' to better understand their needs and expectations.

The next generation of start up family law firms can quickly build scale by connecting with new clients, professional networks, knowledge and information, international markets, suppliers, mentors new skills and the list goes on. I really could write many more chapters about digital productivity and technology market opportunities in the family law sector.

[176.] Family Law Week – 'On 29 July 2010 the Court of Appeal gave its judgment in Imerman v Tchenguiz and others' – http://www.familylawweek.co.uk/site.aspx?i=ed115137

[177.] McKinsey 'A new order for law' August 2015 – Alex D'Amico and Christian Johnson http://www.mckinsey.com/business-functions/operations/our-insights/a-new-order-for-law

As I see it, there are six strategic issues facing the family law market:

1. The total number of UK divorces is declining[178.]
2. The market will remain competitive; family law firms need to create a sustained point of differentiation and competitor advantage
3. Online 'DIY divorces' are increasing; new entrants are coming into the market[179.]
4. Relative high level of complaints made to the Legal Ombudsman about cost and customer service[180.]
5. Ubiquity and growth in new digital technologies such as the 'Internet of Things'
6. Changing customer (family), ethnic and social needs

The photographs below compare the audience at Glastonbury Music Festival of 2005 and the audience of 2013. Perhaps the next generation of family lawyers are in the Glastonbury audience of 2013?

From this 2005…

…to this 2013

Photograph by courtesy of the Glastonbury Festival

[178.] Guardian and Office for National Statistics ' Divorce rates data, 1858 to now: how has it changed' 6 February 2014 http://www.theguardian.com/news/datablog/2010/jan/28/divorce-rates-marriage-ons

[179.] YouGov 'Potential surge in DIY divorce' 25 June 2013 https://yougov.co.uk/news/2013/06/25/potential-surge-diy-divorces/

[180.] The Legal Ombudsman 'The price of separation: Divorce related complaints and their causes' December 2012 http://www.legalombudsman.org.uk/downloads/documents/publications/The-price-of-separation-LeO-report.pdf

Finally, to underpin the need for innovation and change in the family law industry; commenting on the report 'Potential surge in DIY divorces' YouGov Reports Research Director James McCoy says: "The reduction in the number of divorces year-on-year, the loss of legal aid funding for most divorce cases and the likelihood that this will spark a rise in DIY divorce proceedings are all challenging factors for the family law industry. In order to survive this market environment, law firms must innovate and look for new ways to provide legal support outside of traditional divorce proceedings. This could include more legal work associated with the dissolution of civil partnerships, services for co-habiting couples and legal advice beyond divorce for those involved."[181.]

Divorce and social change

We further live in a fast and dynamic world of multicultural change and growing ethnic diversity, which will in time raise a number of new challenges with implications for family lawyers. A growth in the ethnic population and the diversity of cultures, religions and values is now ever-present in the UK, as is an increase in mixed ethnic marriages between spouses from different ethnicity; it is possible, although not conclusive that mixed ethnic marriages are at higher risk of divorce.

Census figures[182.] shows that the number of people in England and Wales living with or married to someone from another ethnic group jumped 35% to 2.3 million in the ten years up to the last census. The ONS reports that 'almost one in ten people living in Britain is married to or living with someone from outside their own ethnic group'.

The 2011 census reported the following ethnic groups in England and Wales:

[181.] YouGov 'Potential surge in DIY divorces' 25 June 2013 https://yougov.co.uk/news/2013/06/25/potential-surge-diy-divorces/
[182.] The Office for National Statistics 2011 Census – Census Day 27 March 2011 was 56,075,912 – https://www.ons.gov.uk/census/2011census – https://docs.google.com/spreadsheets/d/1y63Iy64jqvvtT1sfSLvcC_ZJNnfNpaMVZTCzzoPSn14/edit?pref=2&pli=1

Diagram 27

% Split

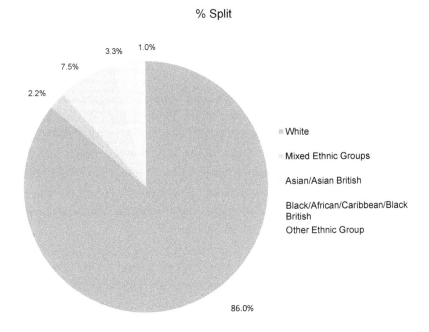

3.3%   1.0%

7.5%

2.2%

- White

- Mixed Ethnic Groups

Asian/Asian British

Black/African/Caribbean/Black
British
Other Ethnic Group

86.0%

Source: ONS

Since the ONS report was published in 2011 immigration has continued to grow in the UK, particularly (pre-Brexit) as the European Union has opened its borders, resulting in increased freedom of movement from Eastern European countries. These changes are likely to bring further ethnic and cultural diversity to UK marriages and ultimately more mixed-ethnic divorce. In London alone, there are 270 different nationalities[183] living in the capital, all with differing family cultures, beliefs, languages and values.

[183.] Evening Standard '270 nationalities and 300 different languages: how a United Nations of workers is driving London forward' 1 March 2011 – http://www.standard. co.uk/news/270-nationalities-and-300-different-languages-how-a-united-nations-of-workers-is-driving-london-6572417.html

The UK as a whole is deeply affected by these drastic population trends. There are significant implications for secularism in the UK, as the balance of religion changes, religious beliefs on families, marriage and divorce will have an impact on our lives in the UK and across the globe.

An article published by the *Daily Telegraph*[184.] states:

"The population figures also underline the scale of immigration during the decade which saw the enlargement of the EU, helping drive an unprecedented 4.1 million increase in the British population to 63.2 million. The number of foreign-born residents of the UK rose by almost two thirds between 2001 and 2011, from 4.9 million to 8 million – now accounting for 13 per cent of the population. The make-up of Britain's minorities has also changed beyond recognition: with the number of Polish-born people living in the UK increasing tenfold in a decade.

Yet the census exposes wide variations in the make-up of Britain. Four in 10 Londoners are from an ethnic minority while in Northern Ireland non-white people account for only two per cent. And it gives a glimpse of lifestyles have changed even more than the population."

In the US it is a similar picture of a changing population mix; by 2020 it is forecast that one in five marriages will be from mixed nationalities.[185.] A recent report published by Nielsen also finds a continued growth in a multi-ethnic society; primarily driven by younger generation Latinos in their family building years. This trend is set to continue to 2050.

[184.] The Telegraph 'Britain's married minority' 12 October 2013 – http://www.telegraph.co.uk/women/sex/divorce/10373894/Britains-married-minority.html
[185.] Nielsen Insights 'Uncommon sense: back to the future: perspectives on "Thriving in 2020"' Posted 1 July 2015 – http://www.nielsen.com/uk/en/insights/news/2015/uncommon-sense-back-to-the-future-perspectives-on-thriving-in-2020.html

Diagram 28

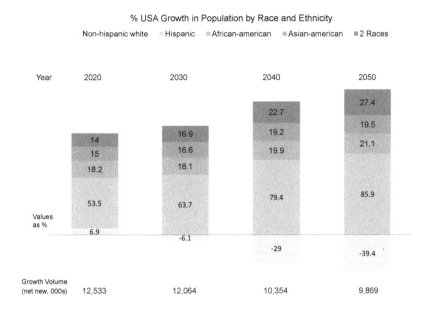

% USA Growth in Population by Race and Ethnicity

Non-hispanic white   Hispanic   African-american   Asian-american   2 Races

Year	2020	2030	2040	2050
				27.4
			22.7	19.5
	14	16.9	19.2	21.1
	15	16.6	19.9	
	18.2	18.1		
	53.5	63.7	79.4	85.9
Values as %	6.9	-6.1		
			-29	-39.4
Growth Volume (net new, 000s)	12,533	12,064	10,354	9,869

Source: U.S. Census Bureau, Population Projections, December 2012

Interestingly or maybe coincidentally, the US report states that:[186]

"Technology provides both a bridge across cultural and national borders and a platform on which to explore, share and celebrate new forms of multicultural identity as well as sustaining native culture. In an age where social media, instant language translation software and personalized online avatars are melding and blurring the boundaries between race, ethnicity and nationality, multicultural consumers are not so much melting as they are morphing, merging and mashing.

[186.] Nielsen 'The multi-cultural edge: rising super consumers' July 2015 – http://www.ethnifacts.com/THE_MULTICULTURAL_EDGE_RISING_SUPER_CONSUMERS_2015.pdf

Technology is the great equalizer, the platform for expression, and access to information and new opportunities. Multicultural consumers see no contradiction in being many things at once, and they can reinvent themselves at will, instantly and globally."

Returning to the UK, earlier we made reference to the impact on social change as a result of the UK's age population; the over 60s age category was showing one of the fastest increases in the number of divorces.

A report published by International Longevity Centre–UK (ILC–UK) stated:[187.]

"While divorce is difficult at every age it throws up particular challenges for those in later life who may find themselves struggling financially and without a salary. They could be forced back to work or into protracted legal battles to gain access to asset – especially pensions. Older people may also find themselves socially isolated following divorce, which can have a significant impact on their mental and physical wellbeing, a cost borne by society in providing care, social and health services. When it comes to financial battles and wellbeing, prevention is better than cure and steps can be taken to make it easier to divide retirement assets and to ensure older people are not alone when they split from their spouse."

The ILC report further stated:

"The impact of rising divorce rates in later life need to be more fully understood and factored into government planning.

- Financial products, particularly pensions, and the rules surrounding them need to better cater to the situation of those divorcing in later life
- Societal attitudes to divorce, remarriage and the impact it has on individuals need to change to be more sympathetic to the needs of individuals on their own

---

[187.] ILC-UK 'The rise of silver separators – divorce and demographics in later life' January 2015 – Downloads/The_rise_of_the_silver_separators%20(1).pdf

- Care needs should incorporate the impact divorce has on mental and physical wellbeing
- Prevention of loneliness and social isolation after divorce, or the breakdown of other relationships including long-term partners and other family relationships, should be key for communities, local authorities and charities."

To conclude, the constant pace of change, whether that is technological change, changing client-needs, social and cultural change or financial change; requires family-law firms to adapt. The family-law market is competitive, where customers have a choice they will seek and demand the very best legal value and service, whilst controlling their costs; no longer is it 'one size fits all' when dealing with growing ethnic and social diversity. This dynamic market within which family lawyers operate represents a significant commercial opportunity for progressive family-law firms to grow and differentiate themselves from their competitors.

In a nutshell, as one international lawyer posted to me on social media:

> *"I agree that the field will change and lawyers certainly need to change*
> *to fulfil the needs of divorcing clients, including advising them on costs,*
> *their finances and emotional needs and the myriad of choices available!"*

100% legal compliance and full disclosure

Throughout, I have emphasised the unconditional requirement to maintain 100% legal compliance and full disclosure, right up to the final divorce financial settlement. A reminder, do not attempt to hide any assets, no matter how small they are or tempted you may be, in fact avoid any enticement to engage in unscrupulous activity; this could be deemed in the eyes of the law as fraud and dishonesty with proportionate consequences.

For example, there was a case brought before the Supreme Court in early June 2015 as reported in the *Guardian*;[188] an ex-spouse sought to re-open her case, following allegations that her ex-husband misled the divorce courts about the true value of their assets. The original financial settlement awarded to the ex-wife included a payment of £10 million; however, she now claimed that her settlement should have been substantially more from her former husband on the grounds that it emerged later that the value of the shares in his company were an estimated worth of £656 million. At the time of the original divorce settlement the lawyers acting for the ex-husband told the court that the shares in the company were worth between £31m and £47m. The ex-husband was found in an earlier case to have "laid a false trail by his dishonest evidence" and to have hidden the fact that he was considering floating the firm. The judges agreed that the ex-wife had been misled and it paved the way for new proceedings. It is now possible that the ruling could open the floodgates for previous divorce cases to be re-opened. A salutary lesson – make full and honest disclosure throughout any divorce proceedings; if you don't it's bound to come back and bite you at some time in the future. Maintain and fully respect the legal and moral high ground is much wiser; you will have a clear conscience and sleep easier in your bed.

"Honesty is the first chapter in the book of wisdom".[189]

Thomas Jefferson

"No legacy is so rich as honesty."[190]

William Shakespeare

---

[188] Guardian 'UK supreme court to consider impact of fraud in divorce settlements' 8 June 2015 – http://www.theguardian.com/money/2015/jun/08/supreme-court-divorce-settlements-alison-sharland-varsha-gohil-ex-husbands
[189] Brainy Quote http://www.brainyquote.com/quotes/quotes/t/thomasjeff101007.html accessed 27th April 2016
[190] Brainy Quote http://www.brainyquote.com/quotes/quotes/w/williamsha101008.html accessed 27th April 2016

A divorce of attrition

It was Winston Churchill who said:

"If you are going through hell, keep going."

On the 23rd August 2006, just one month after my mum had passed away; my ex-spouse and I committed to a shared intention to reach an amicable divorce settlement, in order to protect our daughter, who had recently left school and started her studies at university. We agreed to commence legal proceedings the following January, allowing us both time to prepare for the legal procedures, also, and more importantly provide our daughter time to adjust into university life, without too many distractions caused by our divorce. With all the best and human intentions to reach an amicable divorce settlement; our divorce quickly turned to acrimony, conflict and high cost; all against our initial and best laid plans.

My email requesting that we do not pursue the hostile route:

"Thanks for getting the info. I too want to get divorced amicably & then get on with life. Can we please reconsider going the court & barrister route as this will cause much more stress, hostility and cost for us all.

My solicitor has proposed an alternative to your solicitor to avoid the court & barrister route…"

In January 2007, I received the divorce petition. When reading the petition, it was clear that our agreed intentions of reaching an amicable divorce settlement had got off to an unplanned start, which, over the passage of time became a protracted and acrimonious five years of divorce proceedings. Despite the unplanned start of proceedings in January 2007 my immediate concern was to protect my daughter, ensuring after her working hard in school to achieve good A-level results her university studies were not affected, and I was able to provide her with the necessary financial support. My objectives and 5-point divorce strategy were firmly in place and would not be affected by the unexpected beginnings. However, I reconsidered my tactics as there had been a shift from an intended amicable divorce to one of confrontation and acrimony.

Over the following weeks, my ex-spouse had instructed a new lawyer. In the early dealings, my tactics were to maintain a consistent approach of finding a resolution, which would protect my daughter's university studies and minimise both parties' legal costs. I proposed a 'no fault' divorce be filed on a 2-year separation by consent, which would allow my daughter to complete her university studies, without too much distraction caused by the divorce proceedings. According to 'Relate',[191.] it is interesting to note that 32% of divorces granted to men and 22% of divorces granted to women were settled following 2 years of separation and consent.

Extract from my email sent to my ex-spouse requesting a non-confrontational approach to our divorce:

"It again remains my wish to avoid progressing the court route, which will be acrimonious and at a high emotional cost.

The less acrimonious route will avoid the high emotional effect on our daughter. My proposal; the marriage ends through a two-year separation. My understanding would mean waiting for two years to elapse since you left the matrimonial home. This would be my preferred route, avoiding having yours and my reasons for divorce openly discussed in court.

I am open to discuss the above with you either independently or with our respective solicitors present.

If you are in agreement to progress divorce on the grounds of two-year separation, could you please instruct your solicitor…"

In late March 2007, I received a letter informing me that the other side were not prepared to support my proposed two-year separation, which in my strong opinion would avoid costly court hearings and more importantly to protect my daughter. Within the same letter, I was requested to cease all direct communication with my ex-spouse.

[191.] Relate 'Fact sheet separation and divorce' January 2014 – https://www.relate.org.uk/files/relate/separation-divorce-factsheet-jan2014.pdf

On reflection, I had proposed the divorce be filed on a two-year separation by consent, which in my own view would have saved legal costs, time and stress; further it was my hope that the two-year separation would make matters amicable. I made the proposal nearly one year after separation, which as my understanding meant we would only have to wait a further year for the two-year separation rule to apply. To my complete surprise and with deep held opinion, I felt, not putting the interest of the client first, the other side elected not to accept the proposed two-year separation and pursue an alternative route, which in my judgment and experience took nearly five years, resulting in a very high legal bill at the end of the day. In my opinion, it is such situations, where the legal system requires overhauling to avoid potentially adversarial court action all family lawyers should be held to account, when there is a far less litigious and lower cost route available.

As I see it, this was a classic example in which an 'application of common sense and not an application to the courts' was required. In my heart-felt judgment, I would also question ethics here: I had made perfectly reasonable proposal to protect my daughter, reduce costs and emotion, which would have allowed us to get on with our respective future lives sooner rather than later – yet it was rejected.

In addition to not accepting my proposal at this early stage of proceedings, the other side appeared to 'play hardball' and were in my view not prepared to give any ground. The spirit of our divorce intentions changed from a hope and plans of an amicable split to confrontation and battle. I had met this style many times in my corporate business career; locking horns in hardball negotiations with some of the world's largest companies and some 'heavyweight' negotiators – one thing in my favour I was 'always up for the fight'. Being candid, as the months and years of confrontation progressed, I genuinely felt that my battle became more between me and my ex-spouse's lawyer, rather than directly with my ex-spouse.

The crucial lesson from this change and confrontational approach? Be prepared and have a contingency plan in readiness if the other side choose to pursue the confrontational route. Don't be intimated or fearful of this style of approach, this may show weaknesses. Be and think smart; always be prepared, planned and at least one if not two steps ahead of the other side; maybe similar to a game of chess or poker.

It was Aristotle who said:

> *"Our judgments when we are pleased and friendly are not the same as when we are pained and hostile."*[192.]

My first response to the confrontational style was to file my defence and serve a cross-petition with well-prepared, truthful and compelling evidence. I ensured that my cross-petition was factual and substantiated with hard and objective evidence. In July 2007, one year after my mum had passed away, proceedings were considered and it was agreed that the decree should be granted on my cross-petition and not my ex-spouse's original petition. I received a copy of the Certificate of Entitlement confirming that I had sufficiently proved the contents of my petition, and the divorce was granted.

The Decree Absolute was pronounced in September 2007.

It is critically important that any divorce representations made to courts are 100% true, factual fully disclosed, and supported with substantiated and compelling evidence; maintaining both the legal and moral high ground at all times. As I saw it, it was an effective response to the other side's hardball approach; I felt my cross-petition was a moral win over my ex-spouse. Although the outcome had little or no bearing on the financial settlement, it was my first win, which in my judgment weakened the other side's arguments. The lesson from this situation – secure early wins and weaken the other side's position with hard facts and evidence. Be prepared to change your tactics if the other side employ the confrontational approach.

In April 2007, it was clear that divorce proceedings and hostilities were starting to affect my daughter and her university studies. So much so, that I, rightly or wrongly, broke the request not to communicate direct to my ex-spouse. In my deepest opinion, I felt this was necessary, as any father

---

[192.] Brainy Quote http://www.brainyquote.com/quotes/quotes/a/aristotle691608.html accessed 27th April 2016

would, to protect and put my daughter's interest first. Again, I believe the divorce process should encourage and allow divorcing couples to keep talking and maintain constructive relations, particularly where their children are involved. In my strong opinion, breakdown or enforced legal orders which prevent parents from communicating only adds to further acrimony, stress and emotion for both parents and families; for heaven's sake we are all mature adults. I proposed that the respective parties and lawyers meet early May 2007 to find an alternative route to the confrontation and acrimony we were becoming entrenched in. Under my instruction, attempts were made by my own lawyer to arrange a 'round table' meeting, in order to find alternative divorce routes to protect my daughter. All attempts to achieve this were met with further resistance and confrontation from the other side. I felt such unjustified resistance was an infringement of my right to protect my daughter; I am certain any other law abiding responsible parent would feel the same. Being prevented or restricted to act in the best interest of one's children is simply wrong, and in my strong opinion, family law needs to be changed.

Email from myself to my ex-spouse requesting we meet to resolve matters in the best interests of our daughter:

"I am very concerned over the affect divorce matters are having on our daughter, particularly as she will be sitting exams in May. Her concentration, revision and study time will be important over the coming months. On my solicitor attempting to make the meeting appointment with your solicitor as per your request, my solicitor was advised that your instruction was to proceed immediately with divorce proceedings and no meeting would take place to discuss alternatives, despite the immense risks and deep emotional cost to our daughter. I am sure this is a misunderstanding somewhere along the line."

A further letter was received in July 2007 from the other side stating that they were not prepared to meet under any circumstances in an attempt to resolve matters and help to protect my daughter. In my view, this was a classic example of where a 'grown up round table meeting' would have resolved the relative issues and avoided further and unnecessary legal costs and, most importantly, helped my daughter. I recollect giving my lawyer my full and honest opinion; telling that this approach was ludicrous and unacceptable. I would tell my lawyer that if I had reached an impasse or had an issue with one of my business clients, I would pick the phone up immediately to my client and resolve the problem nine times out of ten by phone. Alternatively, I would drive to meet my client at his or her office as soon as possible, in fact on one occasion where we had hit a financial issue with a client in Brazil; I took a flight to Rio de Janeiro, a 12,000 mile round trip, to sort the problem out. I reminded my lawyer that their office was less than one mile, a five-minute walk to my ex-spouse's lawyer's office vs. my 12,000 mile round trip to resolve the issues.

Further, I genuinely felt that all parties were lacking any 'emotional intelligence' and sympathy to our family emotions and the deep concerns over my daughter. I remember thinking at the time that lawyers must have some compassion when it comes to protecting and helping their client's children.

To reiterate my earlier point; I feel and believe, with deep opinion that some family lawyers could undertake continual skills improvement and practice in managing and demonstrating the 'softer skills' when it comes to the wider sensitivities of family divorce and values, particularly where children are involved, no matter what their age. In my judgement, there should be an 'ethical charter' which all family lawyers need to learn, practice and abide to. Remembering the research carried out by OnePoll reporting that 21% regretted the way they conducted their divorce; in addition the research found 33% regretted the way it affected their children.[193]

To further recap, research from the US suggests there is no such thing as a good divorce where children are involved.[194] An analysis of almost 1,000 families found that children suffer when their parents' marriage ends; no matter how amicable the split. The researchers said their finding contradicts the widely-held belief that it is possible to have a 'good divorce' in which the children and adults emerge relatively unscathed. The research called for marriage counsellors to make greater efforts to save marriages in distress

---

[193] Harrogate law 'One in five regrets the way thy behaved through divorce' 10 February 2016 http://harrogatefamilylaw.co.uk/one-in-five-regrets-how-they-behaved-through-divorce/

[194] The Christian Institute 'No such thing as a good divorce says US study' 5 September 2014 – http://www.christian.org.uk/news/no-such-thing-as-a-good-divorce-says-us-study/

and said that divorcing parents need to do more to protect their children from the fall out. Again, my personal opinion is that not only counsellors but also family lawyers need to make greater efforts in protecting children during the divorce procedures. Emphasising my earlier point and opinion; some family lawyer's need to show 'emotional intelligence', empathy and a more compassionate approach when it comes to considering a client's family and children.

Another US study[195] found that children struggle with maths and making friends when their parents divorce. They often fall behind classmates whose parents stay married, suffering from anxiety, loneliness and from feeling sad, and may never catch up academically. Contrary to some previous research, children through primary school did not show any negative effects before the parents decided to split. As soon as the divorce process started, the children suffered a range of problems that persisted, the American Sociological Review said. The five-year study compared emotional and academic development of children of divorce with those whose parents stayed together, by following 3,585 children from around the age of four.

UK reports[196] claim 'family breakdown is affecting growing numbers of families as a result of the rise in cohabitation and births outside marriage. Cohabiting relationships are much less stable than marriages and even more so when children are involved. The importance for children of the life-long marriage of their parents cannot be overestimated. Far too often separation and divorce are presented as quick-fix solutions without thinking through the longer-term implications'.

Further research, undertaken by state-funded Fathers Direct[197], a campaign group on fatherhood, reports more than 20 million Britons are living in the

---

[195] Living Families 'Divorce 'permanently harms learning and affects their ability to make friends June 2011 – http://livingfamilies.co.uk/divorce-permanently-harms-learning-and-affects-their-ability-to-make-friends/
[196] Centre for Social Justice 'Fractured Families – Why stability matters' June 2013 – http://www.centreforsocialjustice.org.uk/UserStorage/pdf/Pdf%20reports/CSJ_Fractured_Families_Report_WEB_13.06.13.pdf
[197] Mail Online 'British family under threat as one in three lives affected by divorce' 11 September 2007 – http://www.dailymail.co.uk/news/article-481292

shadow of divorce or separation. One in three has seen either their own marriage or relationship break down or that of their parents. If grandparents and step-parents are included, the figure rises to 50%. The report comes at a time of rising concern about the role of family breakdown in crime, violence and disorder. Children whose parents are divorced or separated are more likely to do worse at school or encounter health problems than those who stay together.

In my deepest and heart-felt opinion; considering the volume and weight of all this compelling research and evidence; families and children continue to suffer – this has to change; we really need a fairer and more considered system for children and families.

Returning to my own situation; despite my calls for a 'round table grown up' meeting to attempt to resolve matters and protect my daughter the other side continued with their resistance and confrontational style of divorce proceedings throughout the following months and years. In my opinion, proposed court applications, over matters that could be resolved with a phone call, personal allegations of delaying matters, applications of court orders for costs against me, references of bankruptcy and even a penal notice.

As I saw it, in attempts to apply further pressure, deadlines were set to provide information or a demand an action within an unrealistic time frame. On one occasion, it was arranged that a prospective purchaser would view the matrimonial home just prior to my daughter and I leaving for a well-earned holiday out of the country. All parties were aware that we were travelling to Sri Lanka and under time pressure to leave for the airport by early afternoon, yet it was insisted the property viewing took place just before we left for the airport – fortunately, we didn't miss our flight.

From my side, the ongoing demands became predictable and counter-productive, in my judgment causing escalating legal costs for my ex-spouse. In my own assessment, the tension over time within the other side's legal team, eventually, I am led to believe, placed increasing strain on their relationship.

Over time and paradoxically, the increasing strain on relationships enabled and helped us to reach a direct final financial settlement, which as touched on earlier was achieved 'out of court' and without any of our respective family lawyers.

> *"There was no hostility at the court when I arrived."*[198.]
>
> Sandra Day O'Connor – American Judge

By this stage of proceedings due to confrontation and as I am led to believe with pressure on relationships, both parties were making very little progress in resolving matters – in my own view of matters, I felt the communication between each other were becoming restrictive and hindering. Both sides were continually engaging in a game of 'ping pong' sending and returning letters, faxes and emails to each other, ratcheting up legal costs. My resulting frustration, in April 2008 I emailed my lawyer.

> *"… would it be more effective by picking up the telephone to her and agreeing a constructive way forward, rather than 'ping ponging' faxes to each other; we appear to be going round in circles."*

In my view and as I will cover in a later chapter; the complete irony of this 'going round in lawyer circles' my ex-spouse and I, at a later date, reached a full financial settlement through no more than half-dozen phone calls at zero legal cost. At this stage with a feeling of immense relief, we had now, in my opinion 'stopped going round in circles'.

According to the Legal Ombudsman[199.] some lawyers are failing to advise divorcees to settle courtroom battles before costs rise out of control because of the 'emotional rawness' of those involved. The ombudsman argues, "there

---

[198.] Workedia http://workedia.com/quotes/there-was-no-hostility-court-when-i-arrived-sandra-day-oconnor

[199.] The Legal Ombudsman 'The price of separation: Divorce related complaints and their causes' 31 December 2012 – http://www.legalombudsman.org.uk/downloads/documents/publications/The-price-of-separation-LeO-report.pdf – Researching Reform 'The Legal Ombudsman's Adventure: Tales of Diplomacy' 28 February 2013 – https://researchingreform.net/2013/02/28/the-legal-ombudsmans-adventures-tales-of-diplomacy/

is increasingly a tension between lawyers' financial self-interest in prolonging legal action and their responsibility to offer clients informed advice".

The above report by the Legal Ombudsman only goes to confirm in my earlier opinion that all family lawyers should be held fully accountable; perhaps under a new code of practice or 'Lawyer's Charter' that all reasonable means should be exhausted to resolve matrimonial issues before applying to the courts. This would require lawyers to find alternatives, probably through better negotiation and a more conciliatory approach, which would:

1. Reduce expensive court time.
2. Save taxpayers money.
3. Expedite proceedings by not having to wait for available court dates – sometimes several weeks or months of waiting.
4. Improve client service and collaboration.
5. Reduce hostilities and stress between spouses and lawyers.
6. Reduce client costs.
7. Reduce administration, form filling and paperwork.

In 2012, nearly 7,500 family law related complaints were made to the Legal Ombudsman,[200.] at the time making it the most complained about area of law in England and Wales. To recap on what the Legal Ombudsman's report said:

"The ombudsman report shows that there are legitimate reasons for there to be more complaints about divorce than other areas of law."

The report states, "However, clearly lawyers could be doing more to reduce complaints by providing accurate cost information, providing decent service levels and by taking complaints seriously. The report challenges lawyers to raise their game and make the divorce process less painful for clients".

To further emphasise the need to reduce to complaints, the ombudsman states:

[200.] The Legal Ombudsman 'The price of separation: Divorce related complaints and their causes' 31 December 2012 – http://www.legalombudsman.org.uk/downloads/documents/publications/The-price-of-separation-LeO-report.pdf

"For the lawyer, more work could be done to reduce complaints about cost. Giving proper estimates, updating customers regularly on costs, encouraging customers to manage costs better themselves, ensuring that they put the interests of a customer first: all these are vital to avoiding complaints. Estimates and regular updates throughout a case will become more pressing, not less so. And the reasons for good costs practice stack up: improved reputation, less complaints and potentially more business through recommendations. Though obvious, some lawyers still undervalue good service and effective complaint handling procedures as a means of retaining and gaining customers. With the possibility of more individuals representing themselves in the future, lawyers will be hoping that new ways of funding help to bring in customers. Providing decent service levels will also help to improve consumer confidence, so that those with the means to pay are persuaded to do so. For those seeking a divorce, the lessons are equally important. As hard as it must be to keep emotions in check, the lessons from this report all point towards the necessity for divorcing couples to try to keep emotions at bay. Taking an objective approach and setting realistic objectives at the start of a case could be the difference between £10,000 and £50,000 worth of legal fees."

In support of the ombudsman's findings; an extract from my reminders regarding the importance of keeping legal costs down:

"My deep concern, yet again, is the continued escalation of costs; I would hope both parties and the Court remain mindful of this fact."

"Regarding costs, to be perfectly candid, I remain concerned that neither side seem to be mindful of yet further costs that will be accruing over the coming months."

On a further financial note; This is Money reports investors are even gambling on bitter divorce battles between women and their rich husbands in return for a share of the spoils.[201] Further, venture capitalists, hedge funds and high-end lenders are putting up money to women who want to

---

[201] This is Money 'Shorting on the marriage market: How hedge fund managers gamble on bitter divorce battles' 15 January 2012 – http://www.thisismoney.co.uk/money/news/ article-2087050

fight their husbands in court. In return, the investors take a chunk of the court pay-outs. It is understood that one private company now has loans out to more than 100 'high net worth' spouses. The company charges about 20% interest for up-front divorce financing. It is believed the market is growing rapidly, not least because of cuts to the legal aid budget and the banks refusing to lend money.

In my own case, by using the principles from the DMBO it was not necessary to borrow money or use loan companies. Having a clear set of objectives and a strategy in place gave me a robust structure and cost management. However, looking forward, it was clear the length of the divorce process would increase legal costs beyond my planned budget. The combination of confrontation and a protracted divorce process, which eventually ran into several years, meant I had to re-think my own costs. If unexpected costs do present themselves do not hesitate in re-negotiating terms with your lawyer, explaining your position and reasons for re-negotiation. Considering that my divorce was to become protracted, I needed to put together a 3-point plan to protect my cost position:

1. Re-negotiate payment terms with my lawyer. All future costs would be paid on completion of the divorce financial settlement. The agreement to pay legal costs on completion of the financial settlement would assist with my personal cash flow.
2. Propose to my lawyer and barrister, a percentage of outstanding costs be paid on achievement of my 5 objectives. Unfortunately, this was not accepted.
3. Represent myself; become a 'litigant in person'.

I estimated that I would be saving myself approximately £3000 in legal costs by representing myself, plus the cash-flow benefit of settling my lawyer's bill at the end of the legal process. Representing myself in court and dealing directly with both my ex-spouse's lawyer and her barrister was a calculated risk, it also required me to dig deep into my own resources and, I was under no illusions – it would be a steep and fast learning curve. However, with thorough preparation, sound legal advice and by providing objective, honest and compelling evidence; I felt confident and succeeding as a 'litigant in person'. Throughout the period of acting as a 'litigant in person' I took constant advice and counsel from my family lawyer; I also found a number of online websites and handbooks prepared by various circuit judges, which I found very helpful.

In contrast – and I am sure with some truth – some legal voices describe being a 'litigant in person' in the following way:[202.]

"Representing yourself does come with a great deal of challenges, however. The courtroom will likely be an unfamiliar environment for you, which may make you feel anxious before making your appearance. Standing up in court and representing yourself takes a great deal of courage, especially if the other party is represented by a lawyer."

"Being a highly emotional experience – especially if you do not have the support of a legal professional."

"If you are unfortunate enough to be facing false allegations, it may be hard to fight your feelings of frustration, which can get in the way of your chances of success."

"A living a nightmare and going through the worst experience of their lives."

To overcome such challenges, I knew that I would have to be fully prepared and rehearsed, taking sound legal advice from my own lawyer knowing my facts inside out, supported by compelling evidence. However, I was prepared to learn an awful lot on the journey of being a 'litigant in person'. I personally found hidden strengths and resilience that came to the surface, particularly dealing, in my opinion, with a confrontational lawyer and stepping up to the plate in court and dealing directly against my ex-spouse's barrister – this experience, without any doubt took me (no kicked me) well out of 'my comfort zone' learning so much on the journey.

[202.] Family Law Advice ' Overcoming challenges as a litigant in person' 5 November 2013 – www.family-law-advice.org/overcoming-challenges-as-a-litigant-in-person.

"First you jump off the cliff and you build wings on the way down."[203].

Ray Bradbury

Representing myself against my ex-spouse's legal team could have been fearful; in fact, in a perverse way, I actually enjoyed it. I relied on my values and what I believed in particularly when I was protecting my daughter. Further, I had always taken pride in being able keep my composure when under pressure; something I had become accustomed to in business, being forensically cross-examined by board directors and management of some of the world's biggest companies.

It was Aristotle who wrote:

"The man, then, who faces and who fears the right things and with the right aim, and in the right way and at the right time, and who feels confidence under the corresponding conditions, is brave."[204].

Aristotle, (1115b15-19) NE III.7

To this day, I am unsure whether it was because I was intending to become a 'litigant in person', but the other side filed yet another court claim against me, which was listed for a hearing in early June 2008. As I saw things, perhaps the other side was wanting to test me as a 'litigant in person' – either way I was prepared to step up to the 'courtroom plate' and go head to head against my ex-spouse's barrister. Despite in my view, the attempts to reason with the other side and making progress in resolving the issues raised, we were unable to find settlement without going to court.

In context, one of the provisional claims related to a display of a 'For Sale' sign outside the marital home. Initially, we responded to this request as being an academic requirement; the marital home was situated remotely at the very end of a private road, where no one would see it, with the exception of our very elderly neighbour who would occasionally pass our home. As a matter of opinion, displaying a 'For Sale' outside the marital

---

[203]. Proverbia http://en.proverbia.net/citasautor.asp?autor=10915
[204]. Skills you need http://www.skillsyouneed.com/ps/courage.html

home would serve little or no purpose whatsoever. We took several photographs of the location and even a screen image taken from 'Google Earth'; politely explaining that due to the remote location of the property, displaying a 'For Sale' sign would serve little or no purpose at all. However, as I saw it the other side appeared not see my reason on such a relative minor matter; hence, it was referred to within the court application. To break this impasse, I did display the 'For Sale' outside the marital home; endeavouring not to waste the court's time on something I considered as a relative minor matter; hence this issue was removed by the other side.

As an initial part of my preparation for the court hearing, there were a number of headline checklist points, which I had used to guide me through the legal process, along with the advice and guidance of my own lawyer.

In preparing my 'defence' case against the claims against me, I did have a number of options. I could either accept the claim against me or defend all or part of it. As I had decided to defend the entire claim, I had to file a comprehensive and compelling 'defence' case. My defence document had to set out why I claimed not to be liable or at fault. I was required to file a defence within 14 days of receiving the claim form or within 28 days if I intended to file an 'acknowledgement of service'. I filed an 'acknowledgement of service' within the 28 days permitted. Failing to comply with deadlines to file my defence may have had serious consequences for me. Within my 'defence' I included the following:

1. Which of the allegations set out in the claim form or Particulars of Claim I denied, and why.
2. Which, if any, of the allegations I would admit to.
3. A statement and chronology of my version of events.
4. A Statement of Truth.

During my preparation for the hearing, I had sought regular telephone conversations with my own lawyer; I further passed all court documents and correspondence to him to check and proofread before disclosure.

Engaging my lawyer in the advisory role was a cost benefit, also a reassurance and safety check that I was following the correct procedures and my disclosures would not damage or compromise my position at the hearing – this was my 'safety net'. We will discuss having your own 'safety net' and risk-taking in a later chapter. In addition to using my lawyer in an advisory capacity there was further information available online, which I found very helpful. The Law Society and the Courts and Judiciary Society provide helpful free guidance and relevant handbooks.

When preparing my defence, it was important that I stated exactly what I would be asking the presiding judge for. It was also important that I stick to the facts and get straight to the point, using compelling, objective and relevant evidence from my earlier research; showing why I was right and why the claim against me wasn't true. This is a further example of why it is good to carry out thorough and diligent research. I managed to win a number of arguments against the opposing legal team using my own researched facts and figures; this gave me additional confidence in front of the judge. I remember from a previous court hearing my own barrister telling me that the opposing counsel will try to 'trip you up', intimidate and fluster you under cross-examination, this made me even more determined to remain composed and controlled under pressure.

In readiness, I wrote down in bullet points what I was going to tell the court; I was then able to expand on each bullet point in my own words. Telling the court in my own words rather than through a lawyer not only enabled me to remember all the points I had to make, but I could deliver my statement with genuine and individual expression and feeling, particularly when talking to the court about the issues which would affect my daughter. Before the court hearing, I must have read and rehearsed what I was going to tell the court dozens of times; it is essential that I practised and practised my delivery in court.

Mentally, I had to prepare myself for the court hearing, which had some similarities to the preparation I used when entering into a major business presentation or negotiation. Thoroughly knowing the facts and having them to hand, anticipating likely questions and objections, mitigating the risks, evaluating the strengths and weaknesses, keeping control and composure. Rehearsing and practising time and time again; what I was planning to say was a big element of the preparation, providing me with confidence. I called deep on my value of protecting my daughter, putting her interests first. Fighting for what I had worked so hard for decades, which had provided safety, support, health and wellbeing for my family. I also drew on my mum's values, pride and beliefs, her determination to overcome in the face of adversity. I placed in the inside pocket of my jacket (next to my heart) photographs of my mum and daughter. The court hearing was held in early June; I remember it was a warm summer's day. I sat in the court waiting room listening to the bustling traffic outside through the open windows; our allotted time of 10am was running late. During the extended wait, I began chatting to a lady vicar, who was at court to support a close friend. During the chat, the vicar reminded me very much of my mum's values and beliefs; she also had a similar appearance and demeanour as my mum. When our case was called by the court usher, the vicar smiled and quietly whispered in my ear "good luck, god is with you". All of these factors gave me extra strength and resilience, when entering the courtroom; I also remember singing to myself the theme tune from the film *Rocky* – 'The Eye of the Tiger'. I felt proud and confident with my head held high, shoulders square and chest out; as if I was entering the 'Gladiatorial Arena' – I was defending and protecting my daughter and my family values and beliefs.

I felt empowered by representing my own interests, presenting the facts and my wishes in a way that I felt would be beneficial to the outcome of the hearing.

"The Man in The Arena" Speech at the Sorbonne Paris, France April 23, 1910:

"It is not the critic who counts; not the man who points out how the strong man stumbles, or where the doer of deeds could have done them better. The credit belongs to the man who is actually in the arena, whose face is marred by dust and sweat and blood; who strives valiantly; who errs, who comes short again and again, because there is no effort without error and shortcoming; but who does actually strive to do the deeds; who knows great enthusiasms, the great devotions; who spends himself in a worthy cause; who at the best knows in the end the triumph of high achievement, and who at the worst, if he fails, at least fails while

daring greatly, so that his place shall never be with those cold and timid souls who neither know victory nor defeat.[205]

Theodore Roosevelt

Whether I was entering the 'Gladiatorial Arena', a major business presentation or representing myself in court; I had established a lifetime habit for such occasions of being thoroughly and meticulously prepared, knowing my subject inside out, dotting every 'i' crossing every 't', and being very well-rehearsed. I had left no stone unturned; taking with me to court all back up evidence, ready to be used if required; if I'm honest I was probably over-prepared.

For reasons of confidentiality, for legal reasons and out of respect, I am unable to disclose the details regarding the court hearing held in June 2008. The outcome was mixed for me I won a number of arguments against my ex-spouse's barrister. However, I do remember him knocking over a jug of water at the beginning of the court hearing.

On completion of the court hearing the presiding judge issued a 'Court Order', which set out the steps that each party must take – these are also known as 'court directions'.

To this day my beliefs and the values I held by representing myself in court remain strong and I would, without hesitation, do the same again. However, to reiterate and with a strong opinion, I do believe that divorcing couples and their lawyers should first exhaust all routes to find a solution, without filing for court action; court should always be the last resort. Further, if the impasse remains between spouses and lawyers the issues should be referred to tribunal style hearing; similar to employment cases. The role of the judge may be rather one of an arbitrator as opposed to issuing a 'Court Order' with sometimes financial penalties.

Recapping on what the Legal Ombudsman said:[206]

---

[205] Theodore Roosevelt 'The Main in the Arena' 23 April 1910 – http://www.theodore-roosevelt.com/trsorbonnespeech.html
[206] The Legal Ombudsman 'Costs and customer service in a changing legal services market' March 2012 – http://www.legalombudsman.org.uk/downloads/documents/publications/Costs-Report.pdf

"Here we tell the stories of people who came to the Legal Ombudsman for help. Every day I see cases like these that illustrate the effect that poor service and a lack of a customer service ethos can have on individuals, sometimes with drastic consequences. All of these stories are about costs, but they are also about poor communication. This is a pressing issue for consumers and legal services providers alike."

Adding my own further and final point of opinion on this matter, and to the above opinion of the Legal Ombudsman; some lawyers may inadvertently forget one of the basic fundamentals of a 'win–win' negotiation.

"The aim of a win–win negotiation is to find a solution that is acceptable to both parties, and leaves both parties feeling that they've won, in some way, after the event." Perhaps further training is required for family lawyers in this area of negotiation. Over the decades, not wishing to generalise or be critical, I have found some lawyers in business and/or private cases a tad 'black or white' when it came to negotiations. May I confirm and as the client, this is solely my opinion and experience.

In my further opinion, as negotiations become more and more protracted; some family lawyers may not seem to appreciate the ever-growing financial pressures and consequences on their clients, or if the client fails to keep an eye on the costs as they accumulate. The result could be that the lawyer ends up presenting the client with a bill far higher than they expected and which they simply cannot pay. Being unable to pay a lawyer's bill could possibly result in the lawyer ceasing to represent you. Further, it may lead to them adding interest to your bill of up to 5% above base rates, and the possibility of issuing legal proceedings against you to recover the monies owing. All of which could add up to an inflated bill, which a client is unable to pay – not to mention the stress and anxiety caused. Remembering the earlier research, which quoted 'For the majority, 90% of divorcing couples were surprised by their legal bill, the charge was higher than they expected'.

There were several personal examples, I believe where negotiation added unnecessary legal cost, which in my estimation and judgement required more of a commercial common sense approach rather than negotiation.

The opposing law firm was instructed to handle the conveyancing of the marital home, which was reasonable providing they charged a competitive and fair rate for conveyancing. This was not the case; in fact, their costs were much higher than other local conveyancing firms. We proposed to change the instruction, supported with a lower cost quotation from a local independent legal conveyancer. We were successful and the independent local conveyancing firm was instructed at the significantly lower cost; I estimate that we had saved around £2000 + VAT. In my opinion and with the benefit of hindsight; if there is an order for the sale of the matrimonial home, a reasonable request should be made that the sale of the matrimonial home is handled by an independent conveyancing firm. This instruction avoids any conflicts of interest and allows you and your spouse to negotiate competitive conveyancing fees, again saving you costs in the long-run.

Recapping, in a recent case reported by the *Guardian*[207] a judge described divorce costs as 'madness', the divorcing couple spent £920,000 on legal costs. Nearly a third of the value of the total marital assets, which they spent building up over the 18-year marriage.

The judge added: "The result has been to make a case that was surely so easily settleable almost impossible to compromise." He added: "Such a result should not be allowed to happen again".

"With four out of five divorces ending up before a judge, millions of pounds of taxpayers' money had historically been squandered on legal aid," according to the National Audit Office.[208] "Many cases could have been settled far quicker and with less animosity, if lawyers had not kept their clients in the dark about the mediation option". The spending watchdog calls for an urgent investigation into solicitors who fail to keep enough cases out of the courtroom, and says they should be stripped of legal aid contracts unless they have a convincing excuse. Critics have accused 'fat cat lawyers'

---

[207] Guardian 'Divorcing couple spent nearly £1m on divorce – 1/3 of their assets' 13 November 2014 – http://www.theguardian.com/lifeandstyle/2014/nov/13/divorce-costs-of-nearly-1m-scandalous-says-judge

[208] Evening Standard 'Divorce lawyers 'steer couples to court for profit' 2 March 2007 – http://www.standard.co.uk/news/divorce-lawyers-steer-couples-to-court-for-profit-7254123.html

of exploiting emotionally stressed divorce clients to turn a fast buck and pointed out they are under a legal obligation to suggest mediation. The Commons Public Accounts Committee urged a crackdown on lawyers who are "happy to jump straight into the court room, leaving the taxpayer to pick up the bill". To my best recollection, at no stage during my own near five years of divorce was I made aware by any of my legal team of the options and availability of mediation, ADR or other collaborative processes.

I have made reference to the Legal Ombudsman on a number of occasions throughout my book. They have provided me with excellent and valuable advice throughout my divorce years; without any doubt they deliver an excellent service, which is objective, independent and extremely helpful. The Legal Ombudsman has produced several related reports, including 'The Price of Separation' and 'Using a Divorce Lawyer – Ten Helpful Tips', which can be downloaded from the ombudsman's website; in addition they have provided author permission to quote their relevant reports and research within this book. There is further advice and help available online through the Family Law Advice Centre and McKenzie Friends, who are extensively and legally trained professionals. They are able to provide advice on aspects of divorce, including guidance on being a 'litigant in person'; their services are provided at a lower cost than family lawyers.

Returning to my divorce, it was necessary to keep my costs under review and continually re-forecast my future finances. I needed to make additional cost savings and put yet more contingencies in place, on top of being a 'litigant in person' which had already saved me several thousands of pounds. To achieve further savings – during the winter months I would turn off the central heating and put on an extra layer of clothing to save on costs. I would remember to switch off house lights when not in use; I would only flush the toilet when necessary and park my car off-street rather than pay for car parking. I began writing a shopping list and meal plan; buying only what was needed for the following week. I avoided buying impulse purchase items such as wine, chocolates and non-essentials; in-fact I stopped pushing the super-market trolley down the alcohol, chocolate and non-essential aisles to avoid temptation. I took a packed lunch with me; avoiding popping into expensive coffee shops or Pret a Manger at lunchtime. I put a halt on my social life; the highlight of the week became cleaning the house on a Friday night with a bottle of cheap red wine, whilst listening to classical music. Finally, I continued my lifetime habit to haggle for everything and never accept the first deal; on average I reckon I would save between 10% and 15% on every purchase. During my years of marriage my then spouse would walk out of the store, if and when I started to haggle with the sales assistant; my spouse said it was 'embarrassing'. I must admit during this time of my divorce, acting as a 'litigant in person', cutting back and finding extra savings and living a life of frugality to pay my legal expenses were probably the 'darkest days' of the divorce process. This required me to dig deep and find that extra determination and motivation to keep going. It reminded me of Winston Churchill's quote: *"If you're going through hell, keep going"*.

By my own admission, I had little option but to become frugal. Perhaps, this was my Yorkshire blood or maybe, when I lost my dad in 1964 at a very young age, it was that I had taken responsibility to ensure my mum was able to pay the electricity bill and feed my two younger sisters. I would find ways to save household money during the 1960s and 70s – in addition I had several small jobs, before and after school hours, such as delivering early morning newspapers, and, during the evening, sticking up skittles for the local pub skittle team or fruit picking in the summer months. On my 16th birthday, which was the age I was legally allowed to work part-time, I got a Saturday job working for a large city department store. Perhaps this was character building; today my sister says I am still 'tight with money' – I just tell my sister that it's prudence and wisdom, which has always put me in good stead.

Before closing on the area of self-representation; the Law Society Gazette reports that hard-up couples choosing to represent themselves are putting pressure on the divorce courts.[209.] The 2008 recession and cuts to legal aid are putting immense pressure on family courts as litigants shun solicitors to go it alone. The Legal Ombudsman[210.] further added opinion on divorcing couples representing themselves; "With the possibility of more

---

[209.] The Mail on Sunday 'Rise of DIY divorce' 22 April 2012 – http://www.dailymail.co.uk/news/article-2133418

[210.] The Legal Ombudsman 'The price of separation: Divorce related legal complaints and their causes' 31 December 2012 – http://www.legalombudsman.org.uk/downloads/documents/publications/The-price-of-separation-LeO-report.pdf
http://www.legalombudsman.org.uk/reports/divorce/ conclusion.html

individuals representing themselves in the future, lawyers will be hoping that new ways of funding help to bring in customers. Providing decent service levels will also help to improve consumer confidence, so that those with the means to pay are persuaded to do so".

Returning to my own specific case; it had been agreed in the absence of any offers from purchasers, the marketing price of the matrimonial home shall be reduced in price every six weeks.

In addition, I had considered two further factors here:

Timing wise, we were in the middle of a significant downturn in the UK economy, which had turned into a prolonged recession from 2008 to 2013. Therefore, it was unlikely that we would find an imminent buyer for the matrimonial home.

UK house prices were forecast to decline 20% by 2012; the decline in UK house prices combined with the agreement that we would be reducing the sale price of the matrimonial home every six weeks meant the asset value would rapidly shrink, making the possibility of a 'buy-out' more affordable and attractive for both parties.

However, there was a further factor to bring into consideration, which was the growing financial pressure on both sides. In my own assessment, I was led to believe the increasing financial pressure brought about growing strain to the other side's relationship. Personally, I felt absolutely no sympathy with this situation. I kept reminding and justifying to myself it was their choice to 'play hardball' with me; both underestimated my ability to 'play hardball' as well. As I saw things, it was the other side who had refused my proposal to have a common sense and conciliatory approach; frequently referring matters to court, when they could have been resolved by a 'round table ne-gotiation'. It was the other side who rejected my proposal of divorce by a two-year separation in order to protect and help my daughter in her early years at university.

Subsequently, the combination of economic conditions, falling house prices, timing and financial pressures resulted in my ex-spouse accepting my buy-out of the marital-home significantly below what the other side had origi-nally demanded earlier in the divorce proceedings.

A quick reminder of the quote:

> *"Negotiation is not a policy. It's a technique. It's something you use when it's to your advantage and something that you don't use when it's not to your advantage."*[211.]
>
> *John Bolton*

In summary, my lessons when selecting a family lawyer:

- Take time and patience when selecting your lawyer; it will pay sig-nificant dividends in the long term.
- Carry out thorough research and due-diligence before recruiting your lawyer; remember it's a competitive market.
- Negotiate the best legal value and cost.
- Challenge your lawyer; don't be afraid to complain and fire him or her, if they are not up to the job.
- Prepare and plan for any opposing confrontational lawyer.
- Keep legal and living costs under control; always seek savings.
- Weigh up the pros and cons of becoming a 'litigant in person'.
- Maintain 100% legal compliance and full disclosure; keep the moral high ground at all times.

[211.] Brainy Quote http://www.brainyquote.com/quotes/quotes/j/johnbolton455671.html accessed 27th April 2016

Chapter Four
It's your Quality Financial
Settlement – Step Eight

External Market Conditions

Diagram 29

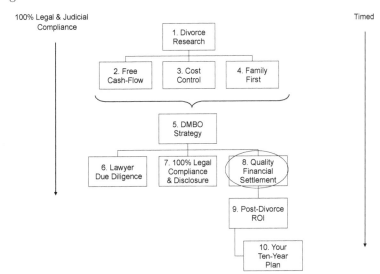

Clearly for most people, 2008 was the beginning of the worst economic recession since the 1930s – fast falling house prices, global financial crisis and future uncertainty was a good reason to put divorce on hold for a while. Paradoxically and for me, I saw the situation differently and as an opportunity to complete my divorce and achieve a quality financial settlement, which secured my financial future.

The demise and eventual collapse of Lehman Brothers in September 2008 almost brought down the world's financial system. It took huge taxpayer-financed bail-outs to support the banking industry. The following credit crunch turned what was already an economic downturn into the worst global recession in 80 years.[212.]

House prices had crashed twice in the last 20 years, between 1990 and 1992, and more recently between 2007 and 2010.

Reported by Economics Online, historically, as the economy came out of recession in 1992, house prices began to rise, and continued for a further 15 years.[213.] Over most of this period, house prices rose well above the general inflation rate, generating a considerable wealth effect. However, during the mid 2000s house price inflation started to slow down, and prices starting falling during 2007. House prices continued to fall throughout 2008 and 2009, and again in 2011. Despite the near economic Armageddon, these market conditions helped me secure a quality financial settlement and achieve my DMBO objectives. Market and economic conditions are constantly changing; assess and analyse the prevailing economic conditions at the time of your own divorce and identify those conditions, which will have both a negative and positive impact on your own financial settlement and respond accordingly.

Diagram 30

Source: Halifax Building Society

[212.] The Economist -www.economist.com/news/schoolsbrief/21584534-effects-financial-crisis-are-still-being-felt-five-years-article 7 Sept. 2013

[213.] Economics Online 'House price volatility' – 27 April 2016 http://www.economics online.co.uk/Competitive_markets/House_prices.html

During the recessionary years, analysts continued to say the economic uncertainty had made couples in unhappy wedlock reluctant to begin divorce proceedings. Falling house prices had forced many to rethink selling their home and dividing the assets in divorce. A family lawyer said: "Current financial woes are bound to cause domestic arguments and put a strain on any relationship, potentially resulting in divorce". He also said, "However, many couples looking to separate are being forced to stay together under the same roof due to the lack of movement in the housing market and also the fact that some simply can't afford to go through divorce proceedings".[214]

Property analysts Savills Research[215] said "historical data from England and Wales showed a 'remarkably strong' link between the property market and divorce rates". Savills further said: "As house prices rise homeowners undoubtedly feel wealthier and our supposition is that they also feel able to afford to get divorced. We forecast that the current falls in property prices, unwelcome and uncomfortable for the majority will result in fewer divorces".

An official ONS commentary[216] said "Recent trends could be consistent with the theory that recession is associated with an increased risk of divorce – but with a delayed impact. This perhaps reflects a couple's wait for an economic recovery to lift the value of their assets or the time lag between separation and obtaining a decree absolute". In 2010 as the UK came out of recession, the ONS reported a 4% increase in the number of divorces.

On Thursday 5 March 2009, the Bank of England announced a 0.5 per cent interest rate, the lowest level in more than 300 years. The historic low interest rate was held for the next 6 years. As of 2015, the Bank of England has signalled that they want interest rates to remain at 0.5% for the foreseeable future.

---

[214] This is Money 'Crunch means couples can't afford to divorce' 31 August 2008 http://www.thisismoney.co.uk/money/news/article-1641019
[215] This is Money 'Crunch means couples can't afford divorce' 31 August 2008 – http://www.thisismoney.co.uk/money/news/article-1641019
[216] The Office for National Statistics 'Divorces in England and Wales 2012' 6 February 2014 – http://webarchive.nationalarchives.gov.uk/20160105160709

Diagram 31

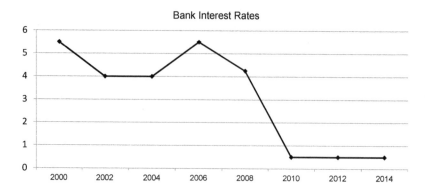

Source: Bank of England

The following economic factors and market trends made me start to think about making a serious move with my buy-out offer:

1. Historically low interest rates, enabling me to raise the capital to fund the buy-out offer at a low fixed rate of interest.
2. Falling house prices and market conditions, enabling me to offer a realistic and acceptable buy-out price.
3. The historic trend that house prices rise after a deep recession as confidence returns to the market.
4. My ex-spouse was willing to sell her share of the matrimonial home to me.
5. My ex-spouse and myself were both committed to achieve a resolution after nearly five years of divorce acrimony.

As a quick comparison with the principles of a successful company MBO, my DMBO 'ticked' the same boxes:

1. A vendor who is willing to explore a sale of their assets.[217.]
2. A vendor who will accept a realistic price and a fundable deal structure.

[217.] Strategic Corporate Finance – http://www.managementbuyout.co.uk/is-an-mbo-feasible 27th April 2016

3. A committed team of people.
4. Good future prospects of a return on investment; without high risks.

Source: Managementbuyout.co.uk

The question now was the timing of my proposed buy-out; the headline news was consistent from 2009 through to 2010:

"House prices 'to crash 20% by 2012"

"Homeowners avoid selling up amid dwindling supplies of houses available to buy."

"House prices fall for second consecutive month."

Considering the housing market and economic conditions, the opportunity to make an acceptable offer to complete the buy-out offer was becoming possible. I continued as a 'litigant in person' with the benefit of reduced personal legal costs – in contrast the other side's legal bills were continuing to increase. In my estimation and opinion, my ex-spouse must have realised that her legal costs were burning an ever bigger hole in her share of the residual marital finances.

Throughout the following months there were further trips to the court. On one occasion, the opposing side called the manager of the incumbent estate agent as a witness to testify against me. They alleged that I had metaphorically speaking 'attacked' him. Thankfully, it was entirely unnecessary to call the estate agent manager as a witness, despite him arriving at court prepared to give a statement.

By now, due to prevailing market conditions, a lack of serious buyers and the agreed reduction in the sale price every six weeks, the marketing price of the matrimonial home had been reduced by 15.75%, probably in line with the overall UK housing market decline. In October 2010, a prospective purchaser made a low offer to purchase the matrimonial home, which I automatically rejected as derisory and as undervaluing the property. However, my ex-spouse accepted the offer; I made my move with 'closing the deal' offering the buy-out at the same price offered by the prospective purchaser. If my ex-spouse accepted the offer there would be the significant financial saving on estate agent and survey fees, conveyancing fees, further legal and court fees and temporary house rental. I estimated my ex-spouse would be saving around £31,000, if she accepted my 'buy-out' proposal. My ex-spouse would receive guaranteed payment from me within eight to ten weeks, whereas, if we were to accept the prospective purchasers offer my ex-spouse would have had a delay of several months before receiving payment. Also, the prospective buyer could have withdrawn from the sale at any time up to Exchange of Contracts, which in my view was adding further risk for my ex-spouse.

> *"The best move you can make in negotiation is to think of an incentive the other person hasn't even thought of − and then meet it."*[218]
>
> *Eli Broad*

I had now put in place 'Objective One and Strategy B' of my DMBO:

Place the marital home on the open market. Obtain a 'preliminary purchase offer' from a prospective buyer; match the 'preliminary offer' to justify a legitimate 'buy-out lump sum' paid as final settlement to my ex-spouse. An estimated £55,000 saving on estate agent, sale and legal fees by retaining the marital home. Re-invest the savings in future property development.

Now, without the involvement of our respective lawyers we could negotiate the buy-out and its detail directly with each other. We completed the buy-out and all the formalities; we agreed on the buy-out figure sharing of the residual equity as per the final court order with neither of us incurring further onerous legal costs or estate agent fees. The buy-out payment would be paid to my ex-spouse within the next eight to ten weeks; I would retain 100% of the matrimonial home contents. The buy-out terms were agreed within a matter of weeks; the irony being that the terms of agreement were achieved without the involvement of lawyers or barristers, court hearings and the usual proliferation of correspondence, which would have resulted in yet even more legal cost, stress and anxiety.

[218.] Brainy Quote http://www.brainyquote.com/quotes/quotes/e/elibroad539552.html accessed 27th April 2016

Effectively, we had turned a complete 360-degree circle from declaring our intention in 2006 to resolve our divorce amicably, with the engagement of lawyers where necessary. We then travelled along nearly five years of legal conflict, acrimony, court hearings and significant costs, to finally find ourselves resolving the divorce issues directly between ourselves, without lawyer involvement and within a matter of weeks. To this very day and with greatest respect, metaphorically speaking, the jury remains out – were lawyers a help or a hindrance– this continues to be my opinion?

In late November 2010; the court ratified the agreement and issued the 'Consent Order', which made the buy-out legally binding. Using the principles of the DMBO; effective negotiation, prevailing property market conditions, tight cost control, full legal compliance and disclosures and having a clear divorce strategy; I successfully secured a quality 'clean break' financial agreement during the worst recession since the 1930s.

Recapping on the earlier statement made by a lawyer:

"However, many couples looking to separate are being forced to stay together under the same roof due to the lack of movement in the housing market and also the fact that some simply can't afford to go through divorce proceedings during the recession."[219.]

As we came out of the worst recession for 80 years, many couples who had waited found that the recession had significantly diminished the value of their properties. This forces major compromises in a couple's lifestyle after a divorce. In my case by using the MBO principles, I had 'bucked the market trend' – my lifestyle after divorce has been far from compromised. It has been one of freedom, positive personal investment, growth and fulfilment after the final 'clean break' divorce settlement.

In summary; evaluating external market conditions will:

- Allow you to assess and decide the trends and market conditions, which will make a difference to your financial settlement.

[219.] This is Money 'Crunch means couples can't divorce' 31 August 2008 – http://www.thisismoney.co.uk/money/news/article-1641019

- Provide collateral and incentives when negotiating the financial settlement – achieve a 'win–win' agreement.
- Provide data and information, enabling you to forecast the future value of the retained marital assets.
- Allow you to plan a timetable, which considers changing market conditions i.e., low interest rates and government legislation.
- Allow you to consider new opportunities as new information becomes available.
- Allow you to better manage and mitigate future risks.
- Provide you with a legitimate and fair competitive advantage when negotiating.
- Allow you to identify and offer financial savings to include and propose as part of the buy-out offer.
- Allow you to select and prioritise market conditions and information that are relevant and bespoke to your own individual divorce and personal financial circumstances.
- Don't be afraid to buck market trends, and don't forget knowledge is power; however, knowledge can become obsolete very quickly.

On the 23 June 2016 the UK voted to leave the European Union, which will probably bring several months or possibly years of economic uncertainty and risk. By comparison, the timing of my own divorce was during deep global uncertainty and the worst recession for 80 years. From my own first hand experience and using the principles discussed in my book – the pursuing years of economic uncertainty post exit from the European Union may just be the time to think, plan and complete a divorce and prepare for a future life of new opportunity and discovery.

Don't be afraid to buck market trends, and use the power of knowledge; however do not forget, knowledge can become obsolete very quickly.

> *"The best advice I ever got was that knowledge is power and to keep reading."*[220.]
>
> David Bailey

[220.] Brainy Quote http://www.brainyquote.com/quotes/quotes/d/davidbaile474005.html

Chapter Five
In to Recovery

Post-Divorce Return on Investment (ROI) – Step Nine ⑨

Diagram 32

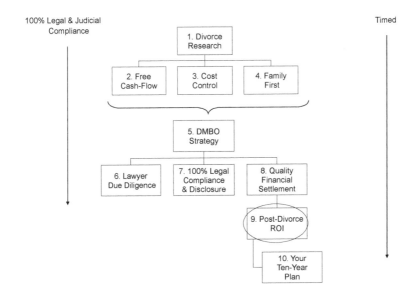

We have discussed the importance of freeing up cash to fund your divorce costs in an earlier chapter. Having set good habits of cost control during your divorce, it is important to maintain and continue the habits and practices after your divorce and financial settlement in order to, as a priority, recover any outstanding legal costs. Always seek new financial efficiencies, particularly if you have retained the marital home as part of the financial settlement. In business we used to say 'sweat the asset' meaning finding asset savings and efficiencies, whilst maximising your financial returns. To briefly remain in business; after an **MBO** of company assets the buyers will seek immediate, sometimes deep, cost savings including job losses to expedite the recovery of their buy-out costs – some even sell-off unwanted assets that may not have long-term value commonly known as 'asset stripping'.

The same principles apply with a **DMBO** 'sweating the ex-marital assets' as hard as possible. These are a few examples of how I managed to 'sweat my assets' immediately after the **DMBO** had been completed, not forgetting that you will no longer now have to disclose the financial gains to your now ex-spouse or their lawyer. First, and prior to making new and more permanent savings to release free-cash-flow, ensure that all the cost savings and efficiencies implemented during the divorce months and years remain firmly in place and you continue to receive the financial benefits and free-cash. A quick checklist on some of the savings we had put in place during divorce proceedings:

- ✓ Cancel unwanted warranties
- ✓ Pay bills by direct debit
- ✓ Cancel unwanted insurance policies
- ✓ Review your satellite TV agreement and cancel unwanted channels
- ✓ Use shopping discount vouchers and loyalty cards
- ✓ Sell unwanted items on eBay
- ✓ Paperless billing
- ✓ Shop online and use voucher codes
- ✓ Switch utility suppliers

Go over any new areas of spending since divorce, to see if you are able to make further savings and efficiencies. Once you have reviewed your own savings checklist; ensure, if you have taken out a new mortgage loan to finance your buy-out, it offers the best interest rate and loan value available. There are hundreds of deals to choose from, it's an intensely competitive market. However, check the small print for hidden catches such as early re-demption penalties, fixed rate interest term, payment holidays, administration fees, property valuation and survey fees.

Once you have secured the best value mortgage loan; give the ex-matrimonial home a permanent energy makeover. There are plenty of things that can be done to improve the energy performance of your home. Install individual room thermostats or programmer also fit thermostatic radiator valves; I estimated you could save up – to £160 a year – I fitted these to all my home radiators.

I switched from oil to gas supply soon after the financial settlement had been completed, resulting in a saving of several hundreds of pounds each year; the average price of oil was well over US$100 per barrel in 2011–12. In addition, I switched telecoms supplier from BT to a much smaller and leaner organisation based in Brighton; saving around £600 a year. Using 'Skype' can be a further way to save money on telephone charges. If you haven't done so already, install a smart meter, which measures your energy use at any moment in time. Most energy suppliers will install your meter free of charge as part of your energy contract. Further, smart meters help you budget your energy use by providing real-time information on energy use, shown in monetary value; providing the ability to manage it. I discovered which appliances were using most energy, such as the microwave oven, boiling the kettle and using the tumble dryer. Smart meters remove estimated billing, you are billed for the actual energy used, which prevents energy companies from overcharging due to inaccurate estimated billing, helping you budget better. In addition to installing a smart meter; energy companies also offer an Energy Toolkit. The Toolkit lets you see how much energy you use compared to other similar customers' homes in your area.

As well as seeing how much energy you use, the Toolkit also lets you;

- See how you're doing compared with the average and lowest consuming customers' homes in your area.
- See how much energy you use across the year and which months you use more or less.
- See a breakdown of your monthly energy costs.

Join community buying groups; such groups pool local residents together to negotiate better group buying prices and consolidate orders when delivered to local communities. One example – if oil is your main energy source, consider joining the 'Oil Buying Club', where members receive the best prices from local oil suppliers, plus a 10% discount. If you have a shower that takes hot water straight from your boiler or hot water tank (rather than an electric shower), then you may be able to fit a water efficient shower head. This can reduce your hot water usage and costs whilst retaining a powerful shower. I fitted two of these to shower heads in the main bathroom and the en suite shower room. Change to LED spotlights, there is a cost to replace halogens, however in the long term they run at a fraction of the cost of more traditional light bulbs. I have since installed LED lights in the rooms, which were most used in the house such as the kitchen, dining areas and new build areas.

To help finance energy efficient installations, there are many grants available to help you improve the efficiency of your home – check out energy saving and government websites. If you are paying a monthly sub-scription to your satellite TV provider, switch to a free no cost provider such as Freeview or Free Sat.; the switch could save you over £600 per year. I have cancelled my Sky TV subscription completely, saving £50 per month; I did find cancelling my Sky TV challenging, the company were continually pressurising me to remain a Sky TV subscriber, which I resisted; today, I still receive regularly invitations and incentives re-subscribe to Sky TV.

Reduce the cost of your fuel, insurance, internet and phone bills; don't be afraid to keep switching your energy suppliers to find the best deal. It is very easy to switch; I have arranged with an independent energy efficiency company to keep me updated and provide alerts of latest energy saving methods and the best deals. The additional benefit offered by the energy company that keeps me informed of the best deals they take responsibility for the actual switch itself including administration and operational changes leaving me to agree the best price with them and sign the energy contract. Many people are in the wrong Council Tax band; it takes ten minutes to check if you're one of them. Dropping a band can result in a saving of £200 a year and a backdated pay-out from when you moved in is often worth £1,000s.

Rent out a spare room, which not only brings in a regular monthly income; it is also tax efficient. The current government 'Rent a Room Scheme' allows you to earn up to a threshold of £7,500 per year tax-free from letting out furnished accommodation in your home. To quickly recap from an earlier chapter; in 2014 more than 60,000 people over the age of 40 placed 'room wanted' adverts with SpareRoom; one of the largest flat-sharing websites in Britain compared with only 20,000 more than five years ago. The 40+ age bracket makes up one in eight of those looking for a room in a shared home.

Pay your credit card balance in full every month to avoid relatively high interest payments. Alternatively, many credit card companies are willing to lend you money at 0% interest, so why not use this cash for everyday spending, replacing all other credit & debit card spending? This means you'll now have debts on your 0% card (make sure you make the minimum repayment each month) and a similar amount in your current account, which you can save in an ISA or high interest savings account. Remember to pay off the full balance before the 0% ends, having earned interest on the money saved.

Use your ISA allowances, which currently is up to £15,240 per year; you can save up to an annual government set amount in an ISA tax-free savings account. It means you save on any tax on the interest accrued. Make sure you claim any benefits and tax credits due to you; if you are entitled to benefits you should still claim them. It could provide several hundred pounds to you. Also, check with your tax authority to see if you are due an income tax rebate.

If you've got or had a loan, credit or store card with payment protection insurance (PPI), you may be able to reclaim thousands of pounds. Banks lost in court after years of systemically mis-selling PPI. Now they've put over £18 billion aside to pay back money wrongly taken from their customers.

If you are paying monthly house and contents insurance premiums: you are probably being charged a premium of between 15% and 20% for the privilege. If you are in a position to pay the annual insurance cost in one go, you could make a reasonable saving. Also, regularly compare annual insurance costs; I have switched again, saving nearly £300 on my annual insurance premium. If you have more than one vehicle in your household you could make savings by insuring them all with one insurer; insuring more than one car will probably qualify for discounts across all vehicles insured. If you are using a car insurance comparison website to obtain new annual quotes, it is likely that you will be required to enter your employment details on the application form. You must disclose the correct employment description, however the comparison website may provide several different job titles to best describe your employment; it has been discovered that differing job titles for the same style of employment can offer preferential and discounted insurance quotations. Hence, checkout all the job titles describing your employment and select the lowest quotation.

If you are in paid employment; you can now ask for a pay rise. Prepare your case and justify your proposed rise through your performance at work; consider individual achievements that have benefited your company financially, you may have taken additional responsibilities or you are managing more people, if you are in a supervisory or management role. Possibly, consider promotion prospects and future increased responsibilities to enhance your salary. Also, check your tax code at the last count it was found that one in three of us are paying either too much or too little in tax, so make sure your tax code is correct.

Interest rates on savings accounts were generally very poor across the board at the time of writing my book. However, there was still a big difference between the top-paying accounts and the worst accounts on the market; shop around for the best savings rates. There are plenty of current accounts that pay respectable levels of interest on balances that are in credit and make sure you use your tax-free savings limit.

As referred to in an earlier chapter; the government has recently changed UK pension rules, allowing far more freedom on how you are able to invest your future pension. Pension savers have always had the freedom to take 25% of their pension in a tax-free lump sum, but have then generally been advised to buy an annuity with all of the rest of the money. From April 2015, savers over the age of 55 will be given the option of taking a number of smaller lump sums, instead of one single big lump sum, and in each case, 25% of the sum will be tax-free. Challenge the performance of your pension; find ways to improve the returns from the remaining pension following your divorce financial settlement. Annuities have come under criticism following reported poor performance; the government has announced further changes in the pension rules allowing you, on retirement, to cash in your pension savings when you retire rather than buy an annuity. It is further proposed that pensioners with existing annuities will also be able to cash in their annuities and benefit from being able to access their pension money when and how they want. Latest government figures report pensioners are withdrawing £30 million a day from their pension pots; many are now re-investing their pension savings in other ways.

In 2014, I decided to invest the 25% tax free pension lump sum into property investment, which gave me a far better financial return with combined yields of 16% through a regular monthly rental income and the continued appreciation of the UK property market. Further, the five year forecast of both the rental and property market was set to grow a further 20%. The 16% yield was providing a much greater financial return than my pension.

The free-cash you continue to generate after your divorce financial settlement can be invested in your future wealth and assets also enjoy some treats; you have earned them by now.

The free-cash I had managed to generate was invested in 3 areas:

1. Growing my company.
2. Increasing financial equity in the ex-marital home and property rental.
3. Travelling the world.

Having new goals to invest in brings a whole new life to enjoy; feeling fulfilment, self-esteem, enjoyment, meeting new friends – personally, I really have had a blast since 2011.

> *"Divorce is the start of a brand new life. Don't lose the chance to redesign it upon your dreams."*[221.]
>
> *Rossano Condoleo*

[221.] Goodreads – http://www.goodreads.com/quotes/789675-divorce-is-the-start-point-for-a-brand-new-life

You are now completely free to spread your wings and literally fly at 30,000 feet, without forensic questions or cross-examination from the other side. In the past few years, I have had the freedom to travel to some of the world's most interesting destinations such as Hawaii, Maldives, Caribbean Islands, Kenya, Sri Lanka, San Francisco, Los Angeles, Mauritius, Mexico and the Cayman Isles. At the time of writing my book I have recently returned from an adventure to Russia. I keep the pictures and memories of these destinations to remind me of the experiences. I am continuing to travel the world; meeting new people, different cultures and learning.

Referring to some of my earlier stories and experiences from around the world; visiting over 60 countries including visits to five of the Seven Wonders of the World. Travelling has provided the opportunity to re-evaluate the 'people facts of life' and human spirit from Third World living of poverty, poor health and education to highly developed economies and lifestyles. These experiences have taught and helped me understand what I see as the new facts of life.

Visiting several Third World African countries – being privileged to visit and meet the people of Soweto, South Africa after years of apartheid. Before making our journey to Soweto we were advised by our South African business colleagues to leave all personal valuables such as watches, jewellery, money and credit cards under safe keeping at the company office. Soweto, and the wider province of Johannesburg, had a very high crime rate; we were told Johannesburg had a reported serious crime every 12 minutes. At this point, prior to leaving for Soweto I became concerned over my own personal safety once in the township. However, I was reassured by my business colleagues that they had taken the company CEO on the same visit to Soweto the previous week and he had survived and returned safely; this did provide me with some reassurance of a safe return.

Experiencing life's devastating effects of HIV, poor education, poverty, crime, corruption and past slavery – whilst staying at the Meikles Hotel in Harare, Zimbabwe, using the hotel gym early one morning before the working day, I met an American lady who was visiting large employers and their workers in Harare. She was on a mission to educate and present to each employer and their staff the precautionary methods available to prevent the spread of HIV. At the time, she informed me that approximately one in three people living in the country were infected. As I understand a similar number were also infected in South Africa. The American lady went on to tell me that some locals feared and saw HIV as a tribal curse, which had no cure and didn't believe simple precautions could be used to prevent the spread of the disease. She understood the first report of HIV was discovered in the Congo jungle after a human had been bitten by a wild monkey. I was further told by a local Zimbabwean, the spread of HIV was not helped by prostitutes visiting miners in remote parts of the country; passing the disease to the miners, who subsequently returned to their wives at home, transmitting HIV, now infecting their families. As so many adults and children born with HIV have died; I was told funerals always took place on a Tuesday and the towns were closed. At the time, the governments of many sub-Saharan countries were in denial of the epidemic, making extensive attempts to cover up the HIV/Aids problem.

Visiting The Great Wall of China on a very cold December morning; looking out to follow the Great Wall snaking into the distance, as far as the naked eye could see and trying to figure out how such an achievement was completed without modern construction equipment and technology. Visiting Tiananmen Square and the Forbidden City; June 1989 saw government military forces crackdown on demonstrators in Tiananmen Square. Events in early June 1989 left an unconfirmed number of young students dead; the demonstrators were protesting for improved pro-democratic rights. Whilst staying in Beijing, I noticed the changing cultural mix from traditional Chinese values and beliefs to modern day and contemporary lifestyles. This is most noticeable in new building design, emerging industries and how the younger Chinese generation aspires to Western lifestyle brands and fashions; most young Chinese knew of the footballer David Beckham.

Looking down on the watery grave of some 1100 sailors entombed in the *USS Arizona*, Pearl Harbour, Hawaii; watching a stingray majestically swim towards us as small bubbles of engine oil rise to the surface from the vessel's fuel tanks – it is said that each bubble of oil represents a tear for the crew who died on 7th December 1941. Hawaii is a popular holiday destination for Japanese tourists; however, during the visit to Pearl Harbour I noted that not one Japanese tourist was present on the bus journey to Pearl Harbour or at the harbour itself.

Following the visit to *USS Arizona*, I was invited to board USS Missouri, nicknamed the 'Mighty Mo.'; 'Mighty Mo.' had recently been decommissioned and was permanently moored at Pearl Harbour. Once on board, our tour guide pointed out a large 'concave dent' on the starboard side of the vessel; the damage was caused by a Japanese kamikaze pilot hitting the ship during the latter stages of World War II. The tour guide further explained Japanese commanders signed World War II surrender documents on board the USS Missouri only after they had been stripped of their *hari kari* knives; it was told that the Japanese commanders would rather kill themselves using these *hari kari* knives than sign World War II surrender documents.

Visiting Sri Lanka with my daughter in May 2009, the same month the Sri Lankan Civil War had just ended with the Sri Lankan army defeating the Tamil Tigers and five years after the tsunami; the island had not recovered. We remember driving past buildings, which had been destroyed by the tsunami, still in ruins five years on. Buddhism is the religion of approximately 70% of the population of Sri Lanka. There are around 6,000 Buddhist monasteries on the Sri Lankan island with approximately 15,000 monks. The locals would tell us of marriage customs, where it is the bride and groom's parents who would make the proposal of marriage. The proposal is guided by the groom's horoscope and only if it is compatible with the future bride's horoscope is the proposal agreed and made. If after the marriage it is found the newly-weds are not suited the married couple and their respective parents blame the stars for the marriage breakdown. A further Sri Lankan custom is for the groom's mother to join the bride and groom during their honeymoon. It is tradition the bride, after her first night of wedlock is required to provide to her now mother-in-law evidence of her loss of virginity to her son on their wedding night.

All of my initial experiences and stories from around the world have shown, not only how people cope and adapt when faced with adversity and disaster, but also their cultures, and which values are relatively important to them.

I have taken on board these first-hand experiences of global tragedies and loss – thinking entire populations face much more adversity than I ever did during my divorce years and beyond. I will hold these profound memories and experiences forever. However, the most moving experience was to witness a grown Dutchman weep and apologise for his country's behaviour whilst visiting a small castle situated on the coast of Ghana. While touring the castle in a small group, the tour guide took us to a dark and very damp dungeon, which was situated deep in the bowels of the castle, adjoining the sea. At the far end of the dungeon was a narrow opening, probably no more than 12" wide, which was used to access ships during the years of slavery. The guide explained how slaves were brought to the castle dungeon and starved to a point that they were able to pass through the narrow opening at the far end of the dungeon to board the slave ships. The process of starvation meant the captors were able to transport many more numbers of slaves on the ships; hundreds of slaves either died in the dungeon or whilst travelling on the ship to their destination. The significance of the story – the reason the Dutchman was weeping and apologising for his country's behaviour and loss of hundreds of lives – was that many of the ships were bound across the ocean to Holland. From the 15th right up to the 19th century, Europeans bought millions of slaves in West, Central and East Africa and sent them to Europe, the Caribbean and America.

It was Martin Luther-King Jnr. who said:

> *"I have a dream that one day on the red hills of Georgia, the sons of former slaves and the sons of former slave owners will be able to sit together at the table of brotherhood."*[222]

---

[222] Brainy quote http://www.brainyquote.com/quotes/quotes/m/martinluth115055.html

The crystal clear waters of the Maldives, whilst on holiday in 2009.

Enjoying evening twilight, whilst in St Lucia, Caribbean in 2010.

On safari at Tsavo National Park, Kenya in 2011. During the visit to Kenya, we learnt about the risks of malaria; the locals told us of the stories of frequent family loss due to malaria. At the time of our visit, we were told by locals that the Kenyan government had only just begun issuing mosquito nets to pregnant women to protect them against malaria.

The magnificent beasts of the Tsavo National Park, Kenya.

The canvas we were under whilst on Kenyan safari; the first night we camped next to a crocodile swamp. We were told by the locals that we were camping in the dry season and the swamp was low, which apparently made it easier for the crocs. to catch their prey. We were assured that when the reptiles crawled onto land during the dry season they were not hungry and we would be safe; we really weren't prepared to test this theory!

After a night of camping; breakfast by the Tsavo River but for who? – the local guide in the photograph assured me that we were safe – he was the one carrying the machete not me; hence the worried look! Check out what crocodile has in its jaws; is it the remains of the last victim?

Watching the sunset on the enchanting Cayman Islands in 2013.

The sun setting over Honolulu harbour, Hawaii in 2007.

The memorial bridge, where I stood above the sunken *USS Arizona* Pearl Harbour, Hawaii in 2007.

Visiting the new Olympic Stadium Sydney, Australia in 2000.

The mighty Victoria Falls during my visit first to Zimbabwe in 1998.

Visiting Tiananmen Square and the Forbidden City, Beijing, in December 2000; remembering the contrast of traditional cultures of China and modern day China's aspiration to Western styles and influence.

Walking the Great Wall of China on a very cold December morning in 2000; it is reputed one million workers died when building the wall.

Sun City South Africa 1999.

First visit to Universal Studios, Hollywood in 2007.

White water rafting on the border of Haiti and Dominican Republic in 1999.

Golden Gate Bridge, San Francisco my daughter's 21st birthday 2008.

On a boat to Alcatraz with my daughter (as tourists) in 2008; the prison's most famous inmate was Al Capone imprisoned in 1934 for tax evasion.

Globe-trotting has, without doubt, been an education and a learning curve; it has also given the opportunity to experience the 'darker side' of international cities and towns. Amongst many stories – whilst visiting Manila in the Philippines our local business acquaintances arranged a visit to a karaoke club. At the time, thinking that this wasn't a visit to a club, where you sang along to words and lyrics on a TV screen, it was something a little different. However, I was always open and broad minded, willing to trying anything new and within reason. On arrival at the karaoke club, accompanied by our local business acquaintances we were ushered into a small room with a few cold beers, and offered a menu of local dishes. After being fed and watered a group of very attractive Filipino girls joined us, each wearing a sarong. On arrival, each girl would walk towards you and as a customary way of personal greeting; she would open her sarong in front of you, what was underneath the sarong left nothing at all to the imagination. What happened afterwards in the Manila karaoke club will stay in the Manila karaoke club; the only clue is that what happened makes the traditional lap dancing clubs in the US and Europe look extremely tame. Of course we had to make a couple of further visits to the karaoke club (as you do), before leaving Manila; what's the saying "when in Rome do as the Roman's do". There was just one caveat when visiting the karaoke club; I didn't take advantage of all the services available – perhaps my old fashioned morals told me what was and was not permissible and safe. If and when I write my second book, I hope to reveal one or two more secrets from the 'darker side' of world travel.

Before departing from stories of world travel; a Dutch entrepreneur has offered couples the chance of a weekend away, staying in a hotel where he will help them finalise their divorce. Jim Halfen's 'Divorce Hotel' [223.] allows couples to work with mediators and family professionals by staying for two days in the hotel. The Netherlands-based company will guide couples through legal rights for children and other outstanding marital issues, and the divorce settlement, to help finalise a separation. The two-day process, normally over a weekend, uses ten principles to draw together documentation by having the two parties, lawyers, and mediators all in the same hotel for a weekend aims to quicken a process, which otherwise could take weeks,

---

[223.] Jim Halfen's 'Divorce Hotel' – http://www.divorcehotel.com/en/team.htm

months or even years. I understand the idea is now being developed in further countries across the world.

Returning home and to the principles of the DMBO, and how to make a return on investment. One of my primary and pre-divorce objectives was to retain 100% shareholding of my fledgling company; since 2010, I have been free to invest and grow the business.

Today, our core business delivers three revenue streams:

1.   Management Consultancy.
2.   Property.
3.   Emerging Market Development.

Our three core business values are not dissimilar to the DMBO values:

1.   Invest using latest research and information.
2.   Be different to the competition.
3.   Have robust cost management.

My company values logo

Diagram 33

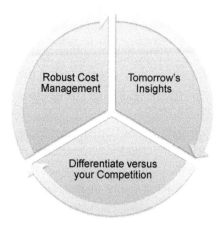

The company's strap line is "Thinking differently for tomorrow's business".

Since the launch of the company, the management consultancy side of the business has secured partnerships with the UK's leading industry associations and financial organisations. Over 3,000 companies have attended our national seminars and workshops. At each workshop we provide latest market research and bespoke management solutions designed to meet future market needs. We operate in the following UK markets:

- Food and Drink
- Retail
- Construction
- Engineering
- Leisure

The company firmly advocates that through constantly changing market conditions, intense competition and increasing customer demands, modern day and successful companies need to be at the leading-edge of strategic change. Existing business plans and strategies rapidly become obsolete; strategic life cycles become shorter. Market boundaries are continually changing; therefore, a business needs to be in a position to respond to such forces. You may have noted some similar parallel's when comparing my business values of research, competition and cost control with my divorce principles; ideas can travel well. We are currently researching and investing in exciting and new projects in growth markets such as digital technology and overseas property. As touched on in an earlier chapter, pre-divorce is not a bad time to think about setting up in business; I have no regrets at all, 'wild horses' wouldn't take me back to corporate life, I guess I have become unemployable.

After 'sweating the retained marital assets' to achieve savings and efficiencies the next phase of the DMBO process is to invest in the ex-marital assets, to provide the best long term returns. After investing in my new company, my next major investment was the ex-marital home. Using DMBO principles and latest markct data, I was confident that the investment would continue to yield a good return.

Applying a combination of free-cash from efficiency savings, tax-free pension lump-sum and company dividends. In 2014, three years after the financial settlement, I invested a six-figure sum in the ex-marital home. After investment, the ex-marital home currently has an estimated market value of £1.3 million. The original purchase price in 2001 was £390,000; arguably the cost of DMBO was some 28% lower than the original purchase price in 2001 and 33% lower than the original buy-out price requested by the other side in 2008. Overall and to date, I am satisfied with the return on investment. Looking to the future figures forecast released by the London School of Economics in early 2016, property values will increase by 21% by 2020 and 91% by 2030.[224] A point of confirmation and substantiated qualification – all property valuations throughout divorce proceedings were conducted, recorded and verified by fully qualified independent property valuers and the courts, also agreed, verified and accepted by my ex-spouse and her legal advisers. The matrimonial sale price of the house and the final buy-out offer was completely transparent, fully disclosed, agreed and protected by all parties, including lawyers, the courts and the 'clean break agreement'. The increase in the value of the ex-marital home has been achieved through the recovery of the property market since the UK recession in 2008, and my own personal financial investment and risk, three years after the divorce settlement. To quickly recap on the importance of having an agreed, transparent and legally binding 'clean break' agreement – where neither party will be entitled to make any further claims for financial provision including property adjustment, such claims shall be dismissed.

The ex-marital home is located in the Cotswolds, in an area of designated outstanding natural beauty; much of the surrounding land is owned by the National Trust. In the spring and summer months there are over 600 cows free-grazing on the common land around the property. We are spoilt by a wide choice of good restaurants and pubs, scenic walks across the National Trust land with a rich history and culture dating back to Roman times. It is also reputed that Tom Long, a famous highwayman, whilst robbing rich travellers was killed and buried nearby. Quintessential English villages and hamlets are within walking distance, offering local traditional food and ales,

---

[224] London School of Economics 'Property Millionaires: The Growing House Divide' 18 February 2016 http://www.santander.co.uk/csdlvlr/ContentServer?c=SANDocument_C&pagename=WCSUKPublicaLte%2FSANDocument_C%2FSANDocumentPreview&cid=1324582166149

which are always a good reason to visit. Many people say to me "having been lucky enough to visit many parts of the world's five continents, where is your favourite place?" – I always say "home"; I guess you can call me old-fashioned. I remember sitting in many international airports up to 9000 miles from home and watching that British Airways 747 taxi to the terminal stand, thinking, "I'm going home now".

Remaining with home – my next move after the completion of the financial settlement was in part as a result of the following early divorce research published by SpareRoom:

> *"More than 60,000 people over the age of 40 placed 'room wanted' adverts with SpareRoom; one of the largest flat-sharing websites in Britain."* [225.]

Using the above data and information, I identified a further niche property market opportunity and customer need.

My customer target markets were:

1. Separating professional couples who are planning to divorce; one of the couple usually plan to move out of the marital home and seeks a good quality rental property for 6 to 12 months. Also, I could offer some free divorce counselling as part of the rental deal.
2. Professional singles, earning an above average salary seeking quality medium to long term rental accommodation.

As part of my post DMBO growth plan and in particular to help in recovering my pension losses: I now rent a two-bedroom apartment with lounge, dining room, kitchen/utility situated on a private road in the Cotswolds, which appears to be much more appealing to divorcing and/or professional singles than a traditional flat or house share in more urban areas. My first tenant was in his 40s and had just separated from his wife, and was

---

[225.] Property Reporter 'Flat sharing for the over 40s on the rise' 29 January 2014 – http://www.propertyreporter.co.uk/landlords/flatsharing-for-the-over-40s-on-the-rise.html?DT=2

beginning divorce proceedings. My 2nd tenant had recently secured a managerial position with a local company and had been required to re-locate to the area. The 3rd and current tenant is a design engineer who is moving with his new wife from Newcastle to Gloucestershire. All tenants were within my target market; the rented apartment met their needs, perfectly. The irony is that I wouldn't have identified the market niche had I not been through my own divorce experience and research.

I did develop the early strap line, albeit very 'cheesy'; however, we decided not to use the strap line after all when marketing the new rental property:

> *"Getting a divorce, need somewhere to stay; don't delay and phone today."*

I said it was 'cheesy'!

The rental market continues to increase; forecasters claim that the number of households in the private rented sector will rise by 1.2 million over the next five years, with more than half of that growth occurring in residents over the age of 35.[226] The value of the rental market is forecast to increase by 20.5% over the next five years, with demand outstripping supply and the average monthly rent is just under £900. Again, this has been a sound investment based on research and wider economic and property trends; it has played its financial part of the DMBO. Recently, my lettings agency has contacted me asking if I have any further properties to rent, due to the high demand for rental properties within the area; this reassures me that my investment will continue to provide healthy future returns and further expansion in the UK property market.

In summary, learning from the Post-Divorce Return on Investment:

- Continually find saving efficiencies and free-cash to invest and grow the retained marital assets.
- Continue to research market trends and gain new knowledge.

---

[226] Savills 'Rental growth in the mainstream market' posted 8 January 2015 – http://www.savills.co.uk/research_articles/186866/185225-0

- Begin to enjoy your freedom after your divorce; start to spread your wings and travel far and wide.
- Use your ability to create your own personal return on investment plan; tailor and design it to meet your individual needs and financial goals.
- Don't be afraid to put some 'spice' and a few risks back into your life.
- Start to live outside your 'comfort zone'.

Your 10-year Plan – living outside your 'comfort zone'

Once your divorce and the financial settlement are completed and you have a post-divorce financial plan in place of savings and investment, it is time to begin planning your new life ahead in readiness for the final part of the DMBO. In the same way as we approached the 'DMBO', we will now journey through the following '10-year Plan' stage by stage with detailed explanations, personal references, case studies and examples each step of the way.

At the very beginning of the plan, we start by setting '10-year Big Goals' – these are the aspirations and desires we aim to achieve over the next ten years. After setting the goals, the next step is to choose any or all of the following 11 personal enablers; the enablers will help build and develop the right skills to help achieve your '10-year Big Goals'. Each enabler is carefully selected to match your individual development needs. I have found the enablers very helpful not only in building my own 10-year plan, but also in the business world. Each is interchangeable, providing you with the right choice and mix of options to best achieve your own personal goals.

The 11 'Enablers' are:

1. Your preferred learning style.
2. Identifying your new skills.
3. The learning cycle.
4. Your moral compass.
5. Your CV (curriculum vitae).

6. Maslow's Hierarchy of Needs.
7. Neuro linguistic programming (NLP).
8. Your own personal development plan (PDP).
9. Identifying your strengths and weaknesses.
10. Your skills and learning plan.
11. Your action plan.

On completing your 10-year plan, the final stage is to convert the plan into multiple income streams. This is where you use the enablers, your new skills and abilities to invest and earn new income and hard-cash returns. In the following chapter we will move through each stage of the 10-year plan.

It's worth mentioning, the 10-year plan and supporting 11 enablers can be used in the sequence of your choice and at any time of your life; you do not necessarily have to wait for your divorce.

The 10-year Plan and the Enablers

Diagram 34

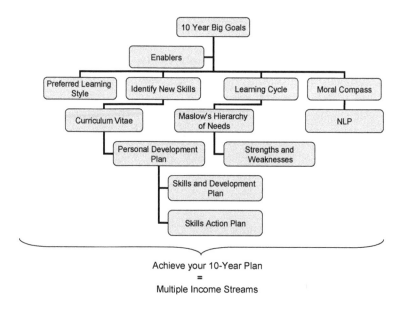

Achieve your 10-Year Plan
=
Multiple Income Streams

Begin by setting new long-term goals

Similar to setting goals and objectives during the divorce process and what you wish to achieve as an outcome, we now set long-term 'big goals' for the next 10 years. Decide what your aspirations and desires are, what you want to do differently, decide how you are going to get there and start now.

My own '10-year Big Goals' were, and still are today:

1. Build a successful and profitable company.
2. Achieve maximum financial return on my assets.
3. Continue to travel the world and visit the remaining two Seven Wonders of the World – the Taj Mahal and the Hanging Gardens of Babylon – and own an international holiday home.
4. Write two books.

It is important to also set some quantifiable financial measures over the next ten years; company profitability and asset value were my two key financial measures. Remember these are my own personal goals and measures; your goals and choices may and probably will be very different.

Remain focused on the four 'big' goals you set. Try not to have more than four goals, otherwise you can lose focus and spread yourself too thin by trying to achieve too many things. Write your goals down and pin them on your notice board at home or in your office as a regular reminder. Having set your four goals, decide how you are going to achieve them. First, use a selection of personal principles, probably not too dissimilar to your divorce principles and practice them daily until they become habit forming.

My own principles are:

- Use free-cash to continually invest in high return assets.
- Continue learning and build your knowledge every day; I regularly ask people 'tell me something I didn't know'.
- Move and live outside your 'comfort zone'.
- Pursue your goals with unrelenting determination.
- Learn from others across the world.

241

- Be prepared to make some mistakes; accept failures, without losing enthusiasm.
- Lead your own destiny and don't wait for others.
- Keep a sense of humour and have fun.
- Uncertainty and change will bring new opportunities and discovery.

Again, these are my own principles and will probably differ from your own. However, you must decide what you want to do, 'nail it' and do it now. We will discuss the more detailed 10-year principles and strategies in the next chapter. When creating your 10-year plan as with the divorce plan, be your own person; I personally found too much advice from others was distracting and sometimes irrelevant, others views tended to be how they saw the future and not how I saw the future. As my step-father used to say 'you can listen to advice, but you don't always have to take it'; again, you need to be your own person.

The reassurance of having a 'clean break' divorce agreement afforded me complete freedom to launch into full flight to build and develop my 10-year plan, and to grow the value of my assets, company equity and income, without the risk or worry of my ex-spouse making any kind of retrospective financial claim against me. If possible – I emphasise again – always endeavour to negotiate a 'clean break' agreement; it provides the protection against any future financial claims from your ex-spouse. A 'clean break' agreement gives you the psychological freedom and confidence to get on with life, without having to keep looking over your shoulder.

We made reference in an earlier chapter to a case where the ex-wife of a now multi-millionaire renewable energy tycoon made a claim for maintenance more than 20 years after they divorced; this is evidence these claims can happen years or decades after divorce.

More recently, and in contrast to the claim, against the energy tycoon, a case was returned to court, no doubt attracting further legal costs after the divorce settlement. As part of the original financial settlement, an annual maintenance package of £75,000 was ordered by the courts. However, now the ex-husband wanted to scale back his contributions on the grounds that he cannot be expected to support his ex-wife indefinitely, into his retirement.

The judge upheld the claim, agreeing with the husband and said "the time had come for his ex-wife to get a job".[227.]

Returning to the '10-year Big Goals'; the next step is to create your own 'Personal Coat of Arms', writing into the coat of arms your 4 goals and your own unique personal motto.

Diagram 35

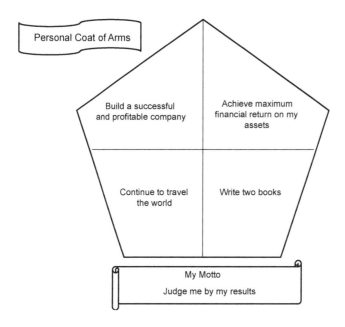

Staying motivated throughout your 10-year plan and achieving your goals will be a big challenge; there will be highs and lows. At each stage of the 10-year plan, I will keep a constant reminder of the importance of staying motivated. Motivation is the critical ingredient and foundation to achieve your 10-year goals. As a reminder, each day write 'Stay Motivated' at the very top of your daily actions and tasks; write it on your PC screensaver or hang it on the office wall.

[227.] Financial Times 'Best of Money: Divorces open up splits in the legal system' 20 November 2015 – http://www.ft.com/cms/s/0/87f690ea-8c79-11e5-a549-b89a1dfede9b.html#axzz46lw1I9SW

Chapter Six
Building your 10-year Plan – Step Ten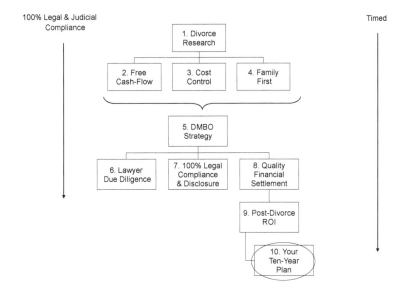

Diagram 36

We now move to the final stage of the **DMBO** model, which is building 'Your 10-year Plan'. We now have the complete freedom to really expand our wings and maximise our financial returns in the ten years ahead.

Having already written your 10-year goals, the 10-year plan provides a strategy of how you will achieve your goals; it's the roadmap of how to get there. Similar to your divorce strategy, your 10-year plan will keep you focused on the parts of your future life that will make a real difference to you. It will provide a framework that motivates and inspires you to achieve your goals.

There are several lifestyle areas you may choose from when first thinking about your 10-year plan. Your selection is unique to you, and you need to take time, and give a lot of thought and consideration before selecting them.

You will probably find that you make a number of changes in the early stages of planning and preparation. Typically, as a starter for ten, you may wish to consider the following when setting out what you want to achieve and the lifestyle and goals you desire.

Diagram 37

You may wish to further sub-categorise your goals:

- Academic goals – what knowledge and/or qualifications do you want to achieve?
- Career goals – where would you like your career to take you, what level do you want to reach?
- Monetary goals – what do you aim to earn at the individual milestones over the next 10 years?
- Ethical goals – do you want to volunteer some of your time to a good cause or get involved in local events, politics, charities etc.?
- Creative goals – do you want to progress creatively or artistically? You may have innovation or entrepreneurial skills to use in help achieve your goals.
- Domestic goals – how would you like your domestic and family life to be in the future?
- Physical goals – do you want to develop your skills in a certain sport or other physical activity?[228.]

[228.] The sub-categories referenced and provided by 'Skills You Need – setting personal goals' http://www.skillsyouneed.com/ps/setting-personal-goals.html

Continue to research and build relevant knowledge which could impact on the achievement of your own 10-year goals. For example, in 2015, the UK held a general election. The result of the election and the respective political party policies will, without doubt, have an impact on the future financial performance of the UK property market. Following a Conservative party election victory; post-election the UK property market rallied, following months of waiting and some caution as to which political parties housing and property policies would prevail. Short-term forecasts were positive, with predictions as high as 6.5% increase in UK house prices in 2015; my own forecast would be a little more modest at around 4%. In further good news, the threat of rent controls suggested by the Labour party have been removed, following their failure to win the election. This will make the rental market more appealing to investors; forecasts suggest that investors could commit to as much as £30 billion as a result of the election.

I referred in an earlier chapter the pension reforms introduced by the UK government in 2015. As a result of the reforms over-55s are able to withdraw cash lump sums from their pension to invest as they choose; one in ten have chosen to invest in the property rental market. This provides an opportunity for banks to introduce new buy-to-let mortgages specifically targeted at the over-55s market. The buy to let mortgage rates offer attractive low interest rates to over-55s, providing they are able make a 25% deposit.

In addition, and post the 2015 general election; sterling has remained relatively strong against the euro, making foreign travel to Europe attractive. Further the strength of the pound makes investing in an international holiday home in Spain that much more attractive.

To review my own position and investment strategy post-divorce in the UK and international property and rental market; the election result and forecasts supported and reassured me to continue with my 10-year plan. However, markets and government policies can change very quickly – therefore keep research continuous and right up to date; don't be afraid to adapt your plan to changing and prevailing market conditions. For example, in April 2016 the government introduced an additional 3% Stamp Duty on the purchase of UK second homes; this change in government policy may potentially move my future property investment overseas, rather than the UK. Further in early 2016, the UK government renegotiated its relationship with the European Union and then gave the British people the choice in June 2016 between staying in the European Union under those terms or leaving the EU. 52% of the eligible British public voted to leave the European Union. The UK's very own divorce from the EU will create market uncertainty and risk, which will probably impact on domestic economic performance, foreign currency exchange rates and investment.

Once you have set your 10-year goals and updated your own research; the next step is to breakdown your the goals into manageable and realistic milestones that you wish to achieve every two years. Typical milestones could be:

1. Financial targets: for example, making savings, paying off the mortgage, stock market growth, personal net worth.
2. Learning a new skill for example; IT skills or a foreign language.
3. Travelling to certain countries.
4. Achieving career promotion.
5. Writing your first book.
6. Learning to play a new sport or musical instrument.
7. Raising a target amount of money and contribute to your favourite charity.
8. Running the London marathon.
9. Completing a free-fall parachute jump.

Draw up a template and record your personal milestones:

Diagram 38

10-year Big Goals	Milestones Year 2	Milestones Year 4	Milestones Year 6	Milestones Year 8	Milestones Year 10
1)					
2)					
3)					
4)					

Having established your biennial milestones; the next step is to start to develop your strategic plan. As with your goals, keep your plan front of mind at all times, pin it on your notice board at home, download it onto your PC. Without specific steps and dates, all you have is a wish list and not a plan. Writing in the details of the plan is essential to your success. This is where you set in place the action steps and deadlines to get you where you want to be and help you accomplish your goals.

Establish detailed personal objectives that are specific to each milestone set. Consider using the SMART acronym when setting your objectives.

Specific
Measurable
Achievable
Realistic
Timed

I have been using the SMART objectives since the beginning of my business career at Coca-Cola in 1987. I found the SMART principles not only helpful in the business world, but also for career planning, in my personal life and even sporting achievements.

Your SMART objectives should be:

Specific

Objectives should clearly state what you are expected to achieve, using actions to describe what you wish to achieve.

For example:
Increase the value of my personal assets by 10% by the 31st December 2018

Measurable

Objectives should include a quality and/or quantity reference so that you can measure whether or not you have achieved them.

For example:
Reduce my energy costs by 20% by 31st December 2018

Achievable

Objectives need to be pragmatic and achieved in a manageable timeframe; however, objectives need to be stretching but achievable. Setting 'bite size' milestones will make your objectives more achievable.

For example:
Achieve an increase in my company profits of 12% by 31st March 2019

Realistic

Objectives should also be challenging but realistic; set objectives within your current capabilities. Take account of the skills, knowledge and resources needed to achieve them. You may need to consider whether you need any training or development (or other support) in order to achieve the objective.

For example:
Learn to speak the Spanish language before travelling to South America July 2019

Timed

Objectives should include a time reference, such as a specific deadline to achieve the objective.

For example:
Become a home based stock market trader by 31st December 2020

Remember, keep your plan under review every 12 months – just as in a strategic plan in business, things can and will change. Life, as we know has a funny way of shifting from time to time, requiring adjustments in timing, actions, and resources. If you do need to make any changes to your plan maintain the overriding rule; will this change make a real difference to my future life. Making incremental changes without good reason you could just end up 'bumbling along'. Use the opportunity to stretch yourself and move outside your personal comfort zone.

> *"Only those who will risk going too far can possibly find out how far one can go."* [229].

> *TS Eliot*

As an example your 10-year plan could be looking something like the following:

Diagram 39

10-year Big Goals	Milestones Year 2	Milestones Year 4	Milestones Year 6	Milestones Year 8	Milestones Year 10
1) Double my net worth by 2025	Increase asset value + 20% by 31.12.17	Increase asset value +15% by 31.12.19	Increase asset value +13% by 31.12.21	Increase asset value +14% by 31.12.23	Increase asset value +13% by 31.12.25
2) Visit 10 new countries by 2025	2x S. American countries by 31.12.17	2x African countries by 31.12.19	Canada and USA by 31.12.21	New Zealand and Australia by 31.12.23	India and Middle East by 31.12.25
3) Become an internet stock trader by 2025	Complete formal training by 31.12.17	Establish UK stock portfolio by 31.12.19	Invest in FTSE 100 stocks by 31.12.21	Invest in Asian stocks by 31.12.23	Invest in US stocks by 31.12.25
4) Run a full marathon under 4 hours by 2025	Run 3 half-marathons by 31.12.17	Run 3 full-marathons by 31.12.19	Run the London marathon by 31.12.21	Run the New York marathon by 31.12.23	Run the Sydney marathon by 31.12.25

Once you have set your objectives; the next step is to create your action plan and individual deadlines. The action plan will further develop and shape and add detail to the next ten years; this is when your plan becomes meaningful and live – it's the things you are going to do. One of my actions was to increase my knowledge of digital technology markets, through continuous research. To keep up with market changes, technology innovation and new companies, I joined commercial networking groups; I further introduced myself to the University of Bristol and University West of England research and academic departments. I was asked to speak to BA students at the University of Swansea.

---

[229]. Brainy Quote http://www.brainyquote.com/quotes/authors/t/t_s_eliot.html accessed 27th April 2016

The following template and examples maybe helpful when building your action plan:

Diagram 40

My Action Plan		
Objective	My Actions	Deadline
Increase asset value +15% by 31.12.19	1) Release pension cash lump sum of £25,000	30.6.17
	2) Obtain buy to let mortgage of £75,000	31.10.17
	3) Purchase small flat for £100,000	31.12.17
	4) Rent flat for £500 pcm	31.1.18
Run three half-marathons by by 31.12.18	1) Train 3 times a week for 6 months	31.12.17
	2) Run the Bath half-marathon	30.6.18
	3) Run the Bristol half-marathon	31.10.18
	4) Complete the Great North Run	31.12.18

Be innovative…

When creating your action plan, be innovative and think of new ideas which take you out of your comfort zone.

As the saying goes:

> *"Great minds discuss ideas; Average minds discuss events; Small minds discuss people."*

If you were to seek the dictionary definition of innovation you will probably come across a number of varying explanations. In its purest sense the word means "To introduce something new" it may also suggest to "to make changes in anything established".

Google describes innovation:

"For something to be innovative, it needs to be new, surprising, and radically useful." [230.]

An innovative mind set doesn't only allow you to stretch your imagination and take you to new areas. An innovative mind will take you to uncharted waters, making new discoveries and adventures; innovation is also an effective personal development tool. Personal innovation will help recreate and re-energise yourself; making yourself a better person than you were before your divorce. Once you find innovative ideas and solutions to successfully achieve your objectives, you will feel self-motivated and confident. You will want to achieve further success; the innovation process becomes addictive, similar to a drug – you will know the addiction when you've got it.

Just like in the areas of technology and products, without innovation you may personally risk being left behind as others realise the importance of innovation and they do something about it. Look at things with a fresh set of eyes and be aware of the changes and trends in your profession; evaluate these trends and identify new opportunities. Continually come up with fresh thinking, generating new possibilities for yourself, options that extend beyond what you already know. Be willing to take action and risks despite your uncertainties; explore and experiment, test your hunches and intuitions. Gather lots of information; make observations of what is happening around you, especially as a result of your own actions. Look for exceptions and surprises that might point you in new directions.

Do things that you haven't done before – be courageous

"Before you can be creative, you must be courageous. Creativity is the destination, but courage is the journey." [231.]

Joey Reiman

[230.] 'How Google Works' 'What is innovation?' page 206 written by Eric Schmidt, Jonathan Rosenberg and Alan Eagle
[231.] Special Dictionary http://www.special-dictionary.com/quotes/authors/j/joey_reiman/before_you_can_be_creative,_you_must_be_courageous_creativity_is_the_destinatio.htm accessed 27 April 2016

When you need new ideas, choose information, knowledge and experiences outside your normal environment; go to new places, meet new people and learn new skills. I obtained much of my personal inspiration from reading books written by authors who had achieved the extraordinary things in life. I would listen to speakers who had overcome massive challenges; I had 'life heroes' such as Nelson Mandela, Winston Churchill and Jim Lovell. As touched on earlier, I have been lucky enough to visit South Africa on many occasions. I visited the home of Nelson Mandela – I took so much inspiration and learning from the great man and the changes he achieved in South Africa.

There was a situation in my post-divorce years, which was most unexpected. My curiosity and internet searching led me to an online Russian dating site, which was definitely uncharted waters; as touched on a little earlier uncharted waters can lead to new discoveries. My research and curiosity established that this was an organised fraud. An attractive Russian lady called 'Veronica' began sending me a selection of personal, yet tasteful photographs along with romantic emails. She would explain how she was mistreated in her home country and desperate to leave and find her new love in the UK; she claimed to be a nurse working in a hospital for sick children.

A copy of some of the words and emails sent to me:

"I live here with my dad. My dad's name is Alexander. He is very strong man not only physique and of course he have a strong character. My mother leave us when I was very little girl. She said that she do not want to have a family she want have good career. Now she lives in Moscow and she is business woman. My dad takes care about me and our family like a real man!!! I love him very very much! He gave me a good education. I graduated from Krasnoyarsk State Medical University and now I work at little clinic. I love my job because my patients are kids. I love kids and therefore I will never understand my mother who left me and my dad. I think that at first women must think about family and kids and only after that she can think about something other things!

I see that you already understand that I simple and cheerful woman. But I need to say to you about my fear. The fact is that I want to give you know about my past relationship. These relations finished about three years ago. I fell in love with one guy. At the beginning all had been perfect. We had common interests. We spend much time together. He bought for me flowers and gifts. I paid the same. We had many common holidays and every time celebrated it together. About one year of relations ago we begin to live together. He had worked a bus driver and finished university and worked already as nurse like in present time. Then he decided to drive bus to other cities of our country and had gone from home for a week. I stood alone at home and missed him much. Then he returned and I was happy that man with me!

But sometimes later he had gone for two or three week in work. Could you imagine this, Paul? I could not stay a month without my second half. I had told him maybe he changes his work and will more time with me. But he wanted more money. I told that we may have enough money together and live in harmony. But he became angry of these words. I did not understand why. Then he began to drink alcohol and became angry and aggressive on me. And one time he became to hit me. I had gone to police but they told me old Russian saying: "hit – mean love" and what do you think? How I may live in such terrible country??? I do not ready to suffer this one more time. And in the end of this story I had seen that my man had gone with my girlfriend on the street like a couple. After all I had learnt that he did not in bus trips! He spends that time with my girlfriend!!! Paul, could you imagine this??? I hope that you had not ever felt such pain."

After receiving further emails from 'Veronica' over a period of three to four weeks, she wished to travel to London and meet. However, the travel arrangements had to be made through a Russian travel agent called Almika Travel. 'Veronica' whose real name, as I had now discovered, was 'Nicky' asked me to pay for her flight and would I provide my credit card details to a specific email address.

Alarm bells rang loudly – I immediately checked out the travel company and their alleged website. To no real surprise by now, the travel company and website were false and was part of an organised fraud. I replied to 'Veronica' with the following:

"Hey Veronica
Nice try – your travel agent is fake.
I may be the most 'caring guy in the world' – I'm also pretty smart and street wise!!!
Paul."

The lesson learnt here – be cautious of internet dating sites and attractive Russian women who send you romantic messages and photographs for four reasons:

1. You could end up being parted with your hard-earned cash fraudulently, post-divorce.
2. Married couples who meet online are three times more likely to divorce than those who met face-to-face. [232.]
3. The growing number of internet dating scams. The ONS reports a 27% increase in the number of reported frauds from 181,000 to 229,000 in 2013. A spokesman for the ONS said "The figures are showing that this is a new area of crime that is on the rise".[233.]
4. If you receive online speculative invitations from attractive women from any part of the world that 'looks too good to be true', it is probably just that.

Staying in Russia; I have recently returned from a remote part of Western Russia. To access the region we had to travel through Europe by air and road to cross the Russian border. Entering the region, little appears to have changed since the days of the Cold War; there is a strong military presence everywhere and reminders of communist times. Some buildings still bear the communist 'red star' on their frontage. In the main town square there is an imposing statue of Lenin; I was told by the locals that traditionally newly married couples lay their wedding flowers at the foot of the statue. The newlyweds then travel to a nearby bridge to place a padlock bearing each other's name; the lock is closed and the key thrown

---

[232.] The Telegraph 'Couples who met online are more likely to divorce' 26 September 2014 http://www.telegraph.co.uk/news/science/science-news/11124140
[233.] Office for National Statistics 'Crime Statistics announcement, period ending March 2013' http://webarchive.nationalarchives.gov.uk/20160105160709/
http://www.ons.gov.uk/ons/rel/crime-stats/crime-statistics/period-ending-march-2013/vid-crime-statistics-announcement—period-ending-march-2013.html

into the river below. It is alleged that the tradition 'locks' the couple's life and love together to eternity. As a paradox, Russia has the highest divorce rate in the world. Statistics from Russia's social registry office show that the majority of marriages end in divorce. Ten years ago, every third Russian marriage ended in divorce; today it is every second. In 2012, about 650,000 couples divorced while 1,213,000 got married.[234.] Russia had the highest divorce rate in the world in 2012 according to the United Nations.[235.] Sociologists say that the main causes of broken marriages are alcoholism, financial difficulties and crowded living conditions; in many cases, all three.

Statue of Lenin in the town square, where newly married couples lay their wedding flowers at the foot of the statue, as a mark of respect.

[234.] Russia beyond the headlines 'Divorce, Russian Style' 16 October 2013 http://rbth.com/society/2013/10/16/divorce_russian_style_30845.html
[235.] Divorce Science '2012 Updated Divorce Rates' https://divorcescience.org/2015/01/18/2012-updated-world-divorce-rates-70-countries-reporting/

 Russian bridge, where newlyweds place a lock bearing each other's name; then throw the key into the river.

During my 7-day visit to Russia, I was able to see, first hand, the family and living conditions, which clearly contribute to the world's highest divorce rate. Further, sanctions imposed in 2014 and new government policies are now adding to family pressures, which will no doubt serve to further increase the national divorce rate.

I was told that everyday Russian families have to find ways to make financial ends meet due to extraordinarily high food inflation, which runs at + 28%, and with the cost of medicines increasing by up to 50%. The average monthly Russian wage is 20,000 roubles, which at the time equated to around £200 per month. Considering the low monthly wage, high inflation versus the price of food in the shops, which are commensurate to UK food prices; families are being forced to extreme measures to survive. The family I was visiting had two small children; their father was required to work away from home in the north of Russia to earn enough money to support them and his wife. Some families are illegally importing household goods from Poland, where prices are cheaper. Employers are illegally paying their staff in cash to avoid government taxes; many high street shops only accept cash to avoid taxes. Ironically, the only products that have remained cheap in the shops are cigarettes, which cost less than £1 per packet and vodka, which cost under £5 per bottle. The relatively low cost of cigarettes and vodka have contributed to rising levels of alcoholism, shorter life expectancy and the highest divorce rate in the world.

Housing and family living conditions are deteriorating; homes are over-crowded with sometimes three generations living in a small three-room apartment. Some homes are unsafe; during my visit TV reports were broadcast of large cracks appearing in a multi-story apartment block in Kaliningrad, the homes were at risk of collapsing into a nearby river. A further incident occurred; a friend of the family we were visiting had been fatally electrocuted by faulty wiring in his home. Families are not insured or protected against such risks of homes collapsing and electrocution from faulty wiring. Families are unable to afford the move to safer and better homes; the average cost of a new apartment is 3.6 million roubles (£45,000) and current mortgage interest rates are at 15%. New buildings stand empty or unfinished due to the crippling economic situation and lack of invest-ment and credit.

Due to the restriction on food imports, imposed by the Russian government and high inflation, many families are now growing their own vegetables and fruit; some families are growing vegetables illegally on spare land in towns and cities. The government is reclaiming privately-owned land to be used for agriculture and growing; the government's intention is for Russia to become agriculturally self-sufficient over time.

These poor family living conditions, where more and more families are falling into poverty, can only add to family pressures and strain on marriages. However, I discovered that the majority of Russian families are tolerant of high inflation, low wages, deteriorating living conditions. The Russian government tell everyday ordinary people that these living condi-tions are much better compared to the years of communism and the Cold War era; the Russian president describes the current situation as 'belt tight-ening'. Most Russian people accept this and are tolerant at the moment; however, few see the situation improving in the future. The paradox is that the majority of Russian people support the current president Vladimir Putin; they expect him to be re-elected as president in 2018; Russians see no credible opposition to him or his policies. There is further acceptance of the Russian government's high spending on military hardware and nuclear weapons development. I learnt, whilst talking to another Russian family I visited, that the Russian government are selecting school leavers with high-end mathematic qualifications to attend university in Moscow and undertake a five-year training course in the next generation of nuclear weapons design; the Russian government are paying for the five-year university training. The 18-year-old son of the family I was visiting had just completed his first year's training in nuclear weapon design at Moscow University of Engineering; the son boasted that he could solve the Rubik's Cube in 32 seconds, whilst the record completed by one of his university peers, studying the same nuclear weapon's design course was solving the Rubik's Cube in an astonishing 14 seconds; these are smart and intelligent students, potentially designing future nuclear weapons. Incidentally, the mother of the family I was visiting was a school mathematics teacher; to earn extra money she was inundated with demands from her pupils for extra mathematics lessons outside normal school hours in the hope of achieving top grade qualifications and selection by the Russian government for paid university training in nuclear weapons design.

There are distinct characteristics re-emerging from the Cold War years; not only the significant investment in the military and nuclear weapons, also children are again required to wear Russian national dress to school. I visited a residential area where a Cold War bunker had recently been renovated to operational level. Every man under 28 years old is required to complete one year's national service training. New government and state controls had been implemented over high value retailers such as jewellers; there are further government controls on private company profit margins. Russian media regularly report on western news and events; I found the Russian news reports to be inaccurate, negative and out of date; western news was almost reported as propaganda rather than real-time news.

After spending several hours at the local police station; my visit to Russia was curtailed to 7 days. I was advised by Russian police that I would only be permitted to stay until 12 midnight on the 21st August. I managed to cross the road border to Europe on the 21st August at 11.50pm (ten minutes before my visa registration lapsed).

Following my adventure to Russia; I was left without any doubt why the country has the highest divorce rate in the world. The economic future and living conditions will not improve, which will only compound family breakdown.

Photographs taken during my visit Russia

Deteriorating housing conditions.

Overcrowded three-room apartments – often three generations live in one apartment.

Locals selling fruit and vegetables to help pay the bills.

Wooden house on the outskirts of the local town; the owner is unable to afford food in the shops; she has to live off the land.

'Cold War' bunker situated in the centre of a large family residential district; the bunker was recently restored to operational use.

Taking some calculated risks

There will come a time in your 10-year plan when you are faced with choices that involve risk. Risk can be scary and sometimes involve 'taking a leap into the dark'; it brings uncertainty and unpredictability. By contrast, risk can bring excitement, thrills and new energy as the adrenalin rushes through your veins.

Taking risks within your 10 year-plan:

- Provides you with an opportunity to open up to your talents, learn new skills, meet new people and have new experiences.
- Builds new interests, abilities and creates ambition.
- Allows you to feel powerful and proactive, making things happen rather than waiting for them to happen to you; puts you in control of your life.
- Gives you new ideas, innovation and creativity.
- Allows you to grow and build your strengths and develop new responsibilities.
- Allows you to build confidence, self-esteem and overcome fears.
- Takes you out of your comfort zone and discovers new oceans.

It is important that you manage the risks you take. Diligent preparation and planning will help mitigate risk and improve your chance of success. Analyse the risks you take; evaluate the research and information you gather – it will help you be better prepared. If it's a financial risk, work out how you can create a contingency for yourself; build a financial safety net to fall back on if things don't go to plan.

In the early days of my new company, I recollect attending a seminar at Cheltenham Racecourse. One of the keynote speakers was the entrepreneur and co-founder of the coffee chain Coffee Republic and confectionery brand Skinny Candy, Sahar Hashemi OBE.[236] She spoke about taking business risk and the need to have a safety net to catch you if things do not go to plan. Sahar told the seminar audience of how she had a picture of a safety net pinned to her office notice board.

Briefly referring back to the Divorce Strategy, where each of the 5 strategies had a 'Plan B'. 'Plan B' acted as a safety net, if circumstances changed or we were blown off track for any reason.

> *As Jim Lovell said:*
> *"Always expect the unexpected."*

Building your own personal safety net:

Diagram 41

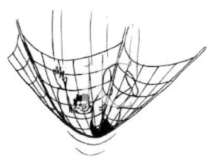

When building your personal safety net. Think about the timing of your plan; your plan may be less risky if it is timed over a ten year period, you do not have to rush – 'Rome wasn't built in a day'. A longer time period,

---

[236] Sahar Hashemi OBE – https://en.wikipedia.org/wiki/Sahar_Hashemi 27th April 2016

without procrastination will give you more time to prepare, save money, learn new skills, research and adapt to life's changes. Look at different scenarios; what are the worst and best cases that could happen if you take this risk? Adapt your plan or acquire additional knowledge or resources to further mitigate risk. Test your risk; you don't have to dive straight in at the deep end. Carry out research and due-diligence, gather all the information you can before jumping in. Carry out a rehearsed run for example buy a small financial investment to see how it performs over time. Gain advice from others who have taken this or a similar risk; try to learn from their mistakes and successes. Learn, learn and learn to increase your knowledge and skills; read books, research online, join discussion groups, obtain advice from reliable sources. Don't let mistakes or failures stop you; learn from your mistakes.

It was Winston Churchill who said:

> *"Success is the ability to go from one failure to another with no loss of enthusiasm."*

Don't become risk averse and make excuses. You will hit brick walls, frustrations, hard challenges and have bad days; put your energy and passion in to finding solutions to the challenges and frustrations. Don't spend too much time on the post-mortem, over analysing why things may have gone wrong; don't be guilty of 'analysis paralysis'. You will find lots of reasons not to do or try new experiences. Keep things in context, sort out what is urgent and what is important then prioritise the important ones and deal with them; don't put them off until tomorrow, nail them now. Keep your objectives in clear focus; single-mindedly plan to achieve them and visualise them as your future real life.

Remember – the biggest risk in life is 'doing nothing'.

Do not risk regrets in later life. Avoid sitting there wondering what your life could have been like if only you took a couple of risks. When your story closes, you're going to find out that it's not what you did that you regret the most, it's what you didn't do.

Remember the earlier quotation:

> *"Don't fear failure so much that you refuse to try new things. The saddest summary of a life that contains three descriptions: could have, might have, and should have."*[237.]
>
> Louis E. Boone

Keeping Motivated

It is important to continually stay motivated throughout your 10-year plan; it's what gets you out of bed every morning. However, ten years is a relatively long time; a test of endurance.

To keep your motivation levels up:

1. Again, constantly learn and acquire knowledge. Read, study and talk to people; knowledge and information is important for feeding your mind and keeping you curious and motivated.
2. Keep the company of enthusiastic and like-minded people. Try to avoid negative people 'doubting Thomases' and seek out positive, well-motivated people. It's a lot easier to stay motivated if the people around you are equally motivated and enthusiastic. Attend networking events, where you will meet and chat with people who are positively like-minded and resourceful.
3. Keep a positive attitude; see problems and setbacks as learning opportunities. Always have a plan B to overcome problems and setbacks.
4. Be pragmatic and adjust your plan to changing circumstances and conditions.
5. Continually review and find new strengths and weaknesses. Constantly work on improving your weaknesses and building on your strengths.

[237.] Brainy Quote http://www.brainyquote.com/quotes/quotes/l/louiseboo170206.html accessed 27th April 2016

6. Get on with it; try not to procrastinate, assess the risks but keep working towards your goals.
7. Get help from the relevant people such as a mentor. Don't be afraid to ask others, who may be experienced and knowledgeable for help and advice and don't hold back if you can help them too. Seeing other people succeed will help to motivate you to do the same.

During my corporate career, one of the many projects that I had developed was a UK business growth strategy for a well-known international company called Ferrero. The business plan was complete and ready for launch; we had decided to launch the plan to the company and its employees at a venue just outside London. To support the launch, we asked Kriss Akabusi,[238.] the former British athlete and the winner of three Olympic medals, to speak at the launch conference. Kriss is a truly inspirational and charismatic speaker, who delivers his story with enthusiasm, energy and lots of passion. He told the conference about his early life; being left in care at the age of four years old when his Nigerian parents returned to their homeland. He joined the Army in 1975, before moving to professional athletics. During Kriss's army life his superior became his mentor, providing him with inspiration, advice, confidence and motivation to build a career after his Army life in athletics. He tells the story of how the Great Britain 4x400m men's relay team changed their strategy at the eleventh hour to beat the American team at the 1991 World Championships in Tokyo. In my opinion, Kriss was a 'role model mentor'[239.].

Coincidentally, I was fortunate to meet Kriss's wife Monika a few years later; enjoying an evening of conversation about the parallels between sport motivation and management. Monika is an expert in her field with a wide range of qualifications ranging from Stress Management Consultant, Nutritional Advisor to Life Skill Coach and Sports Kinesiologist.

Finding a mentor to motivate you is a tremendous help to you and the achievement of your 10-year goals. A good mentor will help you learn to do things, but not do them for you. A good mentor will further:

[238.] Kriss Akabusi – https://en.wikipedia.org/wiki/Kriss_Akabusi http://www.akabusi. com/ accessed 27 April 2016
[239.] Quotation and reference provided with kind permission from Kriss Akabusi.

- Assess your strengths and weaknesses.
- Introduce new perspectives and correct any wrong thinking.
- Boost your abilities and knowledge.
- Introduce you to new resources and people.
- Build your confidence.
- Provide effective and reliable advice and guidance.

Carefully select your mentor; someone who is best suited to help you achieve your 10-year goals and has probably already achieved the same as you are setting out to achieve. Consider:

- A friend, relative or neighbour.
- A sporting acquaintance, coach or trainer.
- Colleagues and business acquaintances.
- An old boss.
- A professional academic such as a teacher or professor.

Without doubt it was someone I have spoken about frequently, my mum, who was my greatest inspiration and mentor. My mum not only raised myself and two younger sisters after the death of my father when he was 31 years old. Being a role model, she worked hard, ensuring we had a roof over our heads, were well-clothed and that food was on the table. She had made sure we had a good school education, encouraging us to learn to be resourceful, independent and to take responsibility. She was a leading example to anyone who is faced with life's cruel losses at a very early age, remaining strong, determined and proud, never complaining and just getting on with it, always, and always everyone's friend.

Obtaining 360-degree feedback

360-degree feedback is a process where you are able to gather feedback from the people you interact with on a daily basis. Again, it is a development tool, which I have used continuously throughout my career, formally and informally; I used to frequently and casually say to my respected old bosses 'how am I doing?' conversely I would say to my direct reports 'how can I help you do your job better?'. We will discuss the application, detail and context of 360-degree feedback as part of your post-divorce personal development a little later in the chapter. There are a number of ways to obtain 360-degree feedback. We have already mentioned the benefits of having a mentor to give feedback. To provide a mix and more balanced level of personal feedback you are able to use additional sources of feedback both at work and at home as the following diagram illustrates:

Diagram 42

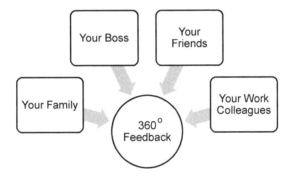

360-degree feedback can provide a number of additional benefits when assessing your strengths, weaknesses and personal development needs:

- It provides an opportunity to find out the opinions of the people you work with and compare them with your own opinions.
- It means feedback is more likely to be accepted, as it is coming from a variety of sources.
- At work, it can improve the dialogue and relationships between yourself and the feedback provider.
- 360-degree feedback encourages increased self-awareness and a focus on personal development.
- Feedback may lead to increased job satisfaction and a feeling of being valued.
- You are able to improve teamwork, by raising awareness of how others perceive individuals as a contributor to a specific group.

As touched on earlier, in my corporate life I always wanted to know 'how I was doing'; today, running my own business, I always ask my clients to complete a formal feedback form, I want to know how and what I can do better. Whilst working for Cadbury Schweppes and Coca-Cola; 360-degree feedback was used extensively as part of the company annual appraisal system. Personally, both the appraisal system and 360-degree feedback identified my strengths and, more importantly, the development areas on which to focus; thus improving my job performance and enabled me to plan my career ahead. Addressing the development areas involved a combination of formal training courses, on-the-job experience including new projects, one-one coaching and mentoring from some much-regarded bosses and colleagues across the globe.

To demonstrate 360-degree feedback in action; here are some examples of my own, while working for my past corporate employers.

My own personal strengths:

✓   Providing leadership and vision
✓   Pursuing new opportunities with determination, energy and enthusiasm
✓   Challenging the status quo
✓   Professional under pressure
✓   Willing to learn, analyse situations and then make recommendations that are realistic and achievable

My personal development areas:

✓   Seek more feedback from my manager
✓   Manage and presenting detail rather than the 'big picture'
✓   Identify key drivers that motivate people
✓   Pursuing my own and personally focused agenda

The 360-degree feedback process identified eight development areas, which my reports, peers, manager and clients assessed me on.

1.   Accountability
2.   Determination
3.   Adaptability
4.   Assertiveness

5.   Motivating
6.   Forward Thinking
7.   Business Maturity
8.   International

Each of the eight development areas had a definition and specific examples, which helped when completing the feedback process. The following diagram provides my own specific score rating, on a scale from one to five for each of the above development areas. It looks as if I rated myself higher than my colleagues and clients in seven of the eight development areas. I quickly learnt that 360-degree feedback tells you that others can see you differently to how you see yourself.

Diagram 43

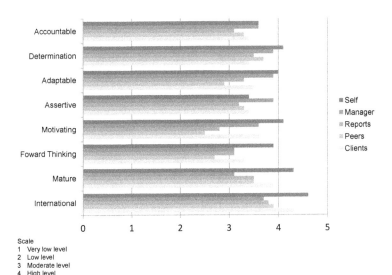

The 360-degree feedback was completed by a mix of 15 people in total. If I am honest, reading the feedback now, which is many years after it was completed – it is a fair reflection of my career history. Having finished my schooling and further education with reasonably good qualifications; I then lived a few more years of my misspent youth enjoying most things that were important to me at the time partying, rugby and girls, which was when I met my ex-spouse in the late 70s. My corporate career began in earnest in 1979. First employed as a sales representative, through to 2004 my final corporate job was Business Development Director for the Italian company Ferrero. I guess my motto through corporate life must have been:

"Work hard and play even harder."

One of my 'play even harder' sporting and career highlights was representing team Coca-Cola at Wembley in 1994; playing as a midfield sweeper. Privileged and honoured to play on the 'hallowed turf', walking up the famous tunnel and to use the same changing room as England's 1966 World Cup winning team. Also, to have the team photograph taken under the famous Wembley scoreboard:

I had a tremendous corporate life of experience, responsibility and continuous learning, without doubt being fortunate to work for some of the best and well-known companies in the world. I also learnt how to use the corporate political system to my advantage, which did come in useful when using one or two legitimate tactics and principles during my divorce years.

Sport and Divorce

"To keep the body in good health is a duty... otherwise we shall not be able to keep our mind strong and clear." [240]

Buddha

Experiencing the painful emotions occurring during divorce, mental wellbeing can be reduced. It is common for people to become depressed over a divorce, and untreated depression is the number one cause for suicide. Thus, a divorce can significantly increase a person's risk for suicide. One study by the National Institute for Healthcare Research indicates that divorced people are three times as likely to die by suicide as people who are married. A study of 13 European countries by the regional European office of the World Health Organization found that divorce was the only factor linked with suicide in every one of the 13 countries. [241]

One way to enhance your mental wellbeing is through participating in physical activity and sport. Physical activity has been shown to have a strong and positive influence on mental wellbeing. There are a huge number of different types of physical activity from which to choose to suit your fitness level, your motivations and lifestyle. Pre-divorce my own physical routine had been reasonably intense, playing four squash matches per week, having two or three visits to the gym each week and the odd cross-country run, weather permitting. I maintained the same level of physical activity and fitness through my divorce years and well beyond. Without a shadow of doubt, participation in regular physical activity increased my confidence and self-esteem, it also reduced stress levels and anxiety during and after the divorce, helping me to get a good night's sleep.

Getting the endorphins and adrenalin pumping through my body from physical exercise not only lowered my stress levels, it improved cognitive thinking and cleared my head. I found playing regular squash was a healthy and welcomed distraction from divorce and the hostile battles against the

[240] Brainy Quotes http://www.brainyquote.com/quotes/quotes/b/buddha387356.html accessed 27th April 2016
[241] Divorceinfo.com 'Suicide and Divorce – http://divorceinfo.com/suicide.htm undated

other side. It brought out all of my personal competitiveness – 'to never give up' and 'failure is never an option', positive thinking and resilience; re-sourcefulness to find solutions and new ideas. Finally, sheer bloody determination to keep going to a successful end and ultimate victory.

> *Remember, it was Winston Churchill who said:*
> *"If you are going through hell, keep going."*

I started my sporting years at school, playing rugby until my early 30s; I have recently completed my 40th year of playing squash, my last game was at the age of 56. Unfortunately, knee injuries have forced me, with great reluctance, to hang up the squash racket to avoid long term and permanent injury. I have now taken up road cycling, which avoids too much pressure on the knees; I cycle around 120 kilometres a week, enjoying the Cotswold countryside, where we live. Cycling is also good thinking time; many new ideas, problem solving and themes for this book were generated whilst out on my bike. I guess the enjoyment of cycling goes right back to my childhood; I loved cycling right up to my late teenage years, I cycled every-where. Today, cycling is still paralleled with a couple of visits to the gym each week; I am now heading to my 30th year as a gym member. All the sports I have played over the last 50 years have helped to build additional people skills such as camaraderie, developing team, leadership and social skills. There was always plenty of banter and 'piss-taking' between team mates. After playing rugby, the team would get in to a large bath together to celebrate the win or if we lost drown our sorrows with a few beers. Whilst in the bath together, there was the rule of 'no peeing', however, you would never know who kept to these rules, I guess it was all part of team and ca-maraderie building. Playing sport was also 'character building' whether team camaraderie, improving individual performance to compete better or just a social event; sport plays its part in shaping the person you become and the choices you make in life.

Playing sport can also make you smarter.

Researchers have known that physical education and exercise changes the structure of the brain, resulting in improvements in concentration and creates new brain cells. Physiologically, it appears that blood flow to the brain stimulates brain growth as a result of physical activity and exercise by oxygenating the brain. Movement and exercise increase breathing and heart rate so that more blood flows to the brain, enhancing energy production and waste removal.

A study reported by stack.com[242] found that top sportsmen and women excel with their mental abilities like working memory, creativity and multitasking. Researcher Joceyln Faubert developed the 3D-MOT procedure, a complex motion system that measures the mind's ability to process an action scene. To test it out, Faubert took professional athletes from the English Premier League, National Hockey League and French Top 14 Rugby League, along with 173 elite amateur athletes from the NCAA and European Olympic Training Centre, and pitted them against 33 non-athlete university students. The study found that the athletes' brains had greater visual perceptual range and possessed more cognitive abilities than their non-athlete peers.

I am not suggesting that you need to become an elite athlete after your divorce, however sport and exercise can not only make you smarter, it can also:

- Increase energy levels; the more you exercise, the more energised you will feel, thinking clearer and coming up with new ideas. On many occasions after a visit to the gym, I would return with the solution to a problem. Remember the saying "great minds discuss new ideas".
- Sharpen your focus; before any important business meeting, client presentation, attending court hearings or meetings with my lawyer; I would play squash or make a visit to the gym.
- Help provide a positive approach to resolving issues and problems, by tunnelling your energy to find a positive solution to a problem.

I also found sport and exercise makes you more disciplined and organised, resulting in a more productive day and better achievements.

---

[242] Stack 'Study: playing sport makes you smarter' 13 February 2013 – http://www.stack.com/a/sports-smarter

Overall, playing sport makes you feel better, improves your mood, helps sort out your priorities and gets things done. As touched on a little earlier, I found it also helps you get a good night's sleep. However, studies by scientists have discovered those who lose sleep worrying over their divorce show increased blood pressure. A growing body of research links divorce to serious negative health effects and even early death, yet few studies have looked at why that connection may exist; divorce-related sleep troubles may be partly to blame, reports the *Daily Mail*.[243.] On a slightly lighter note and as a possible alternative way to exercise; I will readily confess that God did not put me on this planet to dance – I'm certainly no born dancer. Without any doubt, I have 'two left feet' and the TV series *Strictly Come Dancing* has nothing to worry about, whatsoever. During our marriage, my ex-spouse sometimes refused to attend any social events, where there was the remotest chance that, after a couple of glasses of Malbec, I would end up on the dance floor; my daughter would say 'Oh no, dad's on the dance floor' – surely my dancing wasn't that bad. Or perhaps it was; a company colleague was a retired dancer from the world acclaimed musical *Riverdance*, she attempted to correct my dancefloor shortcomings; without success and eventually, despite her best efforts and some persistence, she gave up on me.

On a more serious note, further research claims divorce causes real health problems for men. The research published by the *Mail Online* called for doctors to refer more male divorcees to therapists and said more work is 'urgently needed' to investigate the damaging effects of relationship break-ups on their health.[244.] Further, if you do decide to take up a new sport or increase exercise, it is worth asking your GP for a physical check-up first to confirm that you are physically fit to start a new sport or exercise regime. Over the years, I have known a few squash players, including a close uncle, suffer a terminal heart attack after coming off the squash court.

A differing point of health caution, whilst enjoying your post-divorce life of leisure and sport: it is reported, the rise in divorce is being blamed for an increase in sexually-transmitted infections among the over-50s.

[243.] Daily Mail www.dailymail.co.uk/health/article-2894707/Divorce-really-death-Sleepless-nights-cause-depression-raised-blood-pressure-scientists-claim.html 2 Jan. 2015
[244.] Daily Mail – www.dailymail.co.uk/health/article-2440005/Divorce-mans-health-Separation-increases-risk-death-substance-abuse-suicide-depression.html 1 Oct. 2013.

More and more older men and women are returning to the dating scene, experts say. But many fail to follow the recommendation to use condoms, assuming medical warnings about safe sex are aimed only at the young. As a result, rates of diseases such as chlamydia and gonorrhoea are increasing among the middle-aged and elderly as well as the young, reports the *Mail Online*.[245.]

Divorce and your brain

Diagram 44

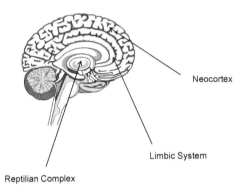

Your brain is responding to the divorce as a threat.

During the years of divorce you will receive many letters, emails and telephone calls from your lawyer or even your ex-spouse's lawyer, if you are acting as 'a litigant in person'. Dr Lisa Gabardi reports:[246.]

"It is highly likely that when you receive such letters, telephone calls etc. your heart rate will increase, also your brain will trigger emotions such as anxiety, stress or even feeling that you are under attack. Your brain is responding to the divorce as a threat; the part of your brain that manages this emotion and the fight-flight-freeze response (the limbic system or mid-brain) kicks into gear; this part of your brain is essential to keeping you alive, it is vigilant for threats and

---

[245.] Daily Mail – www.dailymail.co.uk/health/article-561326/Experts-blame-high-divorce-rates-increase-sexually-transmitted-diseases-50s.html 22 April 2008.
[246.] Dr Lisa Gabardi PhD LLC 'Your brain and divorce: optimize your resilience' 30 May 2015 – http://gabardi.com/2015/05/30/your-brain-on-divorce-optimize-your-resilience/

quick to react. However, this part of your brain is not helpful for planning, making decisions, and considering consequences of your actions. The part of the brain that takes control when you are upset, angry, or scared (during parts of your divorce) is responsible for your racing heart, tight chest, and flushed face; it contributes to your confusion and indecision. When your brain is preparing for a fight or to run for your life, it has shut down access to your pre-frontal cortex (the part of the neocortex behind the centre of your forehead). Unfortunately, it is the pre-frontal cortex that needs to be in charge when ne-gotiating your divorce settlement, making financial decisions, working with your family lawyer, and planning for your future life. This part of your brain is also responsible for imagination, empathy, self-awareness, evaluation, and planning."

Personally, this is where again I found playing sport and exercise a great help in managing your emotions and the brain patterns. As described earlier, sport helped keep things in perspective, it gave me the ability to think clearly and plan during the five years of my divorce, and more im-portantly, plan and look forward to the future ahead. It also kept me motivated and positive about the thoughts of achieving personal change in my years after the divorce settlement was concluded. Briefly returning to receiving letters from your lawyer; a small observation, I seemed to always receive postal letters from the other side's lawyer on either a Friday or Saturday morning. I used to think it was an attempt to spoil my weekend or maybe I was just becoming slightly paranoid.

Achieving Personal Change

Setting your 10-year goals after divorce, presents the real opportunity for personal change. Deciding to do things differently as part of your 10-year plan is energising and motivating; it will give you courage, adventure and confidence to move outside your comfort zone.

> *"God, grant me the serenity to accept the things I cannot change, the courage to change the things I can, and the wisdom to know the difference."*[247.]
>
> *Reinhold Niebur*

[247.] Brainy Quote – http://www.brainyquote.com/quotes/quotes/r/reinholdni100884.html accessed 27th April 2016

Moving outside your comfort zone will take you through a journey called the 'Transition Curve'.

The 'Transition Curve', or 'Change Curve', is widely used and was originally developed in the 1960s by Elizabeth Kübler-Ross [248] to show how people come to terms with life's changes and challenges, such as divorce, illness or grief. The 'Change Curve' shows the changing levels of confidence, morale and effectiveness within an individual, as the change process develops. It shows in the early part of the process how initial ignorance or denial gives way to the feeling of anger. As you progress through the 'Change Curve' your emotions change; feelings then move to exploration of new opportunities and finally accepting a new and changed life. Since its evolution in the 1960s, a number of variations have been developed.

Reflecting on the past months and sometimes years of the divorce procedure; you certainly feel the emotions described in the 'Change Curve'. I was definitely in denial in the very early days; not accepting that our marriage was doomed and trying to convince myself our wedlock was just 'on the rocks'. My quick and reflective learning when at the denial and anger stage was to use the time to obtain information and research in preparing your divorce. Use it to complete the divorce procedure and the onerous legal process – as referred to in the early part of my book divorce procedures spend so much time looking at the past and not the future. This creates confrontation and animosity, which is non-productive and achieves very little. Looking forward, try and pass through the anger and confrontation stage as quickly as possible. Stage three of the 'Change Curve' is setting the direction of your new life ahead; planning how out to achieve your 10-year goals, explore new opportunities, and all the options that exist to achieve your goals. Stage three provides the opportunity to explore new experiences outside your comfort zone, whether that is travelling to different and unusual places, meeting new people or making a career move; some consider it a chance to reinvent yourself. As you quickly experience new opportunities and lifestyle you accept your new life and the ambitions you have made. This is where you 'live and breathe' your 10-year plan; it's in your blood, energising, motivating and rewarding – you feel good!

[248.] Elizabeth Kübler-Ross – https://en.wikipedia.org/wiki/Elisabeth_K%C3%BCbler-Ross accessed 27 April 2016

Diagram 45

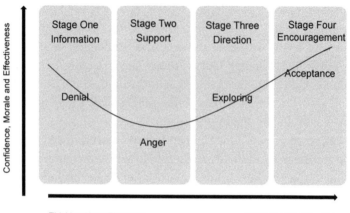

The Change Curve

There are many other models, which demonstrate the process of change, such as the 'change cycle', or Kotter's 8-Step Process. Although there are a number of slight variations, most share a core of:

- Establishing a need for change i.e. divorce, family separation.
- Building leadership for change i.e, taking control, adapting to a new lifestyle and family environment; moving outside your comfort zone.
- Creating a shared vision or direction i.e. planning your future life and how you will achieve your vision and 10-year goals.
- Implementing the necessary change i.e. making it happen, putting your 10-year plan into action.
- Consolidation i.e. reflecting, learning and continually obtaining new knowledge.
- Sustaining the new life and culture i.e. continually building, 'raising the bar' and enjoying life after divorce.

Life after divorce inevitably will mean a high degree of emotional change. Having established your 10-year goals and how you are going to achieve them will bring uncertainty and the discovery of the unknown, which is all part of the process when building your new life. Remember, life's changes are constant; it's a journey and never a destination.

It was JK Rowling who said "Rock bottom became the foundation on which I rebuilt my life".[249.]

After Rowling's marriage ended in divorce; she moved north to Edinburgh with her daughter to enable her to live near and be closer to her younger sister. Whilst she was unemployed, supporting her daughter and herself on welfare benefits, Rowling worked on a book, the idea for which we believe occurred to her while she was travelling on a train from Manchester to London in 1990. Rowling is now Britain's 13th wealthiest woman, in fact wealthier than even the Queen. After her divorce, Rowling developed a skill and an idea in order to become, in 1999, an international literary star, when the first three instalments of her Harry Potter children's book series took over the top three slots of *The New York Times* bestseller list, after achieving similar success in the UK. The phenomenal response to Rowling's books culminated in July 2000, when the fourth volume in the series, *Harry Potter and the Goblet of Fire*, became the fastest-selling book in history.[250.]

I am not suggesting all divorcees will become as successful and wealthy as Rowling. However, developing new ideas and using your transferable skills will play a major contribution to help achieve your 10-year goals.

There are some simple principles and skills you can begin to develop early on to enable you to help achieve your 10-year goals, most of which I have personally used. The next stage of the chapter will take you through each enabling principle.

Personal Development Skills

Personal and self-development is a seamless life process; continually assessing your abilities and skills required to enable and empower you to achieve your personal goals and realise your full potential. Identify the

---

[249.] Simple Reminders 14 October 2014 – http://simplereminders.com/201410140435 44.html
[250.] Wikipedia – https://en.wikipedia.org/wiki/J._K._Rowling accessed 27th April 2016

skills, which you not only need to achieve your 10-year goals also to increase your confidence and lead to a more fulfilling, higher quality life. In my own case, launching and building my own business has taught me new skills and experiences in the property, digital and manufacturing markets. Travelling to Third World countries has provided new experiences of culture, values and education. World travel has taught me and reminds me constantly of Jim Lovell's quote 'everything in life is relative'; gaining an appreciation and respect for international values, beliefs, cultures, human spirit and religion.

Create a personal habit and lifestyle of lifelong learning – lifelong learning is about creating and maintaining a positive attitude to learning both for personal and professional development. Lifelong learners are motivated and always hungry to learn and develop because they want to reach their full potential – as the saying goes 'the glass is always only ever half full'.

> *"The will to win, the desire to succeed, the urge to reach your full potential... these are the keys that will unlock the door to personal excellence."*[251].
>
> *Confucius*

Lifelong learning will certainly enhance your understanding of the world around us, provide you with more and better opportunities and improve your quality of life. One of my future goals is to visit the remaining two of the Seven Wonder's of the World; the 'Taj Mahal' and the 'Hanging Gardens of Babylon'. Referring back to my earlier point 'everything in life is relative' – seeing and experiencing many Third World countries and the poor conditions of health, education and corruption the local people live in, continues to provide me with an endless feeling of gratitude and humbleness – realising how lucky I am.

There can be two main reasons for continuous learning not only in the years after divorce but throughout life as a whole:

[251.] Brainy Quote http://www.brainyquote.com/quotes/quotes/c/confucius119275.html accessed 27th April 2016

1. For personal development.
2. For professional development.

These reasons may not necessarily be distinct; personal development can improve your professional and employment opportunities and, vice versa, professional development can enable personal growth.

Lifelong learning brings many further advantages:

- It boosts your confidence, morale and self-esteem; it makes you passionate and feel good about yourself.
- It makes you more knowledgeable, intellectual and interesting to others; you become more credible and builds your personal stock.
- You are able to help others and provide advice and guidance; this is rewarding and makes you feel valued.
- It helps you meet new and interesting people and networks.
- It makes us less risk averse and more adaptable and prepared to change when it happens.
- You are able to hold wider levels of conversation and improve your intellect.
- Many learning programmes involve travel and visiting new places, meeting new and different people, values and cultures.
- It helps us achieve a more satisfying, fulfilling and rewarding personal life.
- It challenges your ideas and beliefs – you are not always right.
- You become wiser and more experienced.
- It is enjoyable, exciting and fun.
- You are able to take lifelong learning with you; where ever you go in life. No one can ever take away from you learning, knowledge and experience.
- It continually moves you outside your comfort zone.

"If we're growing, we're always going to be out of our comfort zone."[252.]
John C Maxwell

[252.] Goodreads – http://www.goodreads.com/quotes/38432-if-we-are-growing-we-are-always-going-to-be accessed 27th April 2016

There is a common view that continuous learning and having a curious mind throughout life keeps the brain active enabling, a more fulfilling life at any age. Putting the time in for extra learning brings its own rewards as discussed earlier. Within your 10-year plan, build daily time for learning whether that is formal learning, learning at work or on the job, creating new experiences such as travel or working with a life coach or mentor. It means we can get more personal satisfaction from our life and job after divorce; we understand and focus more about who we are and what we do. This can lead to better results and a more rewarding working day in turn. If you choose to learn about another complementary sector, in my own case I have learnt about other industries such as digital technology and manufacturing, this enables opportunities to specialise and potentially earn more money, or to move to a connected industry with good career prospects. In turn this gives you wider experience on which to build our knowledge and more transferable skills in readiness for your next move.

As a member of the Chartered Institute of Marketing[253.] for over 20 years, each year I am required to undertake a minimum number of hours of Continuous Professional Development (CPD). This involves researching new and emerging market sectors such as digital technology, consumer behaviours and world trends; CPD also requires me to attend professional networking meetings and events, where you meet new and like-minded people. Networking with like-minded people is stimulating, obtaining others' point of view, learning by staying connected; new doors open and opportunities present themselves.

From a financial point of view, the more highly skilled and knowledgeable person you become the more of an asset to a company you work for, which can lead to faster promotion with associated salary increases. Someone who can offer more skill and expertise will be of more value, not just to employers but also to customers. Increased skills, expertise and knowledge improves your personal stock to friends, family and peers; you gain respect and esteem from your personal skills and knowledge – it makes you feel good.

[253.] Chartered Institute of Marketing (CIM) – http://www.cim.co.uk/ accessed 27 April 2016

Assess your transferable skills; transferable skills are either existing or new skills and abilities that are relevant and helpful across different areas of life, socially, professionally and at school. They are 'portable skills'. We mentioned JK Rowling earlier in the chapter and how she used her literary skills and imagination to become one of the world's best known novelists, which brought her extraordinary wealth and personal esteem and recognition. When I left my corporate career to set up my own company in 2006, I was able to transfer over 25 years of commercial and business skills to my own company and reap not only the financial rewards, but also great personal satisfaction and love of what I do. People appear to be more interested in you, when you have your own company and the life's experiences that come with it.

The good news is that you probably already have transferable skills; some are more obvious to you, and others maybe hidden. You've developed such skills and abilities throughout your life, at school and perhaps at university, at home and in your social life, as well as through any experience in the workplace. It is important that you can identify and give examples of the transferable skills that you have personally developed – this will be of help in achieving your 10-year plan. Briefly referring back to 360-degree feedback – also having a mentor may well identify some of those hidden transferable skills you possess, and can certainly use to good effect.

Here are some examples of skills that you may be able to transfer to help achieve your 10-year goals:

Team Work

Are you able to work effectively in a group or team to achieve shared goals? Think about times when you have worked well with others in formal or informal groups to achieve results; where you have felt rewarded and satisfied in contributing to the team result. Find examples of how, as part of a group or team, you worked on decision making and problem solving either at work or in your private life; think about how you overcame issues and mention your successes. I've heard on many occasions people say about others 'she's a good team player'. Apply your team skills to enable you to help achieve your 10-year goals; this may be in sport or being part of a team to climb Kilimanjaro, you could be part of a team to raise money for your favoured charity or part of a special cross-departmental project team at work.

Leadership

Do you show initiative and leadership abilities; do you hold a position of leadership at work, maybe as a supervisor, a manager or you maybe captain of your local football or netball team? There are many skills you need to be an effective leader so think about examples when you have helped to motivate, take responsibility for and lead others effectively to accomplish objectives and goals; can you bring others with you when working towards a shared goal or objectives? You should also consider whether you can delegate effectively and whether you are happy to ask for help when needed. Do you possess a charismatic and engaging personality, and what can you do to become more charismatic and build rapport with others? Are you able to pull people together and re-energise them and motivate when things are not going so well or you hit 'brick walls'? Again, thinking about your personal 10-year goals you have to naturally lead the way to achieve your goals.

I have a written reminder hung on my study wall at home, which says:

"Lead the way, life's too short to wait for someone else to."

Communication

Do you have good communication skills where you are able to write accurately, clearly and concisely in a variety of styles? Think of instances of when you have communicated ideas and information verbally or through effective writing, again at work or in your private life. In education you may have produced essays, dissertations or project reports; perhaps you have contributed articles to local or social publications or have examples of your writing ability from past work or voluntary experience. JK Rowling's favourite subjects in school were English and languages; she went to Exeter

University, worked as a secretary and as a teacher.[254.] These early skills no doubt provided her with a foundation of both writing and verbal skills. Humour can be an effective communication tool, can you tell your story with some humour so that people naturally relax and warm to you? Do you communicate with passion, optimism and energy in a way that motivates and inspires people to overcome challenges and to do new things? Over time, think of great and successful leaders; most possess these communication qualities.

Research and Analytical Skills

Gathering, interpreting and analysing useful and relevant information enables you to make the right decisions. A part of your 10-year plan you may be aiming to launch your own business or invent a new product, which will require your ability to research, analyse and critically evaluate market, customer, competitor and financial information. In addition, there could be varieties of complex information that you are required to work with and make sense of, for instance accounting and taxation figures, new product and supplier specifications, technical reports and supply chain information.

> *"Research is creating new knowledge"*[255.]
>
> *Neil Armstrong*

Information Technology

Are you confident using technology and learn how to use new software and gadgets quickly; are you able to troubleshoot basic IT problems? As touched on in an earlier chapter; today, technology is a major part of our lives whether you are at work, home or on the move. The internet is now a global market, work and meeting place that provides a vast array of opportunities not only to learn about the world and access information, but to interact

---

[254.] JK Rowling's Biography – https://en.wikipedia.org/wiki/J._K._Rowling and http://www.kidzworld.com/article/924-jk-rowling-biography accessed 27 April2016
[255.] Brainy Quote http://www.brainyquote.com/quotes/quotes/n/neilarmstr363175.html accessed 27th April 2016

with the world. The future of mobile technology will change the way we all live. The smartphone, which has put a personal computer in everyone's pocket, is now the most widely used consumer electronic product on the planet. I believe for everyone, developing your IT and mobile technology skills can add an awful lot of value in achieving your 10-year goals. In the UK alone, digital technology has created 1.56 million jobs from 2011 to 2014, which is 2.8 times faster than the rest of the UK economy and is currently turning over £161 billion a year, according to Nesta.[256] If you have good IT and digital skills you are in a good position to build and develop your career and income over the next ten years and well beyond; I believe that we are still at the 'tip of the iceberg' when it comes to innovation and technology development. If you plan to enter the technology market, there is plenty of opportunity to provide a freelance service. Around 44 million people worldwide find freelance work across many industries using digital platforms such as Freelancer.com and 'Upwork'.[257]

> *"The rise of Google, the rise of Facebook, the rise of Apple, I think are proof that there is a place for computer science as something that solves problems that people face every day."* [258]
>
> *Eric Schmidt – Chairman and Co-founder of Google*

Entrepreneurial Skills

For me, having the entrepreneurial skills, which I had gained and developed from my corporate career became my most valued and transferable skill. I had a 10-year plan, which I believed in and was passionate about; I was prepared to work hard and diligently to achieve my plan. My vision was set with a clear plan of how I was going to get there.

---

[256] Tech Nation 2013: Transforming UK Industries' report posted February 2016 – http://www.techcityuk.com/wp-content/uploads/2016/02/Tech-Nation-2016_FINAL-ONLINE-1.pdf

[257] McKinsey report 'Digital Globalization: The New Era of Global Flows' March 2016 – file:///C:/Users//Downloads/MGI-Digital-globalization-Executive-summary.pdf

[258] Brainy Quote – http://www.brainyquote.com/quotes/quotes/e/ericschmid460814.html accessed 27th April 2016

It was Howard Schultz Chairman and CEO of Starbucks who said:

> *"I think if you're an entrepreneur, you've got to dream big and then dream bigger."*[259.]

Some corporate organisations have introduced an entrepreneurial process to transfer and develop skills between companies. For example, Procter and Gamble have introduced an employee swap programme with Google to transfer skills and knowledge, in order to build and develop their respective search engine optimization, commonly known as SEO and brand marketing skills. During my employment at Cadbury Schweppes, the marketing department reciprocally exchanged non-conflicting knowledge and research with companies in adjacent industries such as Kimberley Clark and Bass; the knowledge transfer was called 'Project Jigsaw'.

The above are just some of the transferable skills that could be helpful and relevant throughout many different areas of our lives. Think back on your own life and experiences; identify other personal skills that you possess. Obtain 360-degree feedback and ask the trusted people you have close proximity and relationships with to tell you what they see as your transferable skills; you know, you may be surprised by some of those hidden talents.[260.]

Returning to lifelong learning; whether you are using your existing transferable skills or learning new skills, it is likely you will need to undertake some form of formal or informal studying. You will develop your own personal and preferred approach to study and learning in a way that meets your own individual needs and is effective for you personally; attending formal classes or reading books in a library are not everyone's 'cup of tea'. As you develop your study skills you will discover what works for you, and what doesn't. Study skills are not subject specific; they are generic and can be used when studying any area. You will first need to understand the concepts and ideas surrounding your specific subject area. To get the most out of your studies, you'll want

---

[259.] Brainy Quote – http://www.brainyquote.com/quotes/quotes/h/howardschu592284.html accessed 27th April 2016

[260.] Transferable skills referenced and provided by 'Skills You Need – Transferable Skills' http://www.skillsyouneed.com/general/transferable-skills.html

to not only develop your study skills; you will also need to practise and continually apply, develop and improve your skills. This will increase your awareness of how you study and you'll become more confident; once mastered, study skills will be beneficial throughout your life.

Everybody has their own preferred way of learning. Some people may find that they have one dominant or leading style of learning, with far less use of the other styles; others may find that they use different styles in different circumstances. There is no right mix, nor are your styles fixed in anyway. You can develop ability in less dominant styles, as well as further develop styles that you already use well. In reality at some stage of the 10-year plan, we all probably fall into each category, depending on the learning that is taking place. It is also useful to reflect on your own current personal learning styles and methods.

Understanding your own preferred style at this moment in time and then learn about other approaches, which can help to improve your learning skills; this will create a repertoire and mix of learning styles.

Broadly speaking there are seven learning styles:

Diagram 46

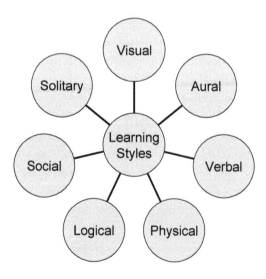

1. Visual: Your preferred style is using pictures, images, and spatial understanding. Technology is playing an increasing visual style of learning such as the use of YouTube, video streaming and social media.
2. Aural: Your preferred style of using sound and music. Learning to play a musical instrument or singing in a choir is an example.
3. Verbal: Your preferred style of using words, combining both in speech and writing. Perhaps the more traditional classroom style of learning would be used or listening and repeating a new language from a pre-recorded tape, CD or online download.
4. Physical: Your preferred experiential style of using your body, hands and sense of touch. Taking up a new sport or craft such as art or sculpture.
5. Logical: Your preferred style of using logic, reasoning and systems. Use of research would be applicable when using this learning style. As touched on in an earlier chapter, I would imagine lawyers and accountants use and prefer this particular learning style.
6. Social: Your preferred style is to learn in groups or with other people. A friend of mine has recently taken up Salsa dancing, she learns in a beginners group every Wednesday evening, followed by a glass of sangria. When I was in Buenos Aries, Argentina one Sunday morning we were stood in a local market square watching some excellent Tango dancing; one of the female dancers made a beeline for me insisting that I joined in. To avoid my embarrassment, I politely declined quietly saying to myself "you haven't seen my dancing"; this was certainly not my preferred style of learning to Tango.
7. Solitary: Your preferred style is to work alone and use self-study. There are many distance or e-learning courses available for home study. This style of learning can fit in with your own lifestyle and commitments. I used to study at lunchtime and Saturday morning.

Once you have identified your own and unique learning style; we need now to think about the key steps of learning itself. There is a short mnemonic called 'MASTER', which again I have widely used and favoured for several years both at work and personal learning. It enables you to use and remember the following key steps when learning new skills. Each stage interacts and in some cases support and overlaps with each other, making the mnemonic integrated and joined up.

The 'MASTER' mnemonic:

Motivation
Achievement
Seek
Trigger
Evaluate
Review

Motivation

We have discussed motivation already at some length and is always worthy of a reminder. Without doubt it is an essential and continuing ingredient to successfully achieving your 10-year goals. Lifelong learning requires self-motivation, gained by quickly establishing the benefits and results of learning as you progress towards your goals. As you achieve each goal, through learning you become motivated to achieve the next goal, each time raising the bar of achievement. The next goal and achievement is bigger and better than the last one; it is a fundamental part of personal growth and self-development.

As an essential part of the overall 10-year plan, it is not a bad thing to recap on the benefits. Motivation not only pushes you to achieve your goals, you feel more fulfilled and improve overall quality of life; self-motivation makes it easier to get out of bed in the morning and start the day positively. People who are self-motivated tend to be more organised, with good time management skills and have more self-esteem and confidence; you feel good about yourself, you are happier and smile more, thinking life is great again!

- Self-motivation is productive; it directs behaviour, passion and energy towards achieving your goals.
- Self-motivation leads to increased commitment and energy; you become action orientated.
- Self-motivation increases initiation of and persistence in activities; you do not want to give up until you have achieved your goals.
- Self- motivation determines which consequences are reinforcing and punishing; the saying goes 'there's no gain without pain'.

- Self-motivation enhances performance and desire; it makes you hungry to achieve more and continually raising the performance bar.

"Desire is the key to motivation, but it's the determination and commitment to unrelenting pursuit of your goal – a commitment of excellence that will enable you to attain the success you seek." [261.]
Mario Andretti – World Champion Motor Racing Driver

Achievement

A major part of self-motivation is the feeling of achievement, which feeds the desire and hunger to achieve even more. By setting key achievement milestones as part of your learning programme you are able to measure your successes. As you progress to each learning milestone, it helps and motivates you take the next step and then the next step and so on towards your 10-year goals. As you progress one step at a time motivation becomes self-fulfilling almost an addictive drug to achieve more and more, which builds continuing momentum – remember success breeds success.

To refer back to our earlier template which breaks our 10-year plan into manageable and realistic milestones 'bite size pieces', allowing you to track and measure our annual progress and grow against the goals you have set:

Diagram 47

10-year Big Goals	Milestones	Milestones	Milestones	Milestones	Milestones
	Year 2	Year 4	Year 6	Year 8	Year 10
1)					
2)					
3)					
4)					

Learning and growth sit together and are continuous; make them habit forming that they become an integrated part of your daily life.

[261.] My Goals and Outcomes – http://valeriecastaneda.weebly.com/my-goalsoutcomes. html accessed 27th April 2016

"Without continual growth and progress, such words as improvement, achievement, and success have no meaning."[262].

Benjamin Franklin

Seek

To briefly recap; again, continually seek new information through reading, listening, observing, practising, experimenting and experience. Information is all around you in copious amounts, on and offline, ensure you acquire relevant and meaningful information and develop this into new knowledge and skills, which will help and support your 10-year plan. Without doubt, information availability on the internet has changed our lives. Availability of information provided online has given us many opportunities to enhance and interact with the quality of our lives, learning, business and communication.

As touched on earlier in the chapter; seek a mentor, discover people who've already 'got the t-shirt' and achieved what you want and then model their behaviour in your own way. Rather than try to figure it all out on your own, find that someone who has already achieved what you desire, determine how this person did it, follow their behaviour, attitude, skill and learn. While you might seek a relationship with a face-to-face human mentor, you could also use a personal coach or read a book or articles by an expert. The important point here is building a network of successful people, who you are able to learn from. Seek and learn from successful people, seeing what they have achieved drives you it is infectious – say to yourself, "I can do that, but better".

"Nothing could be worse than to have been in the same room with several millionaires without asking them some questions..." [263].

Robert G Allen

---

[262]. Goodreads http://www.goodreads.com/quotes/103000-without-continual-growth-and-progress-such-words-as-improvement-achievement accessed 27th April 2016
[263]. Quotewise – http://www.quoteswise.com/robert-g-allen-quotes-2.html accessed 27th April 2016

Time

Create a timetable of learning; ensure you put appropriate time aside in your daily routine. I have heard many times people say "I don't have time; I'm just too busy" – this can become a well-worn excuse not to learn and not to increase personal knowledge; you just end up staying on the same 'hamster wheel' never finding time to jump off and learn something new and different. If you do the same thing you will get the same results: I regularly say to my own business clients "you are good at running your business but not so good at growing and changing it".

You may need to create time to undertake formal evening or weekend classes at college or studying through a distance learning programme. You simply use a lunch break or an hour in the evening to read a book. Join a professional body, which requires a minimum amount of time towards Continuous Professional Development (CPD). CPD refers to the process of tracking and documenting the skills, knowledge and experience that you gain both formally and informally as you work, beyond any initial training. It's a record of what you experience, learn and then apply. The CPD process helps you manage your own development on an ongoing basis. Its function is to help you record, review and reflect on what you learn. Joining a professional body that requires you to complete a minimum number of hours of CPD ensures or even forces you to put the appropriate amount of time aside to complete the CPD process.

The key features of CPD are:

- Provides an overview of your professional development to date.
- Reminds you of your achievements and how far you've progressed.
- Directs your career and helps you keep your eye on your goals.
- Uncovers gaps in your skills and capabilities.
- Opens up further development needs.
- Provides examples and scenarios for a CV or interview.
- Demonstrates your professional standing to clients and employers.
- Helps you with your career development or a possible career change.

As touched on a little earlier, as a member of the Chartered Institute of Marketing, I am personally required to undertake a minimum 35 hours CPD every year. The 35 hours CPD involves a mix of research, reading, attending learning events, knowledge sharing and networking with fellow professionals.

This is what the Chartered Institute of Marketing say about CPD:[264.]

"Continuing Professional Development (CPD) is about improving skills and knowledge, ensuring you remain current and effective as a marketing professional. It's relevant through-out your career – whether you are new to marketing or an experienced professional wishing to keep abreast of the latest trends and techniques."

Benefits of joining the CPD Programme:

- *Learn new skills, develop knowledge, stay up to date with the latest trends.*
- *Track your progress and receive recognition for your achievements.*
- *Remain compliant.*
- *Stand out from others in a competitive job market – impress employers.*
- *Increase your confidence and credibility as a marketer.*
- *It's your route to Chartered Marketer status.*

Source: Chartered Institute of Marketing

A further benefit of CPD; it is structured and disciplined ensuring that your development covers a number of learning areas, for example:

- Qualifications studies
- Short training courses and workshops
- Language training
- In-company development
- Imparting knowledge
- Mentoring
- Conferences and exhibitions
- Community contribution
- Private study

[264.] Chartered Institute of Marketing 'CPD and Chartered Marketer Status' 27 April 2016 – http://www.cim.co.uk/community/cpd-and-chartered-status/

Henry Ford, who was born in 1863, once said:

> *"Anyone who stops learning is old, whether at twenty or eighty. Anyone who keeps learning stays young. The greatest thing in life is to keep your mind young."*[265]

Google quote from Eric Schmidt's and Jonathan Rosenberg's book '*How Google Works*'.[266]

> *"Our ideal candidates are the ones who prefer roller coasters, the ones who keep learning. These 'learning animals' have the smarts to handle change and the character to love it."*

Probably over a century has passed since Henry Ford's statement and Google's more recent quote; however, the importance of learning has not changed one iota.

Evaluate

Evaluate your learning and reflect on what you have learnt and the new knowledge gained. Use the information you have gained and apply it at work and everyday life. Using the earlier template, evaluate your progress at each two year 'bite size' milestone; each milestone achieved is another step towards your overall 10-year goals.

First question, ask yourself where am I now? Evaluate and reflect on any learning experiences over the previous year. Write down what you have learned, what insights it gave you and what you might have done differently. Include both formal training events and informal learning, such as:

- Learning from colleagues at work or shared learning from networking such as professional bodies and universities.

---

[265] Brainy Quotes http://www.brainyquote.com/quotes/quotes/h/henryford103927.html accessed 27th April 2016

[266] Reference 'How Google Works' Page 102 'Hiring Learning Animals' in 2014 – http://www.howgoogleworks.net/img/preview/how-google-works-book-preview.pdf

- Reading about new technologies, new methods of working, legislative changes; so much information and insight is available online.
- Shadowing or assisting an experienced colleague; this is commonly known as 'buddying'.
- Insights and learning points from coaching and mentoring.
- Reflections, insights and learning points from taking on a new responsibility, project or job.
- Organisational or role change; your employer may restructure the workforce or merge with another company.
- Temporary job swaps or special projects within the department/organisation. When in corporate life, I gained invaluable learning by working in sales, marketing, business development and finance.
- Deputising or covering for colleagues or even your boss.
- Insights and lessons learned from mistakes and failures.
- Lessons learned from critical incidents or life changing events such as divorce or bereavement.
- Make a note of any outcomes of each learning experience and what difference it has made to you in helping achieve your 10-year goals.

Next question; where do I want to be?

Look at your overall 10-year goals and evaluate where you want to be at the end of each year. It is useful to refer to the two year milestones already set, and now break them down into annual learning targets.

Final and most important question; what do I have to do to get there?

Now, look at each biennial milestone and write down what you need to do to achieve each one of them. This could include further training, job or role progression or a complete change in direction. For shorter term objectives, include the first step establish what you can do today or tomorrow, there's always some 'low hanging fruit' to pick. For example, having a chat with your manager about a new responsibility or a work related new project; finding out about new technology from a colleague who has experience of it or download a latest report from the internet.

Review

This step is essential; continuously review your learning; questioning whether the new information is helping you achieve your 10-year goals. Review what you could have done differently or better to improve learning. If things are not going to plan, think twice about the learning path you are following, don't be afraid to change it. You'll need to set a date in advance for a review of the goals and the objectives you've set yourself. You can either do this from one review to the next or decide to review regularly. I have found once every six months is good time duration to review your learning; put it in your diary and do it. Finally, use your learning programme to 'shoot the odd sacred cow'. If something is failing to produce results or you have a self-confessed bad habit, which will hinder your learning progress and achievement stop doing it straight away.

Kolb's Experiential Learning Cycle[267.] is a great development tool to help reflect, review and act. I first began using Kolb's model in 1995, when joining Cadbury Schweppes as the Head of UK Business Development. On joining the company, I inherited a team of newly recruited Business Development Managers of all ages, experience, backgrounds, personality and capabilities – some senior colleagues in the company called them 'a right shower'. One of my early priorities was to bring the complete team up to an acceptable level of performance and capability. Due to individual differences, each manager required a bespoke personal learning programme, including the way in which they learnt, individually and as a team. Today, whilst running my own consultancy and management training company, I have continued to use Kolb's Experiential Learning Cycle and techniques. Many of my clients are small businesses with a mix of ages, experience, backgrounds, personality, capabilities and attitude; I discovered that Kolb's principles are very useful and effective with small businesses.

The principles are; Kolb proposes that we all learn from our experience in a cyclical way. People observe something happening and reflect on their observations. This experience and reflection is then incorporated into the

---

[267.] Academic Registrations 'Experiential learning: experience as the source of learning and development – http://academic.regis.edu/ed205/kolb.pdf and http://www.business balls.com/kolblearningstyles.htm 27th April 2016

theoretical knowledge that the person already possesses, or is supported by reading and training, building up a framework into which to fit their experience.

To complete the cycle, people then need to be able to act and practice the new skills they have learned.

Diagram 48

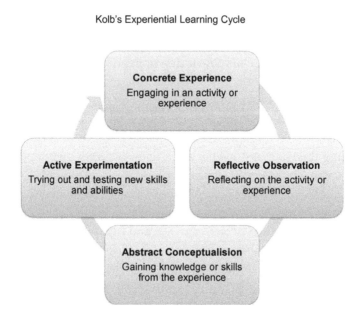

Kolb's Experiential Learning Cycle

Concrete Experience
Engaging in an activity or experience

Active Experimentation
Trying out and testing new skills and abilities

Reflective Observation
Reflecting on the activity or experience

Abstract Conceptualision
Gaining knowledge or skills from the experience

Kolb's Experiential Learning Cycle

The Four Different Learning Styles

Kolb proposed this as a cycle. But there's no question that while we all go through the cycle when we learn something and act on it, we also all prefer to start in different places and to spend more time on some aspects than others.

Two men called Peter Honey and Alan Mumford[268.] noticed this and built on Kolb's work to propose the theory of learning styles.

Honey and Mumford identified four separate learning styles:

1. Activist
2. Pragmatist
3. Reflector
4. Theorist

1. *Activists* learn by doing.

They don't want to hear what they should be doing, they want to dive in head-first and have a go.

Activists are likely to say:
"Let's just give it a go and see what happens."
"Can I try it out?"

I guess if I'm honest, I'm a bit of an 'Activist'; I never fully read all the instructions when buying a self-build piece of furniture; I just open the box and get on with building it. When learning to ski; I really didn't listen to the ski instructor on the nursery slopes, hence I spent most of my time on my backside or rolling in the snow. However, once free of the instructor and almost self-taught, I was nearly ready for the 'black run' by the end of the week, and won a trophy for the most improved skier. The same story when learning to play golf, despite taking half-dozen lessons from a golf-pro – at my first corporate tournament at the Belfry, I managed to hit a tree at the first tee, lose my golf club in the lake at the 18th green. By the second corporate tournament, this time at Gleneagles, Scotland, I again won the prize for the most improved player; managing to keep all my clubs intact and avoid hitting any large trees at the tee.

[268.] Learning Styles: Wikipedia 27 April 2016 https://en.wikipedia.org/wiki/Learning_styles

2. *Pragmatists* care about what works in the real world.

They aren't interested in abstract concepts; they just want to know if it works.

Pragmatists are likely to say:
"How will it work in practice?"
"I just don't see how this is relevant."
"How will this help me?"

Sometimes, Pragmatists can come across negative or narrow minded. I used to have an old boss like this, who at times I just ignored; in fact, on occasion I used to go all out to prove him wrong.

3. *Reflectors* like to think about what they're learning.

They want to understand things thoroughly before they try them out. Reflectors are likely to say:

"Let me just think about this for a moment"
"Don't let's rush into anything."
I used to call this type 'Steady Eddie'.

4. *Theorists* like to understand how the new learning fits into their 'framework' and into previous theories.

They're likely to be uncomfortable with things that don't fit with what they already know.

Theorists are likely to say:
"But how does this fit in with [x]?"
"I'd just like to understand the principles behind this a bit more."

In my experience, I have found that lawyers and accountants falling into the 'theorist' category.

In order to learn effectively, it's important to be able to use all four styles, but most people have a preference for one or two. Particularly common mixtures seem to include Activist/Pragmatist and Reflector/Theorist. People often notice that their learning style has changed in response to different job demands or changes in their life. Thinking about learning after divorce; we are facing a life of change with new and different demands. It is worthy to note if your preferred learning style has changed as a result of divorce, and by setting new goals as part of your 10-year plan.

Further, identifying learning styles is interesting and entertaining, but it also has some important practical implications.

1. You learn best using your own preferred style.
    This follows whether we're talking about Honey and Mumford's four learning styles or Kolb's model. Select your own learning preference and you will also enjoy learning more, and get more out of the experience, if it's in your preferred style and it has to work for you.

2. Choose your very own experiences to fit your preferred style.
    It follows, therefore, that you should use your preferred style to work out what sort of learning experiences will suit you best and which you will feel most comfortable with.

If you're considering a training course, whether for long-term study or shorter-term learning, don't be afraid to call the person organising it and discuss the type of learning. It may be that it could be tailored more to your learning style, or the tutor may be able to suggest a more appropriate course for you. If you can't choose your experiences, adapt them. If you're a visual or kinaesthetic learner, you're not going to get all that much out of sitting in a lecture, listening to someone talk. But don't be tempted to just abandon the experience. Instead, you have an opportunity to tailor it to your preferences. Try taking notes, or drawing a picture such as a mind-map to help you remember it more visually, or organise a discussion session afterwards over coffee with others to consider the learning in a different way. If your learning is examination-based, you also need to think about how you're going to revise the subject matter. For instance, if you're an auditory learner, you're going to love lectures, but you're not going to enjoy reading over your notes to revise them. Maybe you should ask your lecturers if you can record the lecture, or perhaps record your notes onto a Dictaphone or digital voice recorder. Then you can play back your 'notes' afterwards and listen again to revise them. I used to find the use of mnemonics and euphemisms helpful to remember theories, business models and processes when taking exams.

When studying for my marketing exams: I used the following 5 combinations of learning:

1. Each week we had two evenings 6–9pm of formal classroom lectures.
2. Self-study time at weekends, usually three to four hours on a Saturday morning.
3. Learning application in my job as Marketing Manager, whilst employed by Coca-Cola. I was lucky to have a number of new market development responsibilities, where I could apply my classroom learning.
4. Job-related special projects; an example was building new business in the leisure and entertainment market.
5. I purchased learning CDs from the Chartered Institute of Marketing to play and listen to whilst travelling in the car to and from work.

On a point of the financial cost of learning; if you are undertaking formal learning as I did through the Chartered Institute of Marketing, it is likely there will be a cost to undertake the learning. If this is the case, approach your employer and ask if they will financially contribute to the cost of learning, ideally in full or at least in part. This would be justified, particularly if your employer will benefit from your new learning. In my own situation Coca-Cola paid 50% towards my one-year marketing training.

My own experience has discovered that as we grow into our later adult years our learning styles tend to lean towards experiential learning. Adults seem to prefer to learn 'on the job' by interacting with peers and work colleagues to acquire new knowledge and skills.[269]

[269.] Learning styles referenced and provided by 'Skills You Need – learning styles' http://www.skillsyouneed.com/learn/learning-styles.html

In the years following divorce, particularly if it has been emotional and hostile, you can experience times of low self-esteem and feelings of self-doubt. Having in clear focus your 10-year goals and how you are going to achieve them through learning and new skills provides confidence and control of what your future will be. Combine your 10-year plan with improved knowledge, learning new skills and gaining information from self-learning, which will improve your self-esteem and confidence.

Knowing your information, learning and what you want to do is crucial to facing up to your anxieties, and not to walking away from them. Blocking out or refusing to think about fears allows the same fears to take over and damage your self-esteem and confidence; you could 'crash and burn'.

Also, avoid the ostrich effect – do not 'bury your head in the sand'.

> *"Sticking your head in the sand might make you feel safer, but it's not going to protect you from the coming storm."* [270.]
>
> *Barack Obama*

Even the seemingly most confident people may feel insecure, fearful and nervous deep down. Fears and nerves are common and not a bad thing as they can be overcome. I remember in my early days of public speaking, particularly speaking to new audiences, I would overcome my fears and nerves by thoroughly researching, preparing and building in-depth knowledge of the subject matter. I would practise for days, constantly rehearsing my words and what I was going to say, which not only gave me confidence, it provided me with control. I used the same level of preparation and practice when I was representing myself in court and speaking to the judge. It can be the same for everyone, if properly prepared and practiced.

Steve Jobs the founder of Apple would spend hours rehearsing and prac-

---

[270.] Barak Obama at his speech at Georgetown University in Washington DC and reported by BBC News on 25 June 2013 – http://www.bbc.co.uk/news/world-us-canada-23057369

ticing every facet of his corporate presentations and new product launches. Meticulously preparing every slide in fine detail, every corporate and new product presentation was staged like a theatrical experience. He would make his presentations look effortless, but his faultless delivery came as result of hours and hours of practice, practice and more practice.[271.]

A further tip is not to let your nerves show, to appear confident however you feel inside, to learn to channel the nervous energy positively. Once you are in control, the fear will subside and your self-esteem and confidence will improve. Again, quickly referring to my time as a 'litigant in person' and of representing myself in court and in front of the judge, I used the above techniques to overcome my nerves and remain composed. As already mentioned in my book and my view; my opposing barrister did appear to be nervous at the court hearing by knocking over a jug of water at the beginning of proceedings and fumbling with the microphone; maybe I made him feel nervous as a 'litigant in person'.

Do not be critical of yourself to others; don't beat yourself up over failure or mistakes. Whilst it can be useful to self-critique or confide your concerns to someone you trust, telling the world is something else. Be kind to yourself; make a list of your good qualities and believe them, believe in yourself. Carrying out an assessment of your own strengths and weaknesses will tell you your qualities and what you are good at. Don't complain; everyone has problems, so why should yours be greater than others. By being negative you can isolate yourself from others and cut yourself off from solutions to problems. I had learnt the importance of this when seeing for myself people in Third World countries suffering from poverty, disease and disability, their situations were far, far worse than mine.

Relax and allow time for yourself each day; chill-out and create some down time in your personal space. This may only be a few minutes, but it is important to be quiet and to unwind. Find your own sanctuary some discover meditation or yoga as personal space; mine is having a sauna after a hard work out at the gym, I also find driving and cycling a good time for

---

[271.] Presentation Genius of Steve Jobs – www.timbaynes.co.uk/blogImages/184150_ PresentationGenius undated

thinking. Boost your morale by allowing yourself a treat from time to time, especially if you have overcome a hurdle in your personal life or you have had a good week at work; it's that 'Friday feeling' – have dinner at a favourite restaurant, go to the movies or simply treat yourself to a good bottle of wine, a soak in the bath and a box of chocolates.

Congratulate yourself on an individual job or task done well; perhaps tell a trusted friend. Do not always be the one to give out praise, you need some too. Positive feedback and justified praise from others is a good boost to morale. Celebrate together, it makes you all feel good.

If you undertake the 360-degree feedback process discussed earlier, look for the positive feedback as well as the development feedback; work and improve on the development areas and turn them into positive attributes through learning, new skills and practice. A friend of mine would go to great lengths to help anyone out. In his late 50s, he has been a bus driver most of his life; he is also responsible for training new recruit bus drivers. He told me the story, whilst one time waiting to start his afternoon shift the company managing director, who was visiting the local bus depot called him over; his heart sank, thinking he was about to be reprimanded. No, the managing director told him that he had been reading through some of his training reports and obtained feedback from some of the trainees; he thought the reports were excellent and helpful but more im-portantly the 'rookie' trainees had nothing but praise for the way they had been trained. My friend the bus driver felt 10 feet tall, following the positive feedback and personal recognition from his superior. Hence, he is now regularly asked how the bus company can further improve their training of 'rookie' bus drivers. You can definitely teach both young and old dogs new tricks.

We touched on overcoming nerves a little earlier; learn to channel nerves and tension into positive energy. When you are nervous, adrenalin is pumped through the body and you feel more keyed-up and alert. This extra energy can be used to good effect; enabling you to communicate with greater enthusiasm, passion and intensity. Learn to be assertive, always stand your ground and what you believe in; do not be pressured by others. Do not be a 'shrinking violet' call on your values, beliefs and knowledge to argue your corner; it makes for good debate. Briefly returning to the divorce process; make sure that you stand your ground on the key issues and claims, particularly the ones that will make a difference to the financial settlement and your future life.

Improving your confidence as you enter the unknown − we have talked a lot about moving outside your comfort zone and pushing out the boundaries with new experiences and learning. People often feel less confident about new or potentially difficult situations. Perhaps the most important factor in developing confidence is planning and preparing for the unknown. If you are applying for a new job as part of your 10-year plan, you would be wise to diligently prepare for the interview. Plan what you would want to say in the interview and think about some of the questions that you may be asked. Practice your answers with friends or colleagues and gain their feedback. Learning about and thoroughly researching the job and the company you are applying to will help you to feel more confident about our ability to handle new job situations.

Through obtaining information you are in a better position to know what to expect and how and why things are done, which will add to your awareness and usually make you feel more prepared and ultimately more confident. Learning and gaining knowledge makes us feel more confident about our abilities to perform roles and tasks, when this happens we need to combine knowledge with actual experience. By doing something we have learned a lot about, we put theory to practice, which develops confidence and adds to the learning and comprehension.[272.]

"Optimism is the faith that leads to achievement. Nothing can be done without hope and confidence."[273.]

Helen Keller − first deaf and blind person
to earn a BA degree in the US.

[272.] Building confidence process referenced and provided by 'Skills You Need − confidence'
http://www.skillsyouneed.com/ps/confidence.html
[273.] Brainy Quote − http://www.brainyquote.com/quotes/quotes/h/helenkelle164579.html
accessed 27th April 2016

As discussed on a number of occasions and as an important refresher as part of your 10-year plan; know and continually review your strengths and weaknesses. Discuss them with trusted friends, family or your mentor. The importance of obtaining 360-degree feedback, which will tell you how people see you, in addition to how you see yourself is that you will inevitably discover differences, which you can focus on and develop. Celebrate and develop your strengths and constantly find ways to improve or manage your development needs. We all make mistakes whilst learning; don't think of your mistakes as negatives but rather as learning opportunities. Use criticism as a learning experience; everybody sees the world differently, from their own perspective, what works for one person may not work for another. Criticism is just the opinion of somebody else and should be kept in context. Be assertive when receiving criticism, don't reply in a defensive way or let criticism lower your self-esteem. Listen to the criticism and make sure that you understand what is being said, treat it as feedback; use criticism as a way to learn and improve.

Only complain or criticise when necessary and, when you do, do so in a constructive way by suggesting positive solutions to a criticism. Offer others compliments and congratulate them on their successes. As we successfully complete tasks and goals, we gain in levels of confidence and capability. Be courageous and adventurous; gaining experience and taking the first step outside your comfort zone will take courage and confidence. Often the thought of starting something new is worse than actually doing it. Again, this is where preparation, learning and thinking positively will help.

Show courage in what you do:

> *"Courage is what it takes to stand up and speak; courage is also what it takes to sit down and listen."*[274].
>
> *Winston Churchill*

Courage is a highly-prized virtue, many famous and respected people have spoken or written about it over the years. We probably all have an idea of

---

[274]. Brainy Quote – http://www.brainyquote.com/quotes/quotes/w/winstonchu161628.html accessed 27th April 2016

what we mean by courage, or bravery as it is sometimes known. Courageous people stand up against things that threaten them or the things or people that they care about. They take action in a way that is consistent with their values. Sometimes, however, the action required is not necessarily loud, but quiet and thoughtful.

It was Nelson Mandela who said:

> *"I learned that courage was not the absence of fear, but the triumph over it. The brave man is not he who does not feel afraid, but he who conquers that fear."*[275.]

You need courage when going through the divorce procedures; particularly if you are acting as a 'litigant in person'; you need further courage when building your new life after divorce. I took courage and inspiration from those extraordinary people in the world who had overcome their own adversities or had achieved the extraordinary through their own self-determination and desire. Not only heroes and legends but everyday folk such as my mum.

I remember an occasion of courage whilst in the Ghanaian capital Accra. We were stationery whilst in traffic congestion on a sweltering hot day in the centre of Accra. Sitting in the taxi we heard a knocking from the outside of the car, looking through the car windows on all sides we could not see where the knocking was coming from. We heard the same knocking again; this time I looked out the car window and down towards the road, where I saw a small local boy with a big smile from ear to ear offering clothes pegs to buy. The small boy, who was probably no more than ten years old was severely disabled, suffering from polio. He was pulling himself between the stationery cars on a small handmade trolley selling clothes pegs. This young boy was courageous; faced with a life of severe disability; however, his broad smile told us that his spirit and determination was not at all disabled.

[275.] Brainy Quote – http://www.brainyquote.com/quotes/quotes/n/nelsonmand178789.html accessed 27th April 2016

Since my return from Ghana, I have discovered that some small Ghanian babies who have disabilities at birth are disowned by their parents and taken to visit a 'Fetish Priest'; the priest would sacrifice the baby by administering a lethal poison, and then throwing the corpse into a nearby river. The BBC produced a TV documentary in September 2015 called 'The world's worst place to be disabled', which tells the story of how disabled children are treated as a spiritual curse; the children are beaten, shackled in chains and tied to trees and given electric shocks. One boy had been locked in the same room for 15 years due to his disability.

> *"Obviously, because of my disability, I need assistance. But I have always tried to overcome the limitations of my condition and lead as full a life as possible. I have travelled the world, from the Antarctic to zero gravity"* [276]
>
> *Professor Stephen Hawking*

Living by your moral compass

Your 'moral compass' points towards a life that will allow you to flourish as a human being and hopefully, to have few regrets about the way that you have lived. Preparing and setting the goals for your 10-year plan gives you the opportunity to reset your own 'moral compass' after divorce; some take the same opportunity to re-invent themselves, start again and become a new person. We have all made mistakes and poor judgements in life; I have always taken full responsibility for my mistakes, poor decisions and bad judgements, and learnt not to repeat them. My mistakes told me what I was required to change or adjust; some of my mistakes and poor decisions helped me improve my wisdom, maturity and learning. I still say to myself "that was not one of my better decisions" or "not one of my proudest moments to put in the history books". My mistakes and ill-judgement have included infidelity in my years of marriage and poor career judgements, which I took responsibility for and learnt some harsh lessons, never to be repeated.

---

[276] The New Indian Express 7 January 2015 –
http://www.newindianexpress.com/education/student/Its-the-Ability-That-Counts-Not-the-Dis-before-It/2015/01/07/article2607573.ece

"Anyone who has never made a mistake has never tried anything new." [277].

Albert Einstein

When setting your moral compass in order to travel in life's new direction after divorce it is worth referring to your personal coat of arms and your personal motto, which we had discussed and developed earlier.

Diagram 49

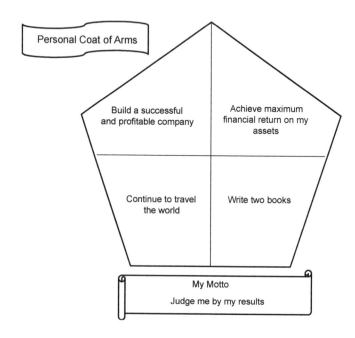

There are three main steps to setting and using your 'moral compass' in order to make key decisions and take the right actions. The steps have similar methods to the ones we have already used when building and preparing the 10-year plan. The process presents the opportunity, if necessary, to reset your own 'moral compass' and change life's direction.

[277.] Brainy Quote http://www.brainyquote.com/quotes/quotes/a/alberteins109012.html accessed 27th April 2016

Step 1 – Again, gathering information, albeit somewhat different information this time.

The main question you should ask yourself before you act is:

'What do I need to know about myself to make a better decision about what to do?'

The answer to this question comes from:

- Your history and memories of past situations that were similar, enabling you to learn from experience, both success and failure. I turned back my history to being a 7-year-old; losing my father and in the pursuing years maturing to be a responsible child and teenager by helping my mum and taking care of my two younger sisters. From here, reflecting on the next 40+ years of my life – learning, mistakes, successes, judgements and ambitions.
- Your understanding of what needs to be done. Here, it will be helpful to refer to your 'Personal Coat of Arms' and the four goals you have set.
- Your values and what you would need to do to act 'well', or how you could use the situation to improve yourself in some way. Again, refer to your 'Personal Motto'. In my own case, I always say 'Judge me by my Results' and measure me against my achievements and what I do.
- Together, these sources of information will help you to understand how you can apply what you already know about yourself. It is vital that you are honest with yourself about your strengths, weaknesses, values, beliefs, misdemeanours and where you need to learn and develop. Do you have an 'achilles heel' a major weakness or flaw that will hinder you?

Step 2 – Evaluate the information that you have gathered.

Now you need to make a judgement about the relative merits and value of all the information that you have gathered. You also need to consider what kind of action or response would fit with your values, and would have a 'good' effect for both you and those around you. It is important to be open-minded in evaluation; you may wish to involve other people at this stage. When my daughter completed her university studies and she returned home, we would discuss our respective plans and future. It's a good thing to seek help with difficult decisions, or when you don't know what to do. However, be aware that if you have a tendency to hesitate or delay decision-making, you may be playing to your weakness; having a mentor can assist and support you with some of the difficult decisions.

Step 3 – Decide and take action

This is action-focused, you need to consider how you will act: boldly, carefully, gently, firmly and with courage. Consider the effects of your actions on yourself and others. Crucially, the action that you take should express the way that you hope or wish to be and how you wish to live your life after divorce. If you have a tendency to hesitate, then concentrate on deciding, and then acting swiftly. Understand that you can't know and do everything as already mentioned "Rome wasn't built in a day" and there will always be an element of risk in any decision. Sometimes, the fact of the decision is more important than its content. Equally, if you have a tendency to be impulsive or rush blindly in, take a moment to pause and consider the likely effects of your actions, including the risks for you and others. Refer to the earlier chapter where we discussed the risks you will probably need to take and how to evaluate and mitigate risk. However, avoid becoming risk averse.

The three-step process referenced and provided by 'Skills You Need – Helping You Develop Life Skills'[278].

A further reminder 'the biggest risk in life is doing nothing''.

How can you avoid looking back at the end of your life with too many regrets? At the time of writing my book, I can candidly reflect on my past years; treating my mistakes and failures with responsibility and also as a character

---

[278]. Skills You Need – Help Developing Life Skills http://www.skillsyouneed.com/ 27 April 2016

building process, which over time has shaped my love and enjoyment for life and ambition. To live my life for my father, who was denied his future life and ambitions at such an early age of 31 years old; I want to make both my mum and dad proud of their son. There is a further moral and standard of pride, which I reflect on and have held since my early school days. During my time at school, there was a school bully called Jimmy who was the same age as me; Jimmy would bully younger school children. Even at a young school age, I had to stop this as it was morally wrong and cowardly to bully someone who may be weaker or disadvantaged than you. After various attempts to stop Jimmy's bullying without success, I took matters of redress onto the rugby field. As school rugby captain, one of my privileges was to select the rugby in-house practice teams; on this occasion, I put Jimmy on the opposing team to me. The colour drained from his face once he knew that he was playing in the opposing team to myself; he did his level best to avoid any physical contact with me during the game by playing on the wing.

However, the moment came when there was the rare opportunity – he had possession of the ball and where I tackled him so hard, that I broke his leg (not something I intended to do nor was particularly proud of). However, you know what, after the injury Jimmy never bullied again. Today, my moral principle remains; if I see anyone being bullied or treated unfairly I will immediately jump to their defence and help them. Recently, a young 'boy racer' parked his 'souped up' car in a disabled parking bay at the local supermarket. Explaining that a disabled driver is likely to genuinely need the parking space, I told him to move his car and park it in a non-disabled parking bay. After much verbal abuse levelled at me he eventually moved his car.

Life's ethics and ambitions are issues which humans have been addressing for hundreds, if not thousands, of years and at least since the days of Aristotle.

Aristotle (384–322 BCE) the Greek philosopher and scientist wrote a number of treatises on ethics. He is considered to be one of the greatest intellectuals in Western history.

Aristotle suggested that there were six basic pursuits or ambitions that might shape individual lives.[279.] He explained these as:

- Pleasure, always looking for the 'feel-good' factor.
- Wealth and material things.
- Status, respect, and fame or influence.
- Power, and being able to persuade others of your point of view, or get your own way.
- Knowledge.
- A morally virtuous and ethical approach.

No life is going to be entirely shaped by any one of these; it is likely that most of us will see one of those approaches as our dominant tendency. I found that life after divorce is a balance of these approaches; friends and family regularly say to me that 'I wear many of life's hats'. Aristotle also suggested that each approach had some drawbacks which might stop those following them from reaching their full potential. For example, he suggested that seeking out only pleasure left no room for thinking or reason, and those who chose to pursue status might find that they were left high and dry when their followers deserted them, for whatever reason. Instead, Aristotle suggested that we should try to live and act thoughtfully. He proposed, we should live in a way that enables us to explore and reflect on the ordinary happenings of life, as well as the extraordinary. We should also try to act out ordinary things in an extraordinary way.

Aristotle suggested that you could look back and say that you had lived a 'good' life if you had shown:

- Courage, and not cowardice or impulsiveness and extreme risk-taking.
- Self-control, instead of self-indulgence or selfishness.
- Generosity, and not wasted resources or opportunities.
- Friendliness and politeness, not rudeness, flattery, or other unpleasantness towards others.
- Tact and discretion.

[279.] Skills You Need 'Living Ethically' – http://www.skillsyouneed.com/ps/living-ethically.html and the Stanford Encyclopaedia of Philosophy – http://plato.stanford.edu/entries/emotions-17th18th/LD1Background.html#Ari 27 April 2016

- Truthfulness and integrity.
- Good temper, even in the face of provocation.
- Fairness.

Aristotle also suggested that there were signs that we could look for in our own and in others' lives, to see whether we or they were flourishing as people. He thought that these signs would mean that a person was growing and flourishing as an individual and living a 'good' life.

Aristotle's philosophies of a good life are:

They are determined to lead the best life possible, and to find the right way to do that. It certainly is true that the virtues discussed by Aristotle are very deep-rooted in the human psyche, particularly characteristics like fairness. Aristotle suggested that if we can live in this way, or at the very least strive to do these things, and occasionally succeed, then we are likely to be happier. He suggested that even if things go wrong, it is still better to act ethically. Overall, we will be happier if we do so. His view was that if all else was equal, he would be happier having lived an ethical life than an unethical one, and he felt that applied to most people: it is a very human characteristic, and that is the basis of his philosophy. This is a philosophy worth referring to during the divorce process; always take the moral high ground. I would further emphasise the ethics of always putting the client and their family, unconditionally first.

Continuing with building your 'moral compass'; again self-motivation is a consistent characteristic throughout the processes and actions. In addition to the motivational points already discussed, understanding and developing your self-motivation can help you to take control of many other aspects of your life. There is a strong correlation between self-motivation, personal goals and achievement. In order to get properly motivated, it helps to spend adequate and regular time thinking about your goals and how you want to achieve them in life; this has been one of the common themes throughout this final chapter.

We all have an inbuilt desire to achieve, what we want to achieve is personal to us and this may change through life. At school you may want to achieve good examination grades or want to be captain of the school rugby team, later you may want to pass your driving test or get a good job. People want to know that they have achieved, or have the ability to achieve something of value, meaning or importance. Generally, the more people achieve the more self-confident they become; as self-confidence increases so does the ability to achieve more. Conversely, when people fail to achieve and meet their goals, self-esteem and confidence can suffer, impacting on their motivation to achieve even more.[280.]

Understanding the relationship between motivations, goal setting and achievement will help you set realistic yet stretching personal goals, which in turn will allow you to achieve more in the longer term; this way you are always 'raising your own personal bar' to go higher and higher by achieving more and more. One of my personal spiritual motivations and continuous desire to achieve is to live and share my moral fibre and achievements with my dad, who was taken from us and denied life's opportunities at the age of just 31 years old.

It is a worthy refresher within the 10-year plan; personal goals will provide long-term direction and short-term motivation. The 10-year goals help us to focus on what we want to be or where we want to go with our lives. They can be a way of utilising knowledge, managing time and resources so that you can focus on making the most of your life potential. By setting clearly defined 10-year goals, you can measure one step at a time your achievements and keep sight of your progress, if you fail to achieve one step you can reassess your situation and try new approaches. Keeping your 10-year goals clearly defined and updated as your circumstances change and evolve is one of the most powerful ways to keep yourself motivated.

A reminder of what Confucius said:

> *"The will to win, the desire to succeed, the urge to reach your full potential… these are the keys that will unlock the door to personal excellence."*[281.]

[280.] Referenced and provided by 'Skills You Need - setting personal goals'
http://www.skillsyouneed.com/ps/setting-personal-goals.html
[281.] Brainy Quote – http://www.brainyquote.com/quotes/quotes/c/confucius119275.html
accessed 27th April 2016

Many of the characteristics and philosophies discussed when building your 'moral compass' are already integrated into the 10-year planning process. This is a reassurance that your plan will be morally and ethically taking you in the right direction.

Using Neuro-Linguistic Programming to help reset your 'moral compass'

Neuro-Linguistic Programming[282] or NLP is an area many of my business peers refer to and promote; some are qualified practitioners having undertaken formal training. NLP provides practical ways in which you can change the way that you think, view past events such as divorce, and how you approach your 10-year plan and future life. The process does overlap many of the areas and topics discussed within the previous chapters; NLP is a helpful tool and does have a particular relationship with your moral compass. NLP shows you how to take control of your mind, and therefore your life. NLP was co-created by Richard Bandler[283], who noticed that conventional psychotherapy techniques didn't always work and was interested in trying different ways. He worked closely with a very successful therapist called Virginia Satir[284], and NLP was born from the techniques that really worked with patients and others.

NLP works from the starting point that you may not control much in your life, but that you can always take control of what goes on in your head.

The notion being, your thoughts, feelings and emotions are not things that you have, but things that you do. Their causes can often be complicated and self-immersing; for instance, comments or beliefs from your parents or education, or events that you have experienced such as divorce and family break up will influence your emotions and the things you do. NLP shows you how you can take control of these beliefs and influences. Using a range of mind techniques and human senses, you can change the way that you think and feel about past events, fears and even phobias.

---

[282] Neuro-Linguistic Programming by Wikipedia – https://en.wikipedia.org/wiki/Neuro-linguistic_programming 27th April 2016
[283] Richard Bandler https://en.wikipedia.org/wiki/Richard_Bandler 27th April 2016
[284] Virginia Satir https://en.wikipedia.org/wiki/Virginia_Satir 27th April 2016

"You can't always control what happens, but you can always control how you deal with it." [285.]

Richard Bandler

The Power of Belief

What you believe can be extremely powerful. If you believe that you can achieve your 10-year goals, if you believe you can do something outside your comfort zone, you probably can. But you can also challenge limiting beliefs, and change whether you believe you can do something by asking yourself questions like:

1. How do I know I can't do that?
2. Who said that to me? Might they have been wrong?

In my study at home, I have on a bookcase the packaging of a video given to me in the early 90s by a client of mine. In the pack was a video of the film *Mission Impossible* and written on the bright pink packaging is "Mission Impossible…they said it couldn't be done."

I guess these words are a constant visual reminder to me of the 'Power of Belief'; if someone says to me 'it can't be done' it motivates and inspires me to find a way that it 'can be done'. The series of *Mission Impossible* movies starring Tom Cruise are personal favourites of mine. A small claim to fame

---

[285.] Skills you need 'Taking control of your mind' http://www.skillsyouneed.com/ps/nlp.html 27th April 2016

– whilst I was staying at the Renaissance Hotel, Sydney Harbour the film crew was shooting the final scenes of the movie *Mission Impossible II*. Each time I watched the film and the closing scenes of the movie, which was filmed in an area called 'The Rocks' adjacent to Sydney Harbour, it would bring back memories of the good times I had whilst in Australia and the sporting banter exchanged with the Aussies.

Returning to NLP and goal setting – by now, we are familiar with the principles of setting our 10-year goals, but NLP suggests some interesting new insights, focusing on satisfaction, not dissatisfaction. For example, it's helpful to make your goals positive; focus on what you want to have, not what you'd like to lose or not have. You should also think about what it is that you really want; your 10-year goals will set and establish what we really want. NLP suggest it is much easier to get motivated about a goal we want and that really satisfies you.

The Power of Questions

Bandler suggests that our minds actively look for answers to questions.

So if you ask yourself 'Why do I feel so bad after divorce?' your mind will find lots of answers and you will feel worse. With NLP the key is to ask the right questions, for example:

- Why do I want to change?
- What will life be like when I have changed?
- What do I need to do more/less of in order to change?

Questions like these naturally lead to a more positive outlook.

To help me keep positive and as an example; I have the two following picture reminders hung on my study wall:

'Positive Thinking – how else are you going to get there?'

'Lead the Way – life's too short to wait for someone else to.'

Before leaving the topic of visual reminders; at the time of bringing my book to a close, Disney Pixar recently released a film called *Inside Out*.[286] The film is about the inner workings of the mind, which controls how people behave. Each character in the film has five emotions living inside their head – Joy, Sadness, Fear, Disgust, and Anger. The film further tells the story of how our unique backgrounds and life experiences shape our personal values, beliefs, assumptions and biases. When researching the film, I discovered that some family and legal professionals in the US are recommending their clients see the movie.

Polish your Curriculum Vitae (CV)

Your CV or resume not only sets out your skills and career experience; it is helpful to measure your progress and build towards your 10-year goals.

---

[286] Inside Out Film Review Metacritic http://www.metacritic.com/movie/inside-out-2015 19th June 2015

Your CV can also help you have a positive outlook as you plan towards the achievement of your 10-year goals. Keep your CV polished and right up to date by adding your achievements and progress against each goal; keep asking yourself the questions:

- What do I want to do next; will it help me achieve my goals?
- Where is my next career move; will it improve and develop my performance and learning?
- How do I get there; what's my career strategy?
- What do I have to do differently; how do I overcome my weaknesses?
- What needs to change; do I have some bad habits that I need to change?
- What will the rewards be; financial and/or career progression?
- How will it help me achieve my overall 10-year goals?

Your CV is a document to take great pride in, reflecting on your life's achievements. If I was ever having a bad day, I would read through my CV to remind myself of the positives and to continually build on the future – I remember saying to myself 'what am I going to do next?' never being satisfied with the status quo. Regularly update your CV; adding your career achievements, new responsibilities, training and learning achievements. Post your CV onto professional networking websites such as LinkedIn. Circulate your CV to industry contacts and relevant recruitment companies; keep your profile top of their minds. Many opportunities over the next ten years can come from your professional networks and referrals.

Keep your CV brief and to the point; it should be no more than two A4 pages long. Your CV needs to have a PUSP (Personal Unique Selling Point) to stand out from the crowd; what is different about you, what will grab an interviewer's attention, this maybe an extraordinary achievement, a legacy, job experience, expertise or skills. Remember, if you are applying for a new job, you are probably competing against dozens of other applicants; find your competitive advantage and make sure it is included in the first paragraph of your CV.

As no more than an example and for demonstration purposes only, my own CV is something that I look back over time to remind me of the positives in life, but more importantly where and what I want to do next.

My Curriculum Vitae

I have spent over 25 years creating business growth for blue-chip companies worldwide; achieved in excess of £250m in new revenue.

Key career achievements:
- *Creation, development and implementation of corporate growth plans for 3 of the world's most recognised blue-chip companies*
- *New market entry and category growth in 50 international markets*
- *Successful launch of innovative new products and processes*
- *Creation, development & leadership of 3 corporate growth teams*
- *Founder and profitable growth of my own company CBG Ltd.*

CBG Ltd. – Founder　　　　　*2006–present*

CBG specialise in delivering business growth plans using 4 integrated principles:
1. *Free cash-flow to invest in growth*
2. *Real-time industry specific research*
3. *Differentiated and customer relevant growth strategies*
4. *Organisational capability and skills development*

Key achievements:
- *Delivered successful and award winning business growth plans in the consumer, manufacturing, digital and construction markets*
- *Delivered business growth workshops to over 3,000 businesses*
- *Strategic partnerships with leading industry trade organisations*
- *Secured and successfully delivered 3 government contracts*
- *New market entry into high growth property and fine art sectors*

Ferrero UK – Director of Business Development　　*2002–2006*

- *Create, develop and deliver UK business growth strategy*
- *Business growth strategy achieved 22% increase in revenue*
- *Recruited, built and developed a brand new team of 6 managers*
- *Customer responsibility included Tesco, Sainsbury's and Asda*

Cadbury Schweppes – Head of Business Development   *1995–2002*

Positions held:
- *Head of UK Business Development*
- *Head of Global Business Development*

Key achievements:
- *Creation, development and implementation of global commercial growth strategies and organisational capability; achieved in excess of £250m revenue growth worldwide*
- *New market entry; foodservice, travel, designer outlets and retail*
- *New product development and innovation*
- *Global commercial partnerships with Shell, BAA and ExxonMobil*
- *Recruited, built and developed a team of 25 managers*

Coca-Cola Enterprises   *1987–1995*
- *Positions held:*
- *Marketing Manager*
- *Business Development Manager*
- *National Account Manager*
- *Regional Sales Manager*

Cadbury Trebor Bassett   *1979–1987*

- *Area Sales Manager*
- *Field Sales*

Education

- *Graduate of the Chartered Institute of Marketing/Chartered Marketer*
- *Qualified in the following specialist areas; value-based management, competitor strategy, consumer relevance and insights, financial management, mentoring and leadership*

University of Gloucestershire

• Graduate of the Chartered Institute of Marketing	*1995*
• Chartered Marketer	*1996*

Maslow's Hierarchy of Needs

A further and useful support tool you may wish to consider when planning and preparing your moral compass, CV and 10-year plan is Maslow's Hierarchy of Needs.[287] The model helps you see the 'bigger picture' by combining five human needs identified by Maslow:

1. Biological and physiological needs
2. Safety needs
3. Belonging and love needs
4. Esteem needs
5. Self-actualisation

The ultimate aim is to achieve and arrive at stage 5 (see diagram 50) meeting 'self-actualisation needs' at the very top of the pyramid. This is where we fulfil our own potential and ultimately achieve your 10-year goals. However, I have always taken the view realising your own personal potential is never a destination, it's a journey; you should be continuously raising the bar and pushing the boundaries and moving outside your comfort zone to discover new levels of personal potential and growth.

Remember it was Benjamin Franklin who said:

> *"Without continual growth and progress, such words as improvement, achievement, and success have no meaning."* [288]

---

[287] Maslow's Hierarchy of Needs; Wikipedia –
https://en.wikipedia.org/wiki/Maslow%27s_hierarchy_of_needs 27 April 2016
[288] Brainy Quote
http://www.brainyquote.com/quotes/quotes/b/benjaminfr387287.html accessed 27 April 2016

Maslow's Hierarchy of Needs Model

Diagram 50

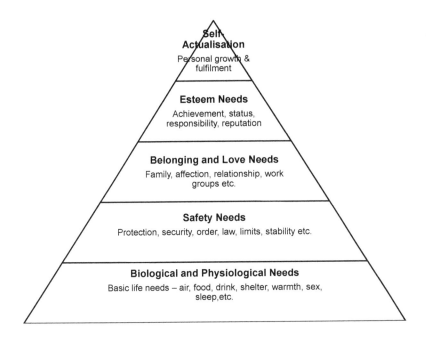

Abraham Maslow[289] developed the Hierarchy of Needs model in 1943; the Hierarchy of Needs theory remains widely used and valid today in understanding human motivation, management training, and personal development. The Hierarchy of Needs model comprises the following descriptors for each of the five human needs. The first three needs are generally the basic needs in life; needs four and five are the more aspirational and needs of ambition, it is these specific needs that are more fitting and relevant to the achievement of your 10-year goals:

1. Biological and physiological needs – air, food, drink, shelter, warmth, sex, sleep, etc.

---

[289] Abraham Maslow; Wikipedia – https://en.wikipedia.org/wiki/Abraham_Maslow 27 April 2016

2. Safety needs – protection from elements, security, order, law, limits, stability, etc.
3. Belongingness and love needs – work group, family, affection, relationships, etc.
4. Esteem needs – self-esteem, achievement, mastery, independence, status, dominance, prestige, managerial responsibility, etc.
5. Self-actualization needs – realising personal potential, self-fulfilment, seeking personal growth and peak experiences.

Maslow states the following description of self-actualisation:

"It refers to the person's desire for self-fulfilment, namely, to the tendency for him to become actualised in what he or she is potentially. The specific form that these needs will take will of course vary greatly from person to person."

Maslow goes on to describe some characteristics and behaviours of 'self-actualised' people and the potential fit with your 10-year plan:

1. Able to look at life objectively – setting your own 10-year goals.
2. Highly creative – being innovative and developing new ideas. Remember "Great minds discuss new ideas".
3. Resistant to enculturation, but not purposely unconventional – moving outside your own comfort zone and taking some risks.
4. Capable of deep appreciation of basic life-experience – everything in life is relative and putting life in context.
5. Democratic attitudes – obtaining 360-degree feedback, having a mentor.
6. Strong moral/ethical standards – having your own moral compass.
7. Trying new things instead of sticking to safe paths – moving outside your comfort zone and continuous learning.
8. Listening to your own feelings in evaluating experiences instead of the voice of tradition, authority or the majority – having your own self-belief and do things differently.
9. Being honest – having your own moral compass and integrity.
10. Being prepared to be unpopular if your views do not coincide with those of the majority – having and practicing your own beliefs, values and determination.

11. Taking responsibility and working hard – being self-accountable for your own 10-year plan and achievements.

Although people achieve self-actualisation in their own unique way, they tend to share a combination of some of the above characteristics.

Using Maslow's self-actualisation model to regularly analyse where your personnel development needs are; your CV should be able to help you identify your personal core strengths and weaknesses. As touched on earlier, regularly review your CV, update a short-list of what you see as your own current personal strengths and weaknesses and what you are able to improve on; even today I review my CV to pinpoint where the gaps are, asking what is missing, what and where do I go next?

Through ongoing analysis, you are continually reviewing and revisiting your own strengths and weaknesses; try to discover the continuing professional and life opportunities that exist for you. Identify your personal barriers and the issues that might hinder your continuous progress. A strengths and weaknesses analysis can also be commonly known as a personal SWOT (strengths, weaknesses, opportunities and threats) analysis. What makes SWOT especially powerful when used regularly is that it leaves absolutely no stone unturned, helping you continually uncover new opportunities that you would not otherwise have spotted before. New opportunities, strengths and weaknesses are always evolving as a result of your own progression and the changing environment around us; keep researching those external conditions, which will impact on your future. Through better understanding of external changes and your weaknesses, you can manage and eliminate threats that might otherwise hurt your ability to be moving forward all the time.

If you look at yourself using the SWOT framework, you can start to develop the new and specialised talents and abilities you need in order to achieve your 10-year goals. Further, refer to your 360-degree feedback to further identify ongoing and new strengths, weaknesses, opportunities and threats; the added benefit of 360-degree feedback it tells you how other people see you and not just your own views. Think of your SWOT analysis as if you were competing against someone similar to yourself. Identify what makes you different and unique, what you can offer, which others can't, what is your personal unique selling point (PUSP). As touched on earlier in the chapter, identifying what makes you different or your PUSP gives you a personal competitive advantage, make sure you include it in your opening paragraph when preparing your CV; it's what grabs people's attention.

Prepare your own personal SWOT; create a template by simply drawing four boxes, each with the respective headings:

Strengths
Weaknesses
Opportunities
Threats

Diagram 51

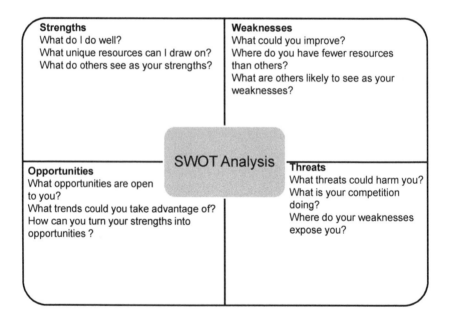

Strengths
What do I do well?
What unique resources can I draw on?
What do others see as your strengths?

Weaknesses
What could you improve?
Where do you have fewer resources than others?
What are others likely to see as your weaknesses?

SWOT Analysis

Opportunities
What opportunities are open to you?
What trends could you take advantage of?
How can you turn your strengths into opportunities ?

Threats
What threats could harm you?
What is your competition doing?
Where do your weaknesses expose you?

Write down in each respective box what you see as your own personal strengths, weaknesses, opportunities and threats; use the sub-headings in each box to guide you; carry out your own SWOT analysis in each year of your 10-year plan.

Strengths

- What advantages do you have that others don't have for example, skills, certifications, education, or connections?
- What do you do better or different than anyone else, what is your PUSP (Personal Unique Selling Point)?
- What personal resources can you access such as a mentor or coach?
- What do other people see as your strengths and abilities; your 360-degree feedback will assist here.
- Which of your achievements are you most proud of such as a university degree, business, a personal legacy or sporting achievement?
- What values and ethics do you believe in that others fail to exhibit?
- Are you part of a professional network that no one else is involved in for example the Institute of Directors, academic networks or alumni. If so, what connections do you have with influential people?

Weaknesses

- What tasks or responsibilities do you usually avoid because you don't feel confident doing them or maybe take you outside your comfort zone?
- What will the people around you see as your weaknesses; again 360-degree feedback will help to identify your weaknesses and development needs?
- Are you completely confident in your education and skills training? If not, where are your training and development needs?
- What is your negative work and personal habits for instance, are you often late for meetings, do you fail to plan ahead, are you poor at handling stress or problem solving?
- Do you have personality traits that hold you back in your field; you maybe naturally introverted, impatient or lacking self-confidence?

Again, consider this from a personal/internal perspective and an external perspective. Do other people see weaknesses that you don't see; do co-workers consistently outperform you in key areas? Always be realistic; it's best to face any unpleasant truths as soon as possible.

Opportunities

- What new technology can help you; can you get help from friends and work colleagues or from people online such as social media discussion groups?
- Is your industry growing; if so, how can you take advantage of the current market changes and new sector opportunities?
- Do you have a network of strategic contacts to help you and offer good advice?
- What trends do you see in your market and company, and how can you take advantage of them?
- Are any of your competitors failing to do something important; can you take advantage of their mistakes?
- Is there an unmet need in your company or industry that no one is filling?
- Do your customers or suppliers complain about something in your company; could you create an opportunity by offering a solution?
- Look for opportunities completely outside your own industry where there maybe a skills shortage. Currently, the shortage problem is particularly acute in construction, engineering, health, marketing and sales; if businesses are unable to fill vacancies it could restrict their ability to grow and prosper.

Threats

- What obstacles and barriers are currently hindering you at work and personal life?
- What events could blow you off your 10-year plan?
- Are any of your colleagues competing with you for projects or career promotion?
- Is your job or your responsibilities changing?
- Does changing technology threaten your position?
- Could any of your weaknesses lead to real threats and seriously prevent you from achieving your 10 year goals?

Performing this analysis annually will often provide key information; it can point out what needs to be done and put problems into perspective; it will also keep you ahead of the game and being proactive. Probing your own strengths and weaknesses will clarify what the best next step is and how further you can improve yourself. It will also tell you more on where you would like to work and where you would be able to prove yourself most at work and in your personal life.

The SWOT framework referenced and provided by 'MindTools – Essential skills for an excellent career[290].

You can search online and find free analysis and tests that can help you with the process of figuring out your strengths and weaknesses. There are tools such as Myers–Briggs [291]Type Indicator (MBTI), based on the work of Carl Jung [292] and Isabel Briggs Myers[293], which provides insights into strengths, weaknesses and preferences in navigating the world.

Throughout my career I have widely used and become familiar with Myers–Brigg; it's a popular choice of analysis tools along with psychometric testing at job interviews. HR departments tend to favour such tools; although I have said to many HR managers over time, such testing must be kept in context as your personality and profiling do change, mine certainly did. Jokingly, I would say to HR managers perhaps there was always a sprinkling of mild schizophrenia in my personality.

By answering a series of questions Myers–Brigg will identify and analyse individual strengths and weaknesses and then characterise them under certain categories. The Myers Briggs model of personality was developed by Katherine Cook Briggs and Isabel Briggs Myers, and is based on four preferences:

---

[290]. Mind Tools – Essential skills for an excellent career https://www.mindtools.com/ 27 April 2016
[291] Myers Brigg; https://en.wikipedia.org/wiki/Myers%E2%80%93Briggs_Type_ Indicator and The Myers & Brigg Foundation – http://www.myersbriggs.org/ 27 April 2016
[292]. Carl Jung – Wikipedia – https://en.wikipedia.org/wiki/Carl_Jung 27th April 2016
[293]. Isabel Briggs Myer – Wikipedia – https://en.wikipedia.org/wiki/Isabel_Briggs_Myers 27th April 2016

- E or I (Extraversion or Introversion)
- S or N (Sensing or iNtuition)
- T or F (Thinking or Feeling)
- J or P (Judgment or Perception)

You are able to combine the preferences to give your Myers–Briggs personality type. eg: having preferences for E and S and T and J gives a personality type of ESTJ (see Diagram 52). There are 16 Myers–Briggs personality types. A frequently used analogy is handedness, where you have a preference for a certain personality on the one hand but on the other you may use other personality types depending on changing circumstances, job responsibilities, or even your personal mood at a given time. When you put these four letters together, you get your personality type code, and there are 16 combinations. For example, INTJ indicates that you prefer Introversion, Intuition, Thinking and Judging:

The 16 profiles are built into the following matrix.

Diagram 52

ISTJ s are dependable and systematic, enjoy working within clear systems and processes. They tend to be traditional, task-oriented and decisive.	ISFJs are patient individuals who apply common sense and experience to solving problems for other people.	INFJs enjoy finding a shared vision for everyone, inspiring others and devising new ways to achieve the vision.	INTJs may come across as cold and distant when focusing on the task in hand. They can neglect to recognise and appreciate the contributions of others
ISTPs tend to enjoy learning and perfecting a craft through their patient application of skills. They can remain calm while managing a crisis, quickly deciding what needs to be done	ISFPs enjoy providing practical help or service to others, as well as bringing people together and facilitating and encouraging their cooperation.	INFPs enjoy devising creative solutions to problems, making moral commitments to what they believe in. They enjoy helping others development to reach their full potential.	INTPs think strategically and are able to build conceptual models to understand complex problems. They can adopt a concise way of analysing the world
ESTPs motivate others by bringing energy into situations. They apply common sense and experience to problems, quickly analysing what is wrong and then fixing it.	ESFPs tend to be adaptable, friendly, and talkative. They enjoy life and being around people. They enjoy working with others and experiencing new situations.	ENFPs are willing to consider almost any possibility & often develop multiple solutions to a problem. Their energy is stimulated by new people & experiences	ENTPs solve problems creatively and are often innovative in their way of thinking, seeing connections and patterns within a system.
ESTJs drive themselves to reach their goal, organising people and resources in order to achieve it. They have an extensive network of contacts and are willing to make tough decisions	ESFJs tend to be sociable and outgoing, understanding what others need and expressing appreciation for their contributions..	ENFJs are able to get the most out of teams by working closely with them, and make decisions that respect and take into account the values of others.	ENTJs see the big picture and think strategically about the future. They are able to efficiently organise people and resources in order to accomplish long-term goals

From my own experience when using Myers–Brigg; it was always helpful to compare, which personality type others saw you versus the personality type you saw yourself and to then explore the reasons for any differences; sometimes the specific differences were quite surprising. You are able to ask your peers, reports and boss to complete Myers–Brigg as part of the 360-degree process.

Your Personal Development Plan (PDP)

Once you have identified and analysed your strengths and weaknesses using a choice of options discussed earlier; you can now begin to create and build your own and unique personal development plan. Your Personal Development Plan (PDP) is one of the key deliverables of the whole process discussed in the final chapters. Your own PDP must give you the right skills and experiences to achieve your long-term 10-year goals; you may also use the PDP to address any further barriers, which may inhibit you achieving your goals.

Your PDP is one of the most important development and improvement tools to enable and empower you with the new skills to achieve your goals. Further, your PDP will provide a structure and a roadmap in which help you realise your goals and self-actualisation, as referred to earlier by Maslow's Hierarchy of Needs. Having a structured approach will bring many benefits in both your professional, academic and personal life; the benefits are:

- Gaining a clearer focus to achieving your 10-year goals.
- Enabling you to address your development needs and weaknesses over the next ten years.
- Enabling you to help remove any threats and barriers to achieving your goals such as a lack of skills.
- Helping to keep you motivated to achieve your goals.
- A better understanding of your preferred learning style.
- How to improve your performance in both professional and personal life.
- Reflective thinking skills that you can take from the learning experiences, particularly learning from failures and mistakes.

- Greater confidence in the skills, qualities and attributes you bring to your 10-year plan.
- Being better able to discuss your skills, personal qualities and competences, possibly with your mentor.
- Better problem-solving and planning skills.
- Developing the positive attitudes and approaches associated with your 10-year plan.
- Being in a better position to make appropriate choices to meet your 10 year goals.
- Developing a positive, forward-looking approach; being self-determined and driven towards your goals.

Create the following template, where you are enabled to record and measure your PDP; keep it updated every six months.

Diagram 53

Personal Development Plan

Areas for Development	Objectives	Method	Measurement
Improve my general business skills in preparation for my new social media company launch in 2019	Achieve a BA degree in business and marketing by 31.12.18	Combination of part-time college study and distance-learning	Achieve a First Class Honours Degree by 31.12.18
Improve my knowledge of social media marketing	Achieve CIM Diploma in Social Media Marketing by 31.7.17	Complete studies online and join a local networking group	Achievement of CIM Diploma with distinction by 31.7.17
Create new business networks and contacts	Achieve a database of 50 new business contacts by 1.1.19	Join the Federation of Small Businesses	Achieve a live database of 50 business clients; made proposals to 25 new business clients by 1.1.19
Improve my business presentation skills and proposal writing	To successfully secure 5 new business contracts by 31.12.19	Complete online training presentation skills and proposal writing course	Secured 5 x three-year new business contracts by 31.12.19

Having now created and built your own PDP; regularly check that the new skills you will be developing support the achievement of your 10-year goals. It is important to ensure that you are developing the right skills and they are aligned and integrated with your overall plan. Use the earlier template shown below, to ensure your goals, milestones and PDP are completely aligned and synchronised with each other.

Diagram 54

10-year Big Goals	Milestones Year 2	Milestones Year 4	Milestones Year 6	Milestones Year 8	Milestones Year 10
1)					
2)					
3)					
4)					

The final step is to create and build your 'Action Plan'

These are the individual and specific actions you plan to do and by when. Examples of specific actions could be:

- Arrange with my local college a part-time training course to improve my social media skills by 31.7.18
- Arrange with my boss a meeting to discuss my 360-degree feedback and training needs by 31.10.18
- Join a local business networking group by 31.8.19
- Attend 4 local social media seminars by 31.1.19
- Attend Internet Retailing Exhibition at the NEC May 2018
- Subscribe to Internet Retailing weekly newsletter by 31.8.18
- Become a member of the Chartered Institute of Marketing by 31.7.18

Diagram 55

My Personal Action Plan

Milestone to be achieved	Action to be taken	By when (specify date)	By who	Measurement

My Action Plan

We have now completed each stage of the 10-year planning process using the framework introduced at the beginning of the chapter. We are now ready for implementation, and to 'make things happen'.

To refresh on the process, we have followed the framework below. We began by setting '10-Year Big Goals'; next, select which of the 11 enablers you will personally use to provide the new skills and experiences to achieve your '10-Year Big Goals'. You may select and use all 11 enablers or just some of them, the sequence and combination of enablers are flexible, and the enablers can be adjusted or merged to suit your choices and lifestyle; remember, it's your plan to meet your needs. It is important to take your time when selecting the right enablers to best meet your individual needs; again, you can select as many or a few as you like – it's your own plan. The next big opportunity is to convert the achievement of your 10-year plan into personal income and revenue.

Diagram 56

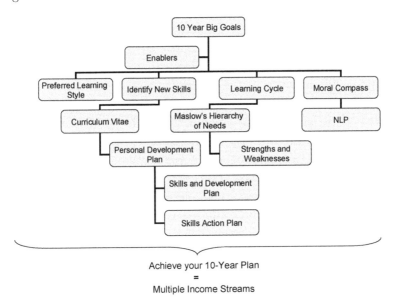

Achieve your 10-Year Plan
=
Multiple Income Streams

In summary, the benefits of having a 10-year plan are:

- It sets the direction you wish to travel to meet your '10-Year Big Goals'.
- It's a journey and not a destination; when you achieve your first set of 10-year goals, establish another set of goals for the next ten years – continuing into perpetuity.
- A 10-year plan provides the appropriate set of enablers from which to select and use; building your own unique plan.
- It provides a set of measurable objectives and milestone to achieve.
- You are able to analyse and evaluate your progress.
- The 10-year plan provides and builds new skills and capabilities; it takes you outside your comfort zone.
- It's a change process, creating new personal behaviours, habits and practices; you are also able to shoot the odd 'sacred cow'.
- The complete process is dynamic and can be influenced by many external factors; keep all components of your plan under review.
- It prepares the foundation to create new multiple income streams.

Creating Multiple Income Streams

The final stage of the process is to analyse your 10-year plan and identify where you are able to earn additional income. Typically there may be an opportunity to create new income through a new skill that you may have developed – for instance you could learn to speak a second language, enabling you to teach others to also speak the language; or you could, with practice become an interpreter. You may already have strong internet skills, which enables you to learn and become an internet trader; a number of entrepreneurs have achieved significant wealth through successful trading on the internet. There are over 2,000 eBay millionaires in the UK; among them is a breast cancer survivor who turned to online trading during her illness, also a city lawyer who changed his job to launch an online shop. The first millionaire used to stack shelves in his local supermarket. The internet offers the opportunity for almost anyone to start a new business from home and create a lucrative new income stream. Knowledge is the one thing you can increase very quickly. Increase your knowledge in a specific area, and you'll simultaneously increase the value that others will pay you for, either to teach them what you know or apply your knowledge on their behalf.

Take advantage of your passions or hobbies. Let's say you are a wonderful artist; use that skill to create multiple streams of income. You could sell your art at local galleries and craft fairs or on the internet, you could offer art training workshops or use your artistic and creative skills to design web sites or apps; all such opportunities will provide new personal income streams. You may decide to improve your IT skills through formal training. Such a skill would open a complete array of new income earning opportunities, which most can be completed from home i.e. technical web design and building, social media management, designing computer games or apps, computer repair and maintenance, even helping lawyers make better use of technology – the revenue opportunities are endless. Providing you have a computer at home, you could train and learn new skills to become an online stock market trader. Once you are successful trader offer to train others, for a fee of course.

Don't quit your full-time job just yet, if you currently have one. As soon as you start implementing your multiple streams, you can cut back on your formal working hours or perhaps work from home, but in the beginning, you'll need to rely on that full-time job income. Think about how you could invest the additional income you are creating to increase your wealth further; think about creating multiple passive income streams. A passive income stream is one where, once you've completed the initial investment, there's little or no upkeep required on that investment to maintain the income stream. Investing in the right passive income streams can give you even further income, without working extra hours. You could invest in long term stocks and equities; you could invest in the property market or become a landlord, as I have done.

Earn royalties from writing a book or music; develop new products or software, which you can licence. A friend of mine invented and designed a special safety knife, which he patented, and he now sells the licence to manufacture it all over the world. He used the transferable design skills he had acquired over many years working in the aerospace industry to invent the safety knife; his design licence has brought him a considerable financial return. Building multiple income streams through using your existing skills and developing new skills not only creates new wealth; it also manages life-risk – if one income stream underperforms you are able to rely on and increase your income from an alternative revenue stream. It is important to prioritise and focus on the income streams that provide you with the best financial returns, otherwise you could find that you are spreading your time and investment too thinly and diluting your returns. Don't be afraid to 'shoot the odd sacred cow'. If an income stream underperforms and shows no signs of improvement then close it down and create a new more lucrative income stream.

Remember:

> *"Money is attracted to great ideas."* [294.]
>
> *Robert G Allen*

[294.] AZ Quotes http://www.azquotes.com/quote/680347 accessed 27th April 2016

Wealth management and the future

At the time of writing and coming towards the end of my book and putting thoughts into context; PricewaterhouseCooper (PwC) stated the following about future wealth management, which, interestingly and reassuringly, features some of the similar themes we have been discussing:

"Wealth managers need to reconsider their business models in light of regulatory requirements regarding transparency and suitability, as well as changing client behaviour, preferences, and expectations. Wealth managers must commit to a 'digital agenda' to enhance the client experience to know their clients better, market products and services more effectively, lower costs in the back office, and improve compliance efforts. Since cost pressures will persist, wealth managers must review their operating model with a systematic effort to separate 'good' expenses from 'bad' (non-strategic) expenses."

The report from PwC went on to say:

"Despite the trials of the last few years and the challenges that lie ahead, wealth management is an attractive growth industry for the long term with return on equity superior to that of any other financial-services segment… Global regulatory trends and evolving client behaviours, particularly around technology, are reshuffling the competitive landscape. Players are consolidating in developed and emerging markets, and innovative digital players are making in-roads."[295]

Returning to my own 10-year plan; pulling everything together along with the many, many learnings since divorce. Today, a brand new and dynamic 'New Life Model' has, without any doubt, definitely emerged. It is inspiring, energising and most of all rewarding; as the saying goes "the output is greater than the sum of the parts".

---

[295] Information and data sourced by Price Waterhouse Coopers (PwC) ' Global Wealth Management Outlook' ' – http://www.strategyand.pwc.com/media/file/Strategyand _Global-Wealth-Management-Outlook-2014-15.pdf This report was originally by Booz & Company in 2014.

The New Life Model

Diagram 57

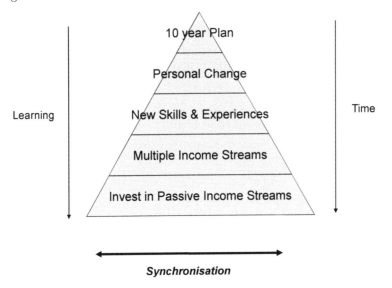

Synchronisation

The new life model has naturally evolved and grown through the five phases shown on the model.

At the top, setting your 10-year goals and plan after divorce, presents the opportunity for personal change. Deciding to do things differently as part of your 10-year plan is invigorating and motivating; it will provide the opportunity to constantly move outside your comfort zone. Moving outside your comfort zone, you will learn and develop new skills and experiences; you will grow and broaden your horizons. Picture yourself reaching those '10-Year Big Goals'. The brain can more easily create new natural pathways when we engage as many of the human senses as possible, so creating a mental movie that is rich in details of what your goals look and feel like. Change your thoughts; everyone struggles with limiting thought patterns from time to time, but because thoughts drive feelings and behaviour, it is important to learn to harness those positive thoughts. Moving out of your comfort zone, learning new skills and experiences, provides the opportunity to create new income streams. As time goes on, the value of having multiple income streams provides a growing return on investment. It is important to remember as one income stream may begin to underperform, replace it with a new and more lucrative income stream.

The final stage of the model is to be in a position in which your multiple income stream investments become passive investments. To confirm, a passive income stream is one where, once you've completed the initial investment, there's little or no upkeep to that investment required to maintain the income stream.

Returning to my own personal 10-year plan, which has now progressed to its fourth year, with six to go; I have created the following four income streams:

1. Property investment
2. Rental income
3. Management consultancy
4. Fine art

Three of the income streams are passive, allowing me more time to invest in the two new potential and different income streams, which are the digital mapping market and writing two books.

In concluding, the London School of Economics (LSE) has published a report called "Property Millionaires".[296] The LSE say "Overall, the number of UK properties worth at least £1 million is expected to more than triple between now and 2030". A further report by Your Move[297] states "the average return for a landlord's property investment in January 2016 was 12% when including both rental income and property price increases; this is best increase since 2014." In addition, Your Move said:

---

[296] The London School of Economics (LSE) and Santander Bank 'Property Millionaires' February 2016 – http://www.santander.co.uk/csdlvlr/ContentServer?c=SANDocument _C&pagename=WCSUKPublicaLte%2FSANDocument_C%2FSANDocumentPreview &cid=1324582166149

[297] International Business Times 'Landlords reap bumper returns as rents and house prices soar' 19 February 2016 – http://www.ibtimes.co.uk/landlords-reap-bumper-returns-rents-house-prices-soar-1544841

"Buy-to-let returns are building and property prices are picking up – as the housing shortage across the UK intensifies. Landlords' balance sheets are looking healthier than at any point since 2014, and property investors are looking at an excellent rate of return from their portfolios. With house prices rising rapidly into the New Year, this acceleration will be a welcome addition to the wealth of landlords on paper, while solid rental yields are underpinning total returns pushing well into the double digits."

This provides me with the confidence and reassurance that my research several years prior and the DMBO was successful; it achieved my first set of objectives and you can 'Profit from your Divorce'. In early 2016, I received an updated preliminary valuation of the ex-matrimonial home; valued at £1.7 million, a 6.7% year on year increase following the overall UK house price recovery, investment in extensive property and building development, and a complete internal refurbishment.

"To get rich, you have to be making money while you're asleep."[298.]

David Bailey

However, a salutary reminder; market and economic conditions can and will change – even when you are asleep.

I guess the one area that I haven't included within my 10-year plan and maybe conspicuous by its absence; finding new and unconditional love, someone to share my future life with.

Maybe I'm old-fashioned, my belief is that finding new love and a lifelong soul mate is something you are unable to plan for. Finding new relationships is like flowing water; it will find its own natural path and in time discover real and unconditional love; again, call it serendipity.

In my early days of post-separation, it was a bit like reliving my misspent youth with a little more money in my pocket. There were dinners, weekends away, theatre trips, holidays and plenty of testosterone with some past and

---

[298.] Brainy Quote – http://www.brainyquote.com/quotes/quotes/d/davidbaile473959.html accessed 27th April 2016

new acquaintances. I remember one new acquaintance; she was attractive and had a professional career. This lady had, to say the least, unusual sexual requirements – I discovered on our first date that she was bisexual; OK I can be forgiven for how my, or any single or possibly married man's mind would work being told by your dinner date that she's bisexual. However, I learnt that informing my date that I was not bisexual but broad-minded, I had travelled the world, seeing the 'darker side' of many cities and I was up for trying most things with the opposite sex was possibly a mistake; her next enquiry was about using anal beads, butt plugs and wearing a gas mask whilst semi-conscious, none of which were on my curiosity list; this relationship didn't last very long.

I mentioned my brief encounter with online dating, discovering fraud and scams. Beyond the unscrupulous activity; to be honest and not wanting to generalise, I found most people using online dating sites as being quite 'shallow' and 'false'; several sent photographs, which were no doubt taken at least ten years ago. One or two online daters wanted an almost immediate commitment to a long-term relationship and even marriage; having just survived five years of divorce hostility, marriage was the last thing on my mind. Turning back the years to my youth and young adulthood, well before online dating, texting or social media; whatever happened to the more traditional ways of getting acquainted with the opposite sex? Again, perhaps I'm old-fashioned. In my more youthful days, I had to pluck up courage and practice my chat up lines before approaching an attractive girl in a bar or at a nightclub.

Alternatively, if I was on a 'lad's night out', where it would be mates before dates; we would all wait for the last dance and hold a bet on which of us would ask the least attractive (ugliest) girl to have the last dance – this was unkindly called 'spot the grot'.

I read in a magazine that your local gym was alleged to be 'a hot bed of flirting and sex'; well I must have been visiting my local gym on the wrong day! Although, I did have a brief acquaintance with a lady at the gym; she worked at the local school. Admittedly, I fast became bored talking about school timetables and educational gossip, which was hardly a 'hot bed of sex'. Another acquaintance had a morbid curiosity; she always kept a home stock of bereavement cards, just in case someone she knew suddenly passed away. A couple of my early acquaintances had conflicting intentions; I was not ready for commitment or long-term relationships. To my surprise when ending these short-term relationships, I was accused by more than one as being 'cold hearted and cruel' for ending the relationship so soon.

However, I soon discovered that the many business and networking events I attended, I was chatting and getting to know 'like-minded' people of the opposite sex. It was some three years after separation, when at a business event in Oxford, where I met my new partner, whilst under a table fixing the electrical plug for my laptop (as you do); now that's serendipity. We immediately discovered shared interest, humour and chemistry; she is intelligent and educated, very witty and beautiful; today, when I wake up in the morning she ignites my day! Perhaps my old fashioned theory is correct; finding true and unconditional love is never planned. However, there is the occasional awkward moment when we are shopping together and inadvertently bump into one of my old acquaintances at the local supermarket.

Keep searching for the next unexpected possibilities – above and beyond your comfort zone

We relish stories of unexpected possibilities; disruptive technologies that create unforeseen benefits. Twitter was born when its creators noticed how alive and engaged they felt when communicating with each other in real time over SMS. The idea has reshaped the way the world communicates. But the initiative arose from brainstorming rather than an elaborate business plan. Brainstorming can be a useful technique, where 'disruptive ideas' such as Twitter, stretch the capabilities of your mind and thinking to what may seem impossible at first to become possible. You may discover that eureka moment; the holy grail to an idea, which could change yours and others lives.

I frequently remind myself of 1990s video packaging, which sits on my study shelf; printed on the packaging is "Mission Impossible – they said it couldn't be done". 'Mission Impossible' can be achieved through brainstorming. Using the technique many times, not only in business but also during my divorce years, in order to not only discover new ideas and solutions, but also find those 'breakthrough moments' that nobody has already thought of. Brainstorming techniques can be further used when facing adversity or even disaster. Returning to the earlier stories about Apollo 13; brainstorming techniques were used by the experts at mission control to save the lives of the three astronauts, by designing and building in a very limited amount of time a carbon dioxide absorber from the few materials available within the Apollo 13 spacecraft, plastic bags, cardboard, suit hoses, and duct tape. The three astronauts survival depended on this makeshift absorber.

Getting back to earth and normal conditions; brainstorming normally combines a relaxed, informal approach to problem solving with lateral thinking; I used to find some of the best collective ideas came up at the pub over a pint or two. Brainstorming at the pub encourages people to come up with thoughts and ideas that can, at first, seem a bit crazy; many ideas are scribbled on the back of the pub beer mat. Some of these ideas can be crafted into original, creative solutions to a problem, while others can spark even more ideas. This helps to get people unstuck by 'jolting' them out of their normal ways of thinking. Therefore, during brainstorming sessions, people should avoid criticising or rewarding ideas. You're trying to open up possibilities and break down incorrect assumptions about the problem's limits.

After a brainstorming session, you'll have a lot of ideas. Although it might seem hard to sort through these ideas to find the best ones, analysing these ideas is an important next step. Prioritise your new ideas by simply asking the following four questions:

1.   Will the idea help me achieve my 10-year goals
2.   Will it create a new income stream?
3.   How much investment will be required to develop my idea?
4.   Will it develop new skills and learning?

From brainstorming, we return to the principles and parallels with the MBO; when businesses are bought through an MBO, all negotiations and the sale is complete the company heads for transformational change. Change, whether you are a business or human being who has just survived months maybe years of divorce, can be hard. However, businesses who have achieved successful transformational change can achieve great things in the future. There are similarities to making personal transformational change, again the opportunity to achieve great things. Probably the critical area and biggest similarity to achieving successful transformational change after divorce are the following five thoughts and principles which I leave you with:

1. Continual investment in your own skills and personal development.
2. Seek continuous self-improvement and financial return on investment.
3. Achieve efficiencies and savings, increasing personal financial wealth and asset value.
4. Do not miss the opportunity to build a new life for yourself; you may just regret it if you don't – remember the 'bucket list' is only ever half-full.
5. If you are going to make a lot of money; it is better to make it after your divorce.

My own 'New-life Model' illustrates what I will be doing for the next ten years; after that, I will without doubt build another 10-year plan. I'm already thinking about my next ten years by expanding property interests in high-growth international markets such as India and China. If property values increase as forecast and interest rates remain low: I may consider releasing a share of equity from existing property to re- invest in further high growth markets and countries. However, there is always the risk of a slow down or even a decline in the property market.

In the 2016 Budget, the government confirmed the 3% addition in stamp duty for 2nd properties and buy-to-let properties will be going ahead; this will now be extended to all investors regardless of size. On the flip side, a reduction in capital gains tax from 28% to 20% for higher rate taxpayers and from 18% to 10% for basic rate taxpayers from 1st April 2016, which is most welcome for investors.

One thing is for sure, change is a constant; don't miss the opportunity to take advantage of it. It is now early July 2016, ten years after my separation, and so much has changed. However, uncertain times are ahead; the economic and political landscape is constantly changing with volatility in the global economic market and particularly in China, the UK's divorce from the European Union (known as Brexit), growth slowing in the UK market, new political leaders and British Prime Minister, interest rates reduced to a record low of 0.25%, Middle East war continues, the refugee crisis in the European Union and elections in the USA; are we heading for the next 'perfect storm'? Hence, always have a 'Plan A' and 'Plan B' to take advantage of the unexpected changes.

On the 13th July 2016; Theresa May became the new British Prime Minster. She has made a commitment within her inaugural speech to address social injustice; she further said "We will make Britain a country that works for everyone one of us" – I do so hope that our new Prime Minister will reform the family law system to help reduce the pain and cost of divorce for British families and children; reform will also help to reduce the financial burden on the British taxpayer. Maybe, now is the opportunity for change and to hold the PM and the British government accountable.

However, there will be one constant; the rate of divorce will continue across the UK and the world - there has to be another way to draw a line under divorce and move on by building a future better life.

Hidden 'between the lines' of my book there is another profound untold story, combined with an uncontrollable personal fear of what the future holds, which over the course of time I may reveal; possibly in another book or even a movie; my alternative true life story could be best described as a hybrid of 'Forrest Gump' and 'Erin Brockovich'.

To learn more about 'How to profit from your divorce' and the further help that is available, please visit: http://www.paul-ross.com/

My 'First' New Life Model

Diagram 58

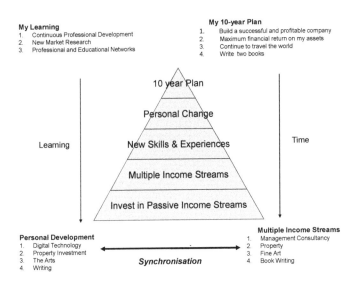

Before I 'rest my case'; I would like to close with four points to remember:

Number One:

It was Martin Luther King who said 'I have a dream'.

Number Two:

Start your journey to your dreams today – never ever let anyone tell you that you can't do something.

> *"The new beginning is right now."*

Number Three:

Keep a sense of humour. Here's a selection of light-hearted 'legal jokes', which I hope the legal professionals reading my book will see equally as being light-hearted.

Q: What's the difference between a good lawyer and a bad lawyer?
A: A bad lawyer makes your case drag on for years. A good lawyer makes it last even longer.

Q: How many lawyers does it take to screw in a light bulb?
A: Three, One to climb the ladder. One to shake it, and one to sue the ladder company.

Q: What's the difference between a lawyer and a herd of buffalo?
A: The lawyer charges more.

Q: Why won't sharks attack lawyers?
A: Professional courtesy.

Q: What's the difference between a female lawyer and a pitbull?
A: Lipstick.

Q: Why does the law society prohibit sex between lawyers and their clients?
A: To prevent clients from being billed twice for what is essentially the same service.

Finally, a quote from one of my modern day heroes; Number Four:

> *"When you are 80 years old, and in a quiet moment of reflection narrating for only yourself the most personal version of your life story, the telling that will be most compact and meaningful will be the series of choices you have made. In the end, we are our choices. Build yourself a great story"* [299.]
>
> *Jeff Bezos – Founder of Amazon*

Thank you for taking the time to read my story.

[299.] Jeff Bezos, commencement of his speech at Princeton University 30th May 2010

The organisations, websites and contacts I have found most useful:

Legal Ombudsman for England and Wales
0300 555 0333
www.legalombudsman.org.uk

Legal Ombudsman
PO Box 6806
Wolverhampton
WV1 9WJ

Citizens Advice
England 08444 111 444
Wales 08444 772020
www.citizensadvice.org.uk

Citizens Advice
3rd Floor North
200 Aldersgate
London
EC1A 4HD

Civil Legal Advice (CLA)
0345 345 4 345
www.gov.uk/civil-legal-advice

DirectGov
ww.gov.uk/divorce

National Family Mediation

0300 4000 636

www.nfm.org.uk/

National Family Mediation
1st Floor
Civic Centre
Paris St
Exeter
EX1 1JN

The Law Society

www.lawsociety.org.uk

Law Society Family Law Panel

www.lawsociety.org.uk/support-services/accreditation/family law
Family Lives
0808 800 2222
www.familylives.org.uk/

15–17 The Broadway
Hatfield
Hertfordshire
AL9 5HZ

Relate

0300 1001234
www.relate.org.uk
Premier House
Carolina Court
Lakeside
Doncaster
DN4 5RA

Resolution
01689 820272
www.resolution.org.uk
Central Office
PO Box 302
Orpington
Kent BR6 8QX

The Ministry of Justice
www.justice.gov.uk

Useful LinkedIn Divorce Discussion Groups
UK Divorce Network
Alternative Dispute Resolution
Divorce Advice
Marketing for Divorce Professionals
Divorce Coaching for Men
Family and Divorce Lawyers
Association of Divorce Finance
Divorce Technology
ALA Marital, Divorce, Family Law & Finance
Divorce Communication

Acknowledgement

To my mum and two little sisters; our family life began with the loss our loving and devoted dad at 31 years old. Our family values and beliefs of hard work, resourcefulness and determination made us what we have become today. You know, although they are no longer with us; I still want to make mum and dad proud of their son.

To my daughter; we share the same family values and beliefs. Call it serendipity; we discovered an even stronger and deeper relationship as a result of adversity and family breakdown in 2006.

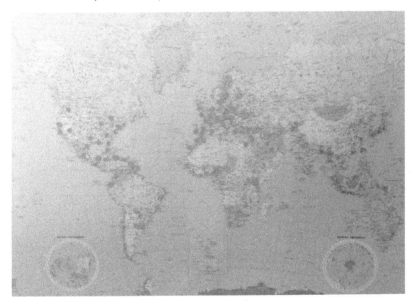

The map of the world, where my daughter and I would place orange stickers on the countries we had been fortunate to visit; learning so much about the 'new people facts of life'.

I thank the many friends, business colleagues and nationals across the globe, who taught me that "everything in life is relative".

About the Author – PA Ross

Born in Sheffield where I lived with my mum, dad and two sisters to the age of seven years old. We moved from Sheffield to the county of Gloucestershire following the tragic loss of my dad. I tell many that I was born in Yorkshire and bred in Gloucestershire.

My school years were 'character building', taking responsibility for and I guess worrying about my mum and two younger sisters; making sure we all helped my mum and were able to pay the household bills. During in my school years; I recollect one of my schoolmasters writing on my school report "If Paul, put as much energy into his academic lessons as he does on the rugby pitch; he would do well". Competitive sport has and remains a big part of my life from my younger rugby playing days; followed by 40 years of playing squash.

Having heeded my schoolmaster's earlier advice; I did 'buckle down' to education in my late teens and early twenties; achieving a reasonable level of educational qualifications to secure my first career position in 1979 as a sales representative. Now channelling my energies from the sports field to my career; I was fortunate to secure commercial jobs with some of the world's most recognised brands, such as Coca-Cola and Cadbury Schweppes. My career progressed rapidly to the latter years of corporate life, where I held the position of Head of Global Business Development at Cadbury Schweppes. I was fortunate to travel the globe partnering and developing new business with clients such as McDonalds, ExxonMobil, Shell, British Airways and BAA. These privileged experiences introduced me to a diverse and fascinating mix of people, cultures and beliefs; from which I learnt so much and a respect for the 'new facts of life'.

The loss of my mum in 2006 and the break-up of my 25-year marriage in the same year – I left corporate life in 2006 to pursue one of my life's ambitions to create and run my own business, which is the centre of my life today; along with my family, sports and continued world travel. At the time of completing this book, I have just returned from Russia this will be the 65th country I have been lucky enough to visit – no doubt, with new stories and experiences to tell; maybe in a second book.

Picture Credits, E-mails and Letters

All photographs, E-mails and letters are from the author's collection with the exception of the following:

Page 173: Glastonbury Music Festival
Page 228: Memorial Bridge, *USS Arizona* Pearl Harbour, Hawaii
Page 277: Lisa Gabardi PhD Brain Systems (Diagram 44).

Every effort has been made to credit all copyright holders of the photographs, diagrams and quotations in this book, but where omissions have been made the author will be glad to rectify them in any future editions.

The Alzheimer's Society

5% of my personal profits received from this book will be donated to the Alzheimer's Society; helping in a small way, their relentless search to discover a cure for this devastating disease.

Research and knowledge are critical tools to defeat dementia and one day, hopefully not too far in the future medical science will discover a cure.

The Alzheimer's Society is the only **UK** charity to fund research into all types of dementia. They are relentlessly searching and improving our understanding of the cause, cure, care and prevention of dementia.

There are many ways you can become involved and help the Alzheimer's Society by becoming a friend of research, taking part in clinical trials, fundraising and donations, joining the research network or simply volunteering a small amount of your time to help those who need support and care.

The society's current strategy for funding research outlines the key priorities over the coming years as well as their unique way of working with scientists and people affected by dementia in partnership. You are able to learn much more about the Alzheimer's Society, dementia and the ways you are able to help by visiting www.alzheimers.org.uk
Telephone:

National Dementia Helpline
0300 222 11 22

Customer Care
0330 333 0804
Or write to the society at:
Alzheimer's Society
Devon House
58 St Katharine's Way
London E1W 1LB
Enquiries@alzheimers.org.uk

Lightning Source UK Ltd.
Milton Keynes UK
UKHW03f1421020418
320407UK00002B/366/P